MAINSTREAMING BASIC WRITERS

Politics and Pedagogies of Access

MAINSTREAMING BASIC WRITERS
Politics and Pedagogies of Access

Edited by
Gerri McNenny
California State University, Fullerton

Associate Editor
Sallyanne H. Fitzgerald
Chabot College

LEA
2001

LAWRENCE ERLBAUM ASSOCIATES, PUBLISHERS

Mahwah, New Jersey London

Lawrence Erlbaum Associates, Inc., Publishers
10 Industrial Avenue
Mahwah, NJ 07430

Cover design by Kathryn Houghtaling Lacey

Library of Congress Cataloging-in-Publication Data

Mainstreaming basic writers : politics and pedagogies of access / edited by Gerri
McNenny ; associate editor, Sallyanne H. Fitzgerald.
    p. cm.
   Includes bibliographical references and indexes.
   ISBN 0-8058-3573-3 (cloth)—ISBN 0-8058-3574-1 (pbk.)
    1. English language—Rhetoric—Study and teaching.   2. Report writing—Study and
teaching (Higher).   3. Basic writing (Remedial education).   4. Mainstreaming in education.
I. McNenny, Gerri.   II. Fitzgerald, Sallyanne H.

PE1404 .M35   2001
808′.042′0711—dc21

00-052149

Books published by Lawrence Erlbaum Associates are printed on
acid-free paper, and their bindings are chosen for strength and durability.

Printed in the United States of America
10 9 8 7 6 5 4 3 2 1

Contents

v

Foreword

This is the right time for this book. This is apparent from the controversy about the best way to meet the needs of those who have been designated basic writers. (The ways in which they have been "designated" raises another issue worthy of serious discussion and debate.) Although, as Gerri McNenny points out in the Introduction to this volume, this issue has been "on the table" since 1992, there is a new urgency to examine the role of basic writing programs and their relationship to mainstreaming issues. As McNenny notes, the arguments for and against mainstreaming are "complicated by the socio-historical moment that we find ourselves in." The question may not turn out to be whether mainstreaming is the best option for basic writers, but whether it may be the case that it is the only option provided to these students, given the moves being made toward the elimination of basic writing classes in many 4-year colleges and university systems.

The complexities in our students' lives are clearly mirrored in the complexities of placement and instruction so prominently delineated in this collection. Students' socioeconomic and educational histories place a growing number of individuals at risk of being denied any higher education at all as political and institutional forces move to restrict or eliminate access to 4-year colleges and universities. Community colleges are increasingly the site where students must quickly obtain the "skills" necessary to pass the required placement tests for entry into 4-year colleges, while simultaneously, instructors at the community colleges are being overwhelmed by gigantic class sizes and teaching loads.

But a larger philosophical issue lies behind the question of what level of writing students should be assigned to. As long as the testing mania controls students' progress in the form of artificial demands from timed, impromptu writing, it will be impossible for students either to be placed properly or to exit from whatever level of writing they have been assigned to. The fallacy in these placement and exit decisions lies in the expectation of what can be accomplished in a single writing, a single semester, or a single year. The support described by Wiley (chapter 10) of the Learning Alliance provides one model of the kind of assistance over all the college years that markedly benefits students.

Having taught courses in basic writing, freshman composition, and a mainstreamed year of composition at an urban college, I find it difficult to unequivocally say that either basic writing or mainstreaming is the best answer for students who would be judged as basic writers using the most frequently used placement instrument, the inappropriately timed, impromptu writing task. This stressful assessment procedure fails to provide students with a fair opportunity to present their best writing. Students have no time for revising or editing their writing. What happens, then, is that many students, especially those with second-dialect or second-language backgrounds, are discriminated against by readers who lack the essential language background to make fair assessments. Such readers are unaware that these interference features in writing are both pattern-centered and amenable to movement toward the "standard" features over time. As long as this inappropriate assessment procedure rules placement, it seems reasonable to encourage mainstreaming classes because "skill" backgrounds at the sentence-level should not hold students back from the challenges of serious reading and writing tasks. These students will profit from the curriculum of a mainstreamed class, while they are provided with opportunities to practice the required conventions of formal writing.

One of the essential keys to proper placement decisions is the knowledge of assessors about second-language and second-dialect features. If readers of placement exams were knowledgeable about dialect patterns and second-language acquisition, they could see the sentence-level features of their students' writing in an appropriate time frame, recognizing that these language features will move over time to the academically required forms. But holding students back because of their language history denies them the opportunity to develop their analytic skills while they are honing their composition skills. Agnew and McLaughlin (chapter 6) point out the problems of overstating the attention to grammatical features produced by some African-American students. And Smoke (chapter 11) focuses on how the immigrant who has likely received poor preparation in an urban high school is discriminated against compared to the international student who received an education overseas.

It is true that students today are being turned away completely from some sites of higher education, and I have no problem abhorring that completely. But I do not think it can be said that every basic writer can be mainstreamed successfully at the moment of admission. The ability level in reading is crucial to placement decisions. For example, Gleason and Soliday refused admission to their mainstreaming program to students who had failed City College's Reading Assessment Test. (But it must be noted that at that time, basic writing classes still existed, and students could be assigned to those classes. This option is being phased out at that college.) Before assessing the success or failure of mainstreaming for all students, it would be necessary to have comparative data on the backgrounds and skills levels of students at a wide range of institutions as Collins and Lynch (chapter 5) argue. At institutions where two or more levels of basic writing classes are offered, it might be more appropriate to mainstream those who had placed into the second level, as Wiley (chapter 10) recommends, while retaining a basic reading and writing semester for those who were to begin at the lower level. (This is the recommendation I made to Gleason and Soliday when I taught in the mainstreaming program at City College of New York in 1995.) Such students may need to increase their reading comprehension skills as well as their writing skills before starting the regular curriculum. But when an institution excludes basic skills instruction entirely, that is, both reading and writing, an intensive curriculum within a mainstreaming class needs to be designed to provide opportunities to practice those processes more extensively than may have been called for previously.

Mainstreaming can be successful for students as long as the expectation is not that one semester or 1 year can provide all the writing needs of students after they exit the course(s). Students will need to continue practicing reading and writing processes, with demands gradually increased to foster growth in cognitive complexity. With concurrent reading and writing instruction in a mainstreaming course, students should not be held back nor denied the opportunity to simultaneously take the core courses of their institutions, because otherwise they would be delayed in their academic progress.

Mainstreaming student writers needs to be seen as the first step in the recognition that using writing as a basis for learning is a long-term proposition. As the basic writer and the conventionally placed freshman writer meet in a challenging course that provides them with the opportunity to practice analytic writing based on thoughtful readings, they will be preparing themselves for the demands of their academic courses. To deny basic writers that opportunity and substitute lower level cognitive demands to allow time for grammatical exercises or lesser writing tasks is to deny them the opportunity to prepare to become full-fledged scholars and potential contributors to the larger society, where their frequently unacknowledged background and expertise can allow them to offer new insights on their disciplines.

As I said at the beginning of this Foreword, this is the right time for this book. *Mainstreaming Basic Writers: Politics and Pedagogies of Access* presents the issues that policymakers must confront when decisions need to be made about access and instruction. The strength of this book lies in its openness and willingness to present a wide range of perspectives from knowledgeable professionals in the field who are grappling with the question of how to best provide opportunities for those students who are increasingly being discriminated against by forces within the larger society who neither understand nor sympathize with the difficult personal and educational backgrounds that have made these students so vulnerable at this time. Believing that knowledge leads to strength, the editor and contributors of this book offer composition professionals a range of options that they can use to help shape policy at their individual institutions. Our students deserve this attention.

—Marilyn S. Sternglass
Professor Emeritus of English
City College of City University of New York

Preface

At a time when various political and administrative bodies are calling for the dissolution of basic writing instruction on 4-year college campuses, the need for information concerning the options available to university decision makers has become more pressing. Anyone familiar with the literature will be aware that even among writing program administrators and composition and rhetoric specialists, a wide range of professional judgments surrounding this situation exists. *Mainstreaming Basic Writers: Politics and Pedagogies of Access* presents many of the various positions taken in response to these recent challenges posed to basic writing instruction and offers alternative configurations for writing instruction that attempt to do justice to both students' needs and administrative constraints. Contributors include for the most part those professionals entrusted with the role of advocating for a student population that has at times been described as "underprepared," "in need of remediation," and "at-risk." In this book, we attempt to give a fair representation of some of the more noted perspectives from nationally recognized scholars and administrators working in the field of basic writing program administration.

Such a wide representation of positions on the issue of mainstreaming basic writers at the college level will, we believe, prove useful to writing program administrators, composition and rhetoric students and scholars, and other key university decisionmakers, from provosts and deans to department chairs. We also hope to provide models of alternative configurations for college writing program curricula and administration to instructors searching for innovative ways to meet the needs of their heterogeneous student bodies. Throughout this book, contributors discuss current institutional developments and curricular designs in basic writing program administration, all of which will undoubtedly contribute to the discussion.

In chapter 1, "Writing Instruction and the Post-Remedial University: Setting the Scene for the Mainstreaming Debate in Basic Writing," the editor of this volume, Gerri McNenny, provides an overview of the cultural, political, economic, and pedagogical forces that have come into play in the discussion surrounding the appropriateness of mainstreaming. Those factors that have given such a strong momentum to the growing need for mainstreaming programs and alternative configurations for underprepared college students are outlined here, along with the exigency that the "post-remedial" university lends to the mainstreaming movement.

"Part I: The Controversy Surrounding Mainstreaming," lays out the theoretical, political, and practical implications of the mainstreaming debate. Here we have chosen a pivotal article by Edward M. White, updated and revised for this book, which originally appeared in the *Journal of Basic Writing* in 1995, concerning the various groups involved in the mainstreaming debate. In this chapter, White defends the role of basic writing courses through a statistical analysis of student retention and improved performance as evidenced in two distinct educational systems—New Jersey State and California State University systems. Both the overview of the oppositional perspectives on basic writing instruction and the statistical analysis of the role that placement and instruction can play in underprepared students' access to higher education provide a useful jumping off point for the mainstreaming debate contained in this book.

Representing a diametrically opposed position, Ira Shor, in his chapter "Errors and Economics: Inequality Breeds Remediation," argues against a system of "mass miseducation" that enforces an unequal status quo via college composition programs through their emphasis on correctness over critical literacy and expression. Instead, Shor maintains, basic writing programs act to reify the cooling-out function of remedial courses that serve to throw up impediments to students lacking the socially correct register that would mark them as members of the more validated social classes. Shor documents the historical progression of gatekeeping classes like basic writing that surge in importance during times of social unrest and upheaval, when immigrant and disfranchised groups start to gain in power. Such courses stabilize the status quo by withholding full membership and privilege through a system of stigmatizing yet questionable placement and testing instruments and skills-based courses that strip writing instruction of any inspiration or power. Instead, Shor enjoins us to set about restructuring our writing courses, taking cues from portfolio assessment recommended by Peter Elbow, Kathy Yancey, Brian Huot, and others, and from the

Writing Studio instructional model established by Rhonda Grego and Nancy Thompson at South Carolina. Altogether, Shor's argument brings up substantial controversies still hotly debated in Composition Studies—controversies that remain at the nexus of the mainstreaming debate.

In "Ideologies of Access and the Politics of Agency," Mary Soliday examines the ways in which the commonly accepted ideology surrounding open access has exaggerated the role of agency that basic writing programs play in assuring student success, thus obscuring the material and institutional factors that often determine students' trajectories through college. By placing so much responsibility on a single program or an entry-level course, those shaping university policy unwittingly avoid a more systemic analysis, thus drawing attention away from the diminishing material and institutional support for students marginalized both economically and culturally through a system of unequal privilege. Soliday traces the ways in which the dominant ideology, through the mechanisms of policy statements, legislative decree, and a conservative press, has given open access a decidedly racial cast and characterized it as politically subversive, despite overwhelming evidence to the contrary. As a result, basic writing programs are targeted as being symptomatic of a tolerance for underachievement and continued support for failed liberal support programs, much like welfare and other "entitlement" programs for the poor. Soliday's analysis enables us to reconsider the place of basic writing programs within the larger institutional and social contexts in which they are contained. What is needed, she argues, is not simply a retrofitting but a revisioning of the ways in which our institutions work with those students designated as being at-risk throughout their college careers.

Arguing for more site-specific criteria for writing program development, Terrence G. Collins and Kim Lynch, in "Mainstreaming? Eddy, Rivulet, Backwater, Site Specificity," caution us to assess our programs mindful of the configurations that define their institutional constraints. Successful writing programs, they maintain, are constructed around the needs of local populations of basic or developmental students and on a critical evaluation of all of the apparati that attend institutional efforts to include high-risk students. By scrutinizing the placement procedures and instruments, the credit or noncredit-bearing curricula, and the place of developmental writing programs within the larger institutional context, they argue, we can make more informed decisions regarding programmatic design.

The need to critically evaluate our programs becomes more apparent when we do uncover disturbing trends in the impact that our basic writing programs have on those they seek to help. Such is the case in the longitudinal study conducted by Eleanor Agnew and Margaret McLaughlin on the impact that flawed placement and exit exams have had on African-American students at a regional southern university. In the chapter, "Those Crazy Gates and How They Swing: Tracking the System that Tracks African-American

Students," Agnew and McLaughlin follow the academic progress of several basic writers, noting the consistently negative evaluations that the presence of African-American Vernacular English dialect in timed writing samples drew from evaluators, thus delaying and in many cases sabotaging students' efforts to receive a college education. Their critique of the placement and assessment process provides a persuasive case for the reconfiguring of basic writing evaluation, along with the entire process that attends institutional writing evaluation.

What happens when decisions concerning writing program evaluation and design are removed from the province of informed academic professionals is the focus of Marti Singer's chapter, "Moving the Margins." Here Singer offers an account of the continual shifting of admissions criteria and raised standards imposed by upper administrators over the 20 years that she has taught and served in the basic writing program at her large urban university. Her narrative documents the vagaries that accompany seemingly arbitrary administrative decisions and their enormous impact on the students served by the affected programs. Blown about by the winds of political exigency and economic need, writing professionals and students alike still find themselves scrambling to adapt to decisions from on high. Singer's documentation of these encroachments on faculty decision making by legislators and trustees lacking the professional perspective that writing program administrators bring to program decisions stand as a cautionary tale, a situation that she makes clear faculty will need to act on in the future.

"Part II: Alternative Configurations for Basic Writing" sets out several innovative approaches to teaching writing to underprepared students. Barbara Gleason, in her chapter "Returning Adults to the Mainstream: Toward a Curriculum for Diverse Student Writers," describes in detail an entry-level writing class conducted at the Center for Worker Education, a program affiliated with the City College of New York. Aimed at mainstreaming returning adult students who would have placed into either "remedial" or "college-level" writing classes, Gleason's course demonstrates the richness with which a writing course can be designed, with a purposeful progression of writing experiences that build on one another while encouraging students to own their own research agendas and processes. Taking students from research situations that focus on one-on-one interviews with peers to later ethnographic fieldwork that encourages writers to synthesize interviews, notes, observations, and interpretations with focused inquiry, this course builds on students' engagement with their own professional goals and interests to help them produce college-level writing. Gleason's position, "that remediation is inappropriate for adults who are returning to college after a 5-, 10-, or even 20-year hiatus" (chapter 8), is well supported in the research and the case studies she presents of two students at seemingly opposite ends of the spectrum in terms of writing competence, yet for whom the

mainstreaming curriculum works equally well, providing challenges and opportunities for growing competence in written expression. Gleason's pedagogical approach capitalizes on two key features essential to a mainstreaming curricula: "(1) the use of oral language and conversational competencies
as resources for developing writers; [and] (2) sequenced assignments comprising more and less difficult tasks." These features, coupled with ample
support and a clear understanding of developmental progress in writing, accelerate students' academic progress and thus challenge notions of remedial
ghettoization.

At Catholic University, a differently conceived mainstreaming effort for
at-risk students is reported in "Rethinking At-Risk Students' Knowledge and
Needs: Heroes' Decisions and Students' Quests for Identity and Meaning in
a Content Composition Course," by Rosemary Winslow and Monica Mische.
Here the authors make the case for a heterogeneous student make-up in
a composition/content course that takes as its focus the hero journey and
subsequent identity quests made by strong individuals. By studying various hero quests, students embark on parallel journeys of their own, relating
the search for meaning and identity to their own identity quests as entering first-year college students. Drawing on the groundwork laid in Jurgen
Habermas' *The Theory of Communicative Action*, Winslow and Mische invite students to read and react to texts that build on the interconnectedness
of the individual with the larger social and cultural domains, through the
study of heroes making choices. By doing so, students confront their own
constructions of purpose and identity in academia, engaging in quests "as
thinkers, readers, and writers, . . . to discover, encounter, and perhaps renew
their various identities" (see chapter 9). By drawing on rich visual and cultural texts in the museums throughout Washington, DC, as well as historical
and literary texts, the authors were able to design a course capitalizing on
multiple modalities in students' knowing and their ability to conceptualize
responses to others' and their own quests.

Although individual courses often provide a means for students to find
their places within academic contexts, other options exist as well.
Mark Wiley, in his chapter "Mainstreaming and Other Experiments in a
Learning Community," reports on the results of a mainstreaming project
through the vehicle of a 4-year learning community initiated at California
State University, Long Beach, within the past several years. As part of CSU
Long Beach's Learning Alliance, a learning community that extends through
the senior year, first-year students share a cluster of three courses the first
semester and two courses in the second. After several years of experimentation, Wiley and others working with learning communities at this primarily commuter campus have found that basic writers who have been mainstreamed into regular first-year composition courses, which in turn share
content with another general education course, do indeed experience a

high success rate. Moreover, Wiley points out, learning communities provide a more substantial support system and address the cultural dissonance that so many first-year students, especially at-risk students, experience by providing an academic community experience.

Whenever mainstreaming alternatives are discussed, perhaps the most problematic student population consists of those students designated as speaking English as a Second Language (ESL). With profiles that vary widely from the highly educated and competitive international students who come here to study for a few years to those immigrants who may have lived in the United States for most of their lives, students whose native language is not Standard English often have the most difficult time understanding and meeting college-level discourse expectations. Trudy Smoke, in her article "Mainstreaming Writing: What Does This Mean for ESL Students?" takes on the complexities of the curricular needs of these students by examining the ways in which special considerations for ESL students are politically manipulated in policy decisions to place immigrants living in the U.S. at a disadvantage. Smoke's research shows that both in placement procedures and through curricular offerings, ESL students pose a special challenge. She then goes on to examine several highly effective approaches to working with nonnative speakers of English (NNSE). These include an extensive discussion of English 110 at Hunter College/CUNY, a mainstream, nonremedial, credit-bearing college writing course that brought together ESL students and native speakers of English (NSE). Smoke also provides a useful review of other programs, including the Stretch Program at Arizona State University, developed by John Ramage and David Schwalm and carried on by Greg Glau; Rhonda Grego and Nancy Thompson's Writing Studio, a mainstreaming program in which small groups of students meet weekly to receive help on writing; California State University, Chico's mainstreaming program, developed by Judith Rodby and Tom Fox; and the Enrichment Course at CUNY, designed and developed by Mary Soliday and Barbara Gleason. Smoke goes on to offer guidelines for structuring writing programs for ESL students that take into account the best pedagogical practices subscribed to at this time. Altogether, her article provides a valuable synopsis of the major issues that program administrators may need to take into account as they seek to keep access to higher education available to growing numbers of immigrant students.

In closing, Sallyanne H. Fitzgerald, in the chapter "The Context Determines Our Choice: Curriculum, Students, and Faculty," gives a much-needed synopsis of the place that the mainstreaming discussion as contained in this book may have for many 2-year colleges. Her interpretation of these issues from the perspective of a dean of Language Arts and Humanities at a well-regarded 2-year college reminds all of us that much of the mainstreaming debate has indeed excluded the voices of 2-year college decision makers.

ACKNOWLEDGMENTS

Many people have helped me in the compilation and editing of this book. Special thanks are due to my colleagues at California State University, Fullerton, the University of Houston, Downtown, and the University of Arizona. These include Mary Kay Crouch, my fellow writing program administrator whose comprehensive understanding of the field of basic writing program administration and instruction have been a valuable resource. I would also like to thank Susan Ahern, a wonderful mentor and administrator whose guidance contributed significantly to this book. She continues to be a powerful advocate for underprivileged students at the University of Houston, Downtown. Duane Roen and Tilly Warnock have also been a tremendous help throughout the process and have tempered all of the work done in this book, even though they may not have been aware of it. Thanks also go to Marvin Diogenes, whose fame as the leader of the Composition Blues Band sometimes overshadows the important work he has done with the Composition Program and the graduate students at the University of Arizona.

Both Sally and Gerri want to thank the Conference on Basic Writing board members who were so encouraging of the undertaking of this book, especially Jeanne Gunner, whose advice and help on this volume have been much appreciated. Finally, my heartfelt appreciation must be acknowledged to all of the contributors to this volume who worked with me in getting this volume together: Ed White, Ira Shor, Mary Soliday, Barbara Gleason, Marti Singer, Trudy Smoke, Mark Wiley, Rosemary Winslow, Monica Mische, Terry Collins, Kim Lynch, Eleanor Agnew, and Margaret McLaughlin.

I would also like to thank the editors at Lawrence Erlbaum Associates for their help in guiding this book through the process of publication. Special thanks must go to Lori Hawver and Naomi Silverman for their extraordinary help and patience.

—Gerri McNenny
California State University, Fullerton

Writing Instruction and the Post-Remedial University: Setting the Scene for the Mainstreaming Debate in Basic Writing

Gerri McNenny
California State University, Fullerton

The issues surrounding mainstreaming are not new. The call to examine the role of basic writing programs was sounded quite competently in 1992, at the meeting of the Fourth Annual Conference on Basic Writing in Maryland, and subsequently debated in the *Journal of Basic Writing* (Bartholomae; Adams; Fox; Greenberg; Berger; Gay; Jones; Scott).[1] And yet the need to examine and reconsider how to meet basic writing students' needs has emerged with a vengeance in recent years. Across the nation, basic writing programs are being scrutinized by numerous audiences—by politicians, boards of trustees, university administrators, and the public alike. Still, the momentum has been building for quite some time. In a report published in 1995 on the political situation facing basic writing programs, the National Association for Developmental Education (NADE) warned that attacks on developmental education in higher education were imminent. NADE political liaison Gerald Corkran noted that, following their efforts to reduce or eliminate affirmative action, some state and national leaders would then move on to dismantle developmental education, believing that because there was no longer a need for affirmative action, there was therefore no need for developmental education. Along these lines, Corkran warned, "some congressional leaders have identified higher education, especially developmental education, as the next major program for review after the welfare debate has concluded" (2). Several states at that time proposed refusing all aid for underachieving students in the belief "that refusing aid for such courses could spark students and schools to improve education" (Corkran 3). At that time, it was clear to many of us in the field of basic writing that the real impact of such actions would more than likely act to further exclude economically disadvantaged students from attending college at all.

Since then, the movement to challenge basic writing instruction at 4-year colleges has gathered further momentum. With it, the need to respond to such challenges, as writing program administrators, writing professionals, and policymakers within 4-year institutions of higher education, has also grown. In this chapter, I present an overview of those factors, both political and pedagogical, that come into play when we consider the issue of mainstreaming basic writers into the typically required first-year writing course. Whether out of absolute necessity triggered by legislative action or out of a desire to address pedagogical concerns, writing program administrators and professionals are increasingly confronted with the alternative to mainstream "at-risk" college students. That decision is further complicated by the complexities of institutional testing and placement, admissions criteria, and the ambiguous nature of criteria used to label the student populations as either "underprepared," "developmental," "inexperienced," "at-risk," or "remedial." Justifications for both the maintenance of basic writing programs that their administrators and instructors see as beneficial, as well as arguments in favor of mainstreaming those students designated as underprepared, are contained in this book. Scholarly research and analysis, as well as studies in which basic writers were included in the regular first-year sequence, support various positions along the spectrum, from substantial justifications and descriptions of basic writing programs that continue to serve their students well to those that propose innovative alternatives for mainstreaming "at-risk" college students into the commonly taken first-year writing course.

A fundamental premise that I work from here is that any decision to mainstream basic writers will always be contingent on site-specific configurations, including the political and economic circumstances that define the mission of the institution and the cultural, social, and intellectual situatedness of the student populations (see Collins and Lynch, chapter 5; Fitzgerald, chapter 12). Lynn Troyka's observations in her foundational article "Defining Basic Writing in Context" concerning the variations on what defines students as "basic writers" in our schools foregrounds any such decision, especially when we consider the wide range of placement procedures and standards for admittance that exist at each institution. At the same time, I want to acknowledge the many valid critiques of basic writing posed in this book, including the economic, ideological, and pedagogical arguments that support mainstreaming. Each has its place and contributes substantially to the ongoing debate.

SETTING THE SCENE FOR THE MAINSTREAMING DEBATE

Although debates on the abolition of composition in general and basic writing in particular are not new, the more recent presence of a political climate unfriendly to the needs of nontraditional college students has forced many writing program administrators to confront the issue of mainstreaming. The events taking place across the nation—at City University in New York, where the Board of Trustees, supported by Mayor Giuliani and Governor Pataki, have effectively discontinued open admissions (Healy A30); in Florida, where only one 4-year institution (Florida A & M University) is authorized to offer basic writing (Corkran); in Georgia, where the Board of Regents for the state university system has passed a motion to reduce Learning Support Programs at the major research universities in the state by the year 2001, thereby serving only 1% of the first-year class (see Singer, chapter 7); and in California, where the California State University system Board of Trustees has determined that by the year 2007, only 10% of all entering students will need to take basic writing, even though more than 60% of the entering freshmen at some campuses place into basic writing at this time—can be interpreted in several ways. Most certainly, they represent the ascendancy of a conservative sentiment toward public education. Legislative efforts to shape educational policy and admissions criteria seem to be following what Michael Apple identifies as the conservative right's agenda on education. The rhetoric of educational reform, Apple points out, has been deftly managed by the conservative right to redefine the very meaning of democracy, as well as access to a college education. Instead of educational goals that place "equity, sharing, personal dignity, security, freedom, and caring" at the forefront of educational policy, we have from legislatures and trustees alike a vision of students "as objects to be manipulated or to be 'freed' to follow the dictates of the invisible hand of the market" (Apple 3). Fortunately, our research and our experience show that basic writers are best understood "as co-responsible subjects involved in the process of democratically deliberating over the ends and means of all of their institutions" (Apple 3).

A closer look at these motions affords a better understanding of their impact. At City University in New York (CUNY), for instance, the trustees voted to dissolve the almost 30-year-old open-admissions policies in the spring of 1998. According to the *Chronicle of Higher Education*'s Patrick Healy, "Under the [new] policy, applicants who are assessed as needing remediation would be barred from CUNY four-year colleges until they completed a summer program or remedial classes at a CUNY community college or elsewhere. In 1997, about 13,000 incoming students at the four-year colleges required remediation" (Healy A30). Such a change would mean a drastic shift in CUNY admissions patterns, resulting in a denial of access for the poor, for students of color, and for the immigrant populations that still define a large demographic population. As Theodore Shaw, the associate director-counsel for the NAACP Legal Defense and Educational Fund, has pointed out, "The CUNY system has long been a door to opportunity for poor people, students of color, and [this move on the part of the trustees] is an attempt to completely remake the City University and abandon that mission" (Healy A30). According to Giuliani's estimates, admissions will be cut by almost 75% (Wright 12), a move that many see as an effort "to downsize the university, rendering it more "cost efficient" along the lines that have become a familiar feature of corporate America" (Gleason "Evaluating" 580), at the expense of minority and disadvantaged populations.

In California, the California State University system plans to phase out developmental education by the year 2007, by requiring college-level skills in English and mathematics as a condition of admission for recent high school graduates. A small number of developmental courses would be available for the returning student who has been out of the educational system for some time, but those students must demonstrate that they can complete their developmental courses within the first year. At this time, though, 47% of entering students must take English developmental courses based on their scores on standardized and institutional placement examinations ("CSU Remediation"). According to NADE political liaison Gerald Corkran, "Many opponents see [the phasing out of developmental education] as an ominous sign of things to come at CSU—doors slamming shut to minorities and disadvantaged students who are more likely to need remedial help" (3).

In Florida, all public universities—except Florida A & M—have been prohibited from teaching "remedial" courses since 1985. The National Association for Developmental Education reports that, in 1995, "Florida's legislators...considered a measure that would fine public school districts whose high school graduates arrived at college unprepared. It has been defeated for now, but some legislators see it as a way to hold K–12 schools accountable" (Corkran). Also at that time, "The [Florida] House of Representatives [were] considering a proposal that would force students to pay for the total cost of developmental courses—typically three to four times more per credit than other classes—for students that have taken the same developmental courses more than twice since they had previously failed or withdrawn" (Corkran).

In Massachusetts, "the Massachusetts Higher Education Coordinating Council...ordered state institutions to use tougher admissions standards starting in 1997." Recent data suggest that 12% to 25% of public-college freshmen in 1994 would not have been admitted. The Council's president, James Carlin, notes that he wants more money spent on academically motivated students and less on remedial-education classes, which are widespread at some campuses. NADE's political liaison Gerald Corkran reports that "Carlin's next goal is to get rid of developmental programs altogether" (Corkran 2).

The common defense for such legislative intervention into educational policy is often framed in a kind of authoritarian populist rhetoric, as a form of common sense dictated by an upper administration that sees itself as strict disciplinarians. "Once is enough," Mayor Guiliani is quoted as saying (Wright 12), referring to efforts to limit the number of times students attempt remediation, when in fact, for many students who come from families whose lives are complicated by poverty and subsistence wage labor, once is not enough. Many a case study in Marilyn Sternglass's book *Time to Know Them* recounts the efforts of students to continue with their coursework, despite poverty-level wages, family obligations, and childcare situations. Moreover, longitudinal studies contained in that book, along with the repeated experiences reported by successful graduates of basic writing programs at 4-year institutions and their instructors (Mutnick; Collins; Soliday and Gleason), all point to an overwhelming number of students whose experiences in basic writing classes at the college level served to initiate them successfully into the culture and expectations of higher education.

What many writing program administrators and other decision makers are faced with, then, is the decision of what to do about existing basic writing programs that may now or in the future be threatened, either by legislative mandate, budgetary constraints, or political pressures. The challenges confronting writing program administrators and writing instructors remain daunting. As cautionary tales, the dismantling of various basic writing programs signals a need for a more public, proactive role for writing program administrators and instructors, to present a convincing and comprehensive picture of the gains that students achieve through their writing programs, and the intellectual work involved for both students and faculty. Although such tactics may have failed at CUNY, despite the heated struggle between political forces and faculty members, at the University of Minnesota's General College, proponents of the basic writing program there, including Terry Collins, Geoff Sirc, and others, have succeeded in rallying support from previous General College graduates and in launching a persuasive public relations campaign to represent the successful work of the College (Collins). The attack on the program, spearheaded by the legislature there in 1996 in an eleventh-hour attack, underscores the importance of the public's perception of basic writing.

The success of the University of Minnesota's General College's efforts in defending a writing program that demonstrably served the needs of its students well underscores the need to address public perceptions of writing programs and the students they serve. Yet, as Harvey Wiener noted following the dismantling of the CUNY open admissions policy, we need to address perceptions among fellow faculty as well as those held by legislators and trustees:

> Those with the responsibility for writing programs have not attended appropriately to public perceptions about the basic writing enterprise. Perhaps we cannot prevent the unenlightened barbs of politicians with an eye on budgets or reelections, but certainly we ought to have educated our University colleagues systematically and thoughtfully about what we do. Yet we have failed here, and, as a result, we continue to suffer uninformed comments and criticisms by the professorate beyond (and unfortunately sometimes within) our English and writing skills departments. Colleagues do not acknowledge basic writing's utility, have little understanding of what it is, and, to a large degree, have undermined our efforts. (Wiener 97)

What Wiener's comment demonstrates is that communication with and support from faculty in other departments within our own institutions are also crucial in counteracting the reductive representation of writing programs as skills based, when in fact the work done in our writing programs contains its own opportunities for interdisciplinary enrichment and critical growth (see also Gleason "Evaluating"; Mutnick; Sternglass; Gilyard; Winslow and Mische, chapter 9).

ISSUES IN MAINSTREAMING

The issues surrounding the choice to mainstream "at-risk" college students are numerous, each impinging on the other and demanding our attention, whether we as program administrators, instructors, and stakeholders in university decision making choose to maintain and enhance basic writing programs or to incorporate them into regular first-year writing programs. They stand at the center of several tensions in the field of composition and rhetoric and include the following:

- The role of institutional testing and placement and the accuracy with which these decisions are made based on the procedures used to determine college readiness.
- The standards with which we measure student preparedness.
- The situatedness of writing programs and the degree to which they take into account their specific student populations—their academic needs as well as their sociocultural orientations to higher education and the middle class institutions it represents.
- The economics of course credits for graduation and the ways in which this contributes to the nullification of students' efforts and motivation.

- The design of our writing programs and the ways in which we provide students with course content that engages them and enables them to participate capably in future academic conversations.

Although each of these elements is covered extensively in this book, I want to focus on two key components here: the role of institutional testing and placement and the design of our writing programs.

ROLE OF INSTITUTIONAL TESTING AND PLACEMENT

The issues of testing and placement have been powerful motivators for many advocates of mainstreaming, precisely because they experience the inaccuracy and lack of validity of these test measures in their own writing classes, in the writing of their students. Although many writing professionals appreciate the improvement that the timed writing test represents in assessing writing competence (White), others find fault with both its reliability and validity as a measure of student writing ability. Some note the inability of some students to perform well in such artificially situated testing situations (Shor; Shaughnessy; Gleason "When the Writing Test"), whereas others note the arbitrariness of the cut-off points selected for placement (Elbow). Calls for a more valid measure of student writing competence for the purposes of placement have increased in the professional literature in recent years (Elbow; Borrowman), and in 1994, the Conference on College Composition and Communication issued a position statement on assessment that integrated current research and scholarship in the field of composition to reflect a more comprehensive understanding of just what it means to evaluate student writing. In addition to acknowledging the social and contextualized nature of language, along with the importance of an authentic rhetorical situation and the ethical uses of assessment, in which assessment instruments are used for those purposes for which they are specifically designed, the CCCC Committee on Assessment also noted the limitations of a single timed writing assessment instrument:

> . . . any individual's writing "ability" is a sum of a variety of skills employed in a diversity of contexts, and individual ability fluctuates unevenly among these varieties. Consequently, one piece of writing—even if it is generated under the most desirable conditions—can never serve as an indicator of overall literacy, particularly for high stakes decisions. Ideally, such literacy must be assessed by more than one piece of writing, in more than one genre, written on different occasions, for different audiences, and evaluated by multiple readers. This realization has led many institutions and programs across the country to use portfolio assessment. ("Writing Assessment")

These findings are supported by other writing professionals who question the validity and reliability of timed impromptu writing assessment. CUNY's Enrichment Program, a mainstreaming project initiated by Barbara Gleason and Mary Soliday as a FIPSE Grant project, was partially motivated by their conviction that the CUNY Writing Assessment Test (WAT) does not accurately predict students' ability to handle college-level work (Gleason "Evaluating" 569). The problem with the WAT, Gleason explains, lies in the test itself:

> The WAT's numerical score itself fails to capture the complex potential of the students. The timed writing test and its interpretative scoring mechanism cannot begin to assess a student's history, motivation, ingenuity, creativity, work habits, sense of self, interpersonal intelligence, or sheer courage in the face of seemingly insurmountable obstacles. ("When the Writing Test" 322)

Gleason supports these observations with discussions of specific students who then went on to take an intersession workshop to help them pass the timed writing test after having successfully completed the basic writing coursework ("When the Writing Test" 313–22). Her findings indicate that test results, with many students failing yet again, were highly influenced by the presence of an ESL accent, regardless of the competence of the writing. In addition, scrutiny of the test provides ample evidence that the cultural bias built into the test, based on assumptions about students' cultural literacy and background knowledge, has a great deal to do with the high failure rate among international students.

Other factors complicate the adequacy of timed writing tests, especially when students speaking Standard English as a Second Dialect (SESD) come into the picture. Research studies conducted by Eleanor Agnew and Margaret McLaughlin document the bias that many test readers exhibit toward the slightest indication of the presence of African America Vernacular English (AAVE) dialect (chapter 6). Concerned with the disproportionate number of African-American students failing the exit exam, they reviewed the testing procedures that framed the basic writing program and found that "many students whose home language is AAVE [are prevented] from ever entering regular college English classes," a consequence, they soon found, of the presence of AAVE markers in students' texts that did not, however, interfere with the fluency of their writing.

Like any high-stakes exam, the timed writing test inevitably influences what is taught in the classroom. Cynthia Lewiecki-Wilson notes the impact that testing has on curricular content, whether as a means of placement or as an exit examination. Despite her efforts to incorporate innovative peda-gogical approaches into her writing classes, she found that "no matter how process-centered a teacher wishes to be, if students must pass (or fail) the course by means of a timed prompt, producing a single piece of writing with no chance for revisions, then a pedagogy emphasizing a few narrow forms of argumentation and surface correctness prevails" (Lewiecki-Wilson and Sommers 448). By limiting course content, she argues, the test, along with the practice of teaching to the test, hardly encourages students to make a commitment to literacy as a lifestyle that students need to succeed in college. Instead, students are placed in a highly artificial testing situation that has little if any correspondence to authentic rhetorical situations. As Mina Shaughnessy noted regarding the timed impromptu essay placement test administered to students at CUNY, "Without strategies for generating real thought, without an audience he cares to write for, the writer must eke out his first sentence by means of redundancy and digression, strategies that inevitably disengage him from his grammatical intuitions as well as his thought" (82). Another critic of the WAT, Ira Shor, argues that "Top-down testing has little to do with bottom-up learning and a lot to do with institutional control" (98), an assertion competently supported by the case studies of students and their responses to the test prompts included in Gleason's analysis of the WAT ("When the Writing Test" 313–22).

Criticism surrounding the use of timed writing assessment has been corroborated in numerous studies. Alexander Astin, in *What Matters in College? Four Critical Years Revisited*, a "longitudinal study of 24,847 students at 159 institutions from 1985–90," found that the strongest predictor of students' success in college "is their high school grades... with SAT verbal scores coming in second at one-half the relative weight of high school grades" (Astin 188 cited in Gleason "Evaluating" 570). Results from Gleason and Soliday's Enrichment Program, the mainstreaming pilot conducted at City College, likewise found that the timed impromptu writing assessment did not accurately reflect students' ability to succeed in college. Remedial-placed students electing to participate in the mainstreaming pilot, a two-semester course, passed the accompanying core course, World Humanities 101, at even higher rates than those who placed into the regular college-ready one-semester writing course (Gleason "Evaluating" 574), findings further supported by the project's external consultant and analytical statistician Michael Janger (Gleason "Evaluating" 578–9). Such findings should lead us to question the weight given to high-stakes tests like the timed impromptu writing exam in determining students' college-readiness and in barring them from admittance to 4-year colleges.

DESIGN OF WRITING PROGRAMS

As numerous contributors to the *Journal of Basic Writing* have noted, basic writing as a space within the academy has enabled many 4-year institutions to honor their highly publicized commitments to diversity and opportunity for those traditionally excluded from the academy, whose voices have not been represented or honored within its halls. Min-Zhan Lu and Bruce Horner, in their reflections on the mainstreaming debate, call on basic writing practitioners and researchers alike to force the issue, in much the same way that Martin Luther King had done in his "Letter from a Birmingham Jail," by calling on administrators and decision makers to honor the ideals with which they publicize their schools by developing and maintaining curricula and the support systems that facilitate students' successful initiation into college life. Along these same lines, Patricia Bizzell urges us to challenge the monolithic status of "academic discourse," refuting its status as an entity outside of time, unaffected by changes in the culture or by contestations to dominance and homogeneity within academe. Instead, we can recognize the process of negotiation and risk-taking that students occupying the borderlands of academe engage in, bringing to bear their home dialects and languages as well as the tools of standardized English, to make sense of the "highly asymmetrical relations of power" that Mary Louise Pratt identifies (34) that constitute the contact zone between the academy and their lived experience (Bizzell 10). By doing so, we will be helping students to carve out a legitimate space for themselves in higher education, one that enables them to voice their own efforts at making sense of a system too often reified and not in their favor. In designing curricula, then, we are in effect "looking for the arts of the contact zone" (35) that Pratt identifies, in which students write themselves into the academic project:

> These will include, we are sure, exercises in storytelling and in identifying with the ideas, interests, histories, and attitudes of others; experiments in transculturation and collaborative work and in the arts of critique, parody, and comparison (including unseemly comparisons between elite and vernacular cultural forms); the redemption of the oral; ways for people to engage with suppressed aspects of history (including their own histories), ways to move *into and out of* [emphasis in original] rhetorics of authenticity; ground rules for communication across lines of difference and hierarchy that go beyond politeness but maintain mutual respect; a systematic approach to the all-important concept of *cultural mediation* [emphasis in original] (Pratt 35).

We see evidence of a growing repertoire of the arts of the contact zone in the curricular experiments of Barbara Gleason, Mary Soliday, Judith Rodby and Tom Fox, Deborah Mutnick, Greg Glau, Terrence Collins, and others. Their research and scholarship into curricular innovations reiterate what many have pointed out: that writing is a task situated by its social, psychological, and cognitive characteristics and requirements and not simply a job that requires a box of tools (Rodby and Fox 89).

To that end, many scholars and practitioners in the field of basic writing have worked to address the needs of students occupying the borderlands of academe. The ways in which we devise writing programs to account for students whose oral skills outpace their writing abilities as well as their varied levels of academic competence and backgrounds are readily reflected in experimental writing curricula (Kells and Balester). Current research into efforts to accommodate heterogeneous student populations indicates that the use of oral strategies and the analysis of the ways in which performative speech, as evidenced in storytelling and autobiography, translated into texts transcribed and revised for academic audiences, can serve as ideal bridging assignments for students with varied strengths in oral and written media. Barbara Gleason, in her description of ethnographic research in both chapter 8 and her account of the Storytelling Project initiated at City University of New York and carried over to City College's Center for Worker Education ("Something of Great Constancy"), demonstrates the ways in which such assignments enable students to develop a metalinguistic awareness of differences in verbal and written forms, observing shifts in register and syntactic structure as well as analyzing text features that distinguish both. Assignments such as these incorporate opportunities for students to make the "sequence of cognitive, linguistic, and social adjustments" (Gleason "Something" 103) that language learners entering a new sociocultural environment, such as college, need to experience. By building on already solid gains in oral literacy, students will be able to make the transition to academic literacies more easily.

Course content that focuses on students' developmental growth in striking out on their own, as evidenced by the course designed by Rosemary Winslow and Monica Mische on heroes and identity quests (chapter 9), also facilitates students' mastery of writing by focusing on areas of research that they can connect to meaningfully and that enable them to make decisions about the directions they want to take in life. By combining the study of heroes and identity quests with exposure to visual and conceptual texts and frameworks, writing instruction, and the necessary reading and response cycles that accompanied the course, Winslow and Mische gave students the opportunity to explore their own journeys and decision-making processes that had led them thus far. The results of the course, an experiment in mainstreaming and in curricular design, proved that "at-risk" students could excel, given content-based writing instruction that engaged them in their own searches for community and identity.

The use of learning communities, with student cohorts sharing writing classes clustered with content courses that then complement each other, can also enable colleges and universities to respond to the local contexts of their student populations, linking writing instruction with socialization and acculturation into the academic community while providing the support that first-year students and especially basic writing students need. Mark Wiley's account of The Learning Alliance, a 4-year learning community that included a mainstreaming experiment, provides evidence for the effectiveness of the coherent curriculum upon which this learning community is structured, in which students enroll in clustered courses "linked by a common theme that is explored differently but in a complementary fashion in each course" (see chapter 10). Wiley's critique of the narrow and somewhat reductive conception of literacy that single, isolated basic writing courses may convey is echoed in Mary Soliday's chapter, "Ideologies of Access and the Politics of Agency" (chapter 4). Too often, basic writing programs are given the sole responsibility for acculturating marginalized students into the university's culture. Wiley's Learning Alliance makes a strong argument for ongoing learning communities that offer a broader vision of the interconnectedness of academic ambitions and students' life goals, with their emphasis on greater student–faculty interaction and more purposeful peer group interactions.

BASIC WRITING, MAINSTREAMING, AND THE FUTURE OF WRITING INSTRUCTION

What does the future hold for basic writing programs? Predictions come from various writing professionals who occupy differing positions along a wide spectrum of opinion. Harvey Wiener sees a future for basic writing in which funding will be drastically reduced, thereby forcing changes in course delivery, perhaps even forcing the issue of basic writing instruction online. With reduced contact hours between instructors and students and ever more reliance on web-based resources and interactions, students typically uncomfortable with university demands on their time may experience an even greater sense of alienation with writing instruction conducted in the impersonal and often daunting medium of e-mail (100-101). Wiener, along with other professionals, foresees basic writing instruction largely removed from the 4-year college environment, with the subsequent loss of diversity at 4-year colleges and universities. The level of professional involvement in basic writing will drop, as employment conditions become even more onerous. Classes will be overenrolled and inadequately trained instructors will be hired to teach what is commonly perceived of as a "skills" course imparting a set of proficiences independent of the sociocultural factors that determine successful learning in an unfamiliar environment. The professional status of writing instructors will drop even further, with fewer hiring lines designated for full-time employment (101). Addressing the impact on students, Cynthia Lewiecki-Wilson and Jeff Sommers warn that, "Time is running short for open admissions students. . . . Decisions about testing, course offerings, and bilingual education are being leveraged by ambitious political figures who use simplified arguments waged against the most vulnerable students in public education to shape opinion and garner support for their careers" (459).

If we are to act effectively to counteract these predictions, we'll need to do so knowledgably. What the contributors to this book and I hope to offer to the field of Basic Writing, then, are numerous perspectives and solutions to the problems that face us. The chapters contributed herein have, we trust, enriched our collective understanding of the arguments for and against mainstreaming, complicated by the sociohistorical moment that we find ourselves in. As researchers and scholars, we can further legitimize the place of traditionally excluded student populations in the academy by documenting our own students' negotiation of these contact zones through our research and scholarship into their own borderlands occupation within the academy. By attending to curricular content that enables students to see the academic enterprise as a meaningful domain that includes them, whether it be through hero journeys in which students learn to identify their own struggles as worthy of notice (Winslow and Mische, chapter 9), through the use of learning communities that link writing instruction with content courses and with academic support programs (Wiley, chapter 10), through the implementation of curricula whose design provides for the heterogeneity of the mainstreamed classroom (Gleason, chapter 8), or through special programs that take into account nonnative speaker status as language learners as well as emerging writers (Smoke, chapter 11), we may more knowledgably construct programs that include nontraditional students in the culture of the university.

NOTE

[1]For an excellent overview of the mainstreaming debate in basic writing, see the spring 2000 issue of the *Journal of Basic Writing* 19.1.

WORKS CITED

Adams, Peter Dow. "Basic Writing Reconsidered." *Journal of Basic Writing* 12.1 (1993): 22–36.

Apple, Michael W. *Official Knowledge: Democratic Education in a Conservative Age.* New York: Routledge, 1993.

Astin, Alexander W. *What Matters in College? Four Critical Years Revisited.* San Francisco: Jossey-Bass, 1993.

Bartholomae, David. "The Tidy House: Basic Writing in the American Curriculum." *Journal of Basic Writing* 12.1 (1993): 4–21.

Berger, Mary Jo. "Funding and Support for Basic Writing: Why Is There So Little?" *Journal of Basic Writing* 12.1 (1993): 81–9.

Bizzell, Patricia. "Basic Writing and the Issue of Correctness, or, What to Do with 'Mixed' Forms of Academic Discourse." *Journal of Basic Writing* 19.1 (2000): 4–12.

Borrowman, Shane. "The Trinity of Portfolio Placement: Validity, Reliability, and Curriculum Reform." *Writing Program Administration* 23.1/2 (1999): 7–19.

Collins, Terrence. *Rhetoric, Ethics, Politics: What Does "Just Teaching" Basic Writing Mean?* Paper given at the Conference on College Composition and Communication. 27 Mar. 1997. Phoenix, AZ.

Cooper, Marilyn. M. "The Ecology of Writing." *Writing as Social Action*. Ed. Marilyn M. Cooper and Michael Holzman Portsmouth, NH: Boynton/Cook Heinemann, 1989: 1–13.

Corkran, Gerald. "Report on the State of Politics in Developmental Education." URL: http://www.umkc.edu/cad/nade/ (12 Nov. 1995).

"CSU Remediation Levels Off." *CSU Stateline* March 1999: 2–3.

Elbow, Peter. "Writing Assessment in the Twenty-First Century: A Utopian View." *Composition in the Twenty-First Century: Crisis and Change*. Ed. Lynne Z. Bloom, Donald A. Daiker, and Edward M. White. Carbondale, IL: Southern Illinois UP, 1996: 83–100.

Fox, Tom. "Standards and Access." *Journal of Basic Writing* 12.1 (1993): 37–45.

Gay, Pamela. "Rereading Shaughnessy from a Postcolonial Perspective." *Journal of Basic Writing* 12.2 (1993): 29–40.

Gilyard, Keith. "Basic Writing, Cost Effectiveness, and Ideology." *Journal of Basic Writing* 19.1 (2000): 36–42.

Glau, Greg. "The 'Stretch Program': Arizona State University's New Model of University-Level Basic Writing Instruction." *Writing Program Administration* 20.1–2 (1996): 79–91.

Gleason, Barbara. "Evaluating Writing Projects in Real Time: The Politics of Remediation." *College Composition and Communication* 51.4 (June 2000): 560–88.

———. "Something of Great Constancy: Storytelling, Story Writing, and Academic Literacy." *Attending to the Margins: Writing, Researching, and Teaching on the Front Lines*. Ed. Michelle Hall Kells and Valeria Balester. Portsmouth, NH: Boynton/Cook Heinemann, 1999: 97–113.

———. "When the Writing Test Fails: Assessing Assessment at an Urban College." *Writing in Multicultural Settings*. Ed. Carol Severino, Juan C. Guerra, and Johnnella E. Butler. New York: Modern Language Association, 1997: 307–324.

Greenberg, Karen. "The Politics of Basic Writing." *Journal of Basic Writing* 12.1 (1993): 64–71.

Healy, Patrick. "CUNY Plan to Phase Out Remediation Faces New Lawsuit." *The Chronicle of Higher Education* 18 Dec. 1998: A30.

Jones, William. "Basic Writing: Pushing Against Racism." *Journal of Basic Writing* 12.1 (1993): 72–80.

Kells, Michelle Hall, and Valerie Balester, eds. *Attending to the Margins: Writing, Researching, and Teaching on the Front Lines*. Portsmouth, NH: Boynton/Cook Heinemann, 1999.

Lewiecki-Wilson, Cynthia, and Jeff Sommers. "Professing at the Fault Lines: Composition at Open Admissions Institutions." *College Composition and Communication* 50.3 (1999): 438–62.

Lu, Min-Zhan, and Bruce Horner. "Expectations, Interpretations and Contributions of Basic Writing." *Journal of Basic Writing* 19.1 (2000): 43–52.

Mutnick, Deborah. *Writing in an Alien World: Basic Writing and the Struggle for Equality in Higher Education*. Portsmouth, NH: Boynton/Cook Heinemann, 1996.

Pratt, Mary Louise. "Arts of the Contact Zone." *Profession* 91 (1991): 33–40.

Rodby, Judith, and Tom Fox. "Basic Work and Material Acts: The Ironies, Discrepancies, and Disjunctures of Basic Writing and Mainstreaming." *Journal of Basic Writing* 19.1 (2000): 84–99.

Scott, Jerrie Cobb. "Literacies and Deficits Revisited." *Journal of Basic Writing* 12.1 (1993): 46–56.

Scribner, Sylvia, and Michael Cole. *The Psychology of Literacy.* Cambridge: Harvard UP, 1981.

Shaughnessy, Mina. *Errors and Expectations.* New York: Oxford UP, 1977.

Shor, Ira. "Our Apartheid: Writing Instruction and Inequality." *Journal of Basic Writing* 16.1 (1997): 91–104.

Sternglass, Marilyn. *Time to Know Them: A Longitudinal Study of Writing and Learning at the College Level.* Mahwah, NJ: Lawrence Erlbaum Associates, 1997.

Troyka, Lynne Quitman. "Defining Basic Writing in Context." *A Sourcebook for Basic Writing Teachers.* Ed. Theresa Enos. New York: Random House, 1987.

White, Edward M. "An Apologia for the Timed Impromptu Essay Test." *College Composition and Communication* 46 (1995): 30–45.

Wiener, Harvey S. "The Attack on Basic Writing—And After." *Journal of Basic Writing* 17.1 (1998): (96–103).

Wright, Scott. W. "The Ill-Prepared and the Ill-Informed." *Black Issues in Higher Education* 15.1 (1998): 12.

"Writing Assessment: A Position Statement." Conference on College Composition and Communication Online. URL: http://www.ncte.org/ccc/ex.html (2 May 2000).

I

The Controversy Surrounding Mainstreaming: Theory, Politics, and Practice

Revisiting the Importance of Placement and Basic Studies: Evidence of Success[1]

Edward M. White
University of Arizona

American education is subject to two contrasting underlying motifs: egalitarianism, the argument that everyone should have opportunities for success, and elitism, the restriction of opportunities to the most "deserving"—which often means to those from a relatively privileged home. At different times, one or the other motif is dominant. The social forces of the 1960s, which led to open enrollment at The City University of New York, for example, produced a generation of egalitarian policies in higher education in general and in writing programs in particular. As we move into a new century, we seem to be cycling back into a time of elitism. Those of us concerned about preserving the opportunities newly opened to the poor and to racial minorities had best prepare arguments to defend these gains against both well-meaning academics arguing for a new elitism and less well-intentioned legislatures and governing boards.

The signs of what I am calling the "new elitism" are everywhere. Budget cuts are the most obvious, and public higher education began suffering these cuts in the last decades of the twentieth century, as competition for tax money increased. But even when budget problems for the states eased, conservative legislatures seemed determined to keep the pressure on higher education, particularly in relation to admission of those not conventionally prepared. In California, for example, the legislature resolved in the mid-1990s to make up the decline in state support for public higher education by raising tuition gradually to one third of the actual costs of instruction—a move which early on caused an absolute drop in student enrollment. [Lavin

19

and Hyllegard report a similar effect at The City University of New York (210).] Although more recent legislative action has backed away from this harsh policy, The California State University remains under legislative mandate to reduce the percentage of those receiving extra help (popularly called "remediation") from approximately 50% to 10% of the entering class. The university campuses of The City University of New York are also being required to cut back or even eliminate the support programs that a dedicated faculty has developed over three decades. Every state has its own horror story, with education perceived by political bodies as an expense rather than an investment, as a personal privilege rather than a public good. Faced with declining enrollments along with tightened budgets, many faculties react by seeking to restrict enrollments to the best-prepared students—further limiting the chances of the underprivileged, already hurt by the increased costs. Thus, with some unintended irony, largely liberal and well-meaning faculties seeking to preserve institutional quality wind up allied to governing bodies intending to restrict the hesitant welcome that has been offered to those whom Patricia Cross has called the "new students."

College and university writing programs are on the front lines of this conflict, because their basic purpose is to induct entering students into the discourse community of higher education. These programs have served both egalitarianism and elitism in their turns. Since the first English Placement Test and required freshman course were developed by Harvard in the 1870s, English programs and assessments have been used to winnow out the "undeserving," often defined as those lacking the right dialect. During the 1950s, the huge freshman English programs of some public universities served in effect as a wing of the admissions office, eliminating those who could not measure up to standards. The intent of those programs was to see to it that those defined as unqualified would quietly disappear from the university—and that intent was met. But during more liberal periods, and during times when sufficient funding could be found, these tests and programs served to help underprepared students succeed instead of washing them out. Thus, the California State University English Placement Test, offered for the first time in 1978, was explicitly separated from the admissions process (only admitted students could take it) and directly connected to a basic writing program with special funding. These programs were explicitly devoted to helping their students succeed, and, as the data below show, their record at doing so has been remarkable.

Among those attacking placement tests and required freshman writing programs these days is an influential group of writing specialists who call themselves "new abolitionists"; they argue that the first-year writing course should not be required and that the course will be much improved if it survives as an elective. A sympathetic history of abolition by Robert Connors appears in *Composition in the 21st Century* (Bloom, Daiker, and White); powerful arguments for it by Sharon Crowley in *Pretext* in 1991 and in *JAC* in 1995 summarize the modern case. Less prominent writing program administrators on the WPA e-mail computer network are widely sympathetic with abolitionism, despite its implications for their jobs. Neither Connors nor Crowley (nor most writing program administrators) consider themselves elitists; Crowley in particular shudders to think herself associated with them. Her 1995 article problematizes the concept of student "need" for a writing course and defends her position, partly on the basis of lack of clear definition and empirical evidence: "It is very difficult to contest it without being written off as either an elitist, a troublemaker, or an insensitive curmudgeon. This is particularly frustrating because support for the claim is virtually unarticulated: no empirical studies have ever been done to test it, and historical research reveals reiterated but unsubstantiated statements of it" ("Composition's Ethic" 234–5). Arguments for abolition are based on genuine curricular concerns, sympathy for students forced to take "the universal course" for vague reasons, and deeply-felt faculty interests, whereas arguments for maintaining the required course have been muted. Unfortunately, until recently, Crowley has been right about the claim that the first-year writing course meets student needs; there has been little published evidence to show that the course does any good for students or that placement, with its negative labeling of those with low scores, actually helps students succeed. Meanwhile, the required course leads to detrimental labor practices on the part of many universities, creating a subclass of teachers with few privileges, low pay, and no chance of tenure or advancement. The new abolitionists argue that if the whole business became elective, students would be motivated to learn and the course would lose its curse as a dreary place for teachers and students to put in wasted time. Complaints that such a change would have drastic effects on English graduate students are dismissed as blatant, even hypocritical disciplinary self-interest at the expense of undergraduates, as long as there is no evidence that the course helps students succeed.

There are, of course, many claimed advantages for the required freshman course: the need to induct first-year students into the higher education discourse community, the discussion of ideas and attention to student performance and student individuality that are common in relatively small classes, the improvements in student writing ability that every teacher observes in strong as well as weak students, and so on. And there are also many claimed advantages from placement testing designed to allow students to enter the composition program in a course that will give them a good chance of success. It is now time to dismiss the claim that no evidence is available to support the value of remedial/developmental programs, because recently considerable evidence has been accumulating to demonstrate their success.

Three studies made available since the data in this chapter were first published in the *Journal of Basic Writing* in 1995 (White) have presented the kind of data-based arguments that Crowley was asking for. In 1997, Richard Haswell prepared a bibliography of 49 quantitative studies to support the developmental approach to writing instruction he takes in *Gaining Ground in College Writing* (1991). In 1997, Marilyn Sternglass published an elaborate case study, showing the gains made by her small sample of students from The City University of New York. Her plea for providing help for underprepared students, based on her qualitative research, is powerful:

> As the title of this book, *Time to Know Them*, suggests, students must not be judged on their early accomplishments (or lack of them) in the academic setting. Consideration must be given to their previous preparation for academic demands, their experience with the formal language and thinking required in the college setting, and, yes, the other demands being made on them in their complex lives. This latter factor is crucial if economically less well-off students are to have a chance to succeed. I am not arguing here for any lowering of standards but instead for the recognition that either additional financial resources have to be supplied so that students can do their best work without having to choose between eating and learning, or else the colleges and universities must be more hospitable to part-time schedules, offering required courses at times of the day to accommodate working schedules. For students like those pictured in this chapter, the college experience and gaining a professional education were their whole life. Such individuals should be valued, encouraged, and honored through societal policies. (293–4)

Although the Sternglass study presents in-depth findings from nine case studies, an authoritative study published in 1998 by Clifford Adelman, a senior analyst in the United States Department of Education, attempts to give a national portrait. His study became part of a volume published the same year by the Institute of Higher Education Policy. Entitled *College Remediation: What It Is, What It Costs, What's at Stake* (Phipps), this volume analyzes a mass of data on the high school graduating class of 1982. The document's conclusion is that "These data seem to indicate that remediation is, in fact, quite effective at improving the chances of collegiate success for underprepared students" (11).

Those arguments and studies have not convinced those under the sway of the new elitism and its (however unintended) theorists, the new abolitionists. They continue to see the first-year college writing course as dominated by trivializing placement tests, poorly trained and rewarded staff, and unprofessional remedial programs. Even though the new abolitionists will admit that pressures from the increasing number of professionals in composition studies and from the WPA have brought about some improvement in the situation, institutional pressures in American colleges and universities, the argument goes, will never allow first-year writing courses to live up to their claims.

Nonetheless, if faculty and socially aware administrators could be persuaded that the required course and responsible placement testing do in fact help underprivileged students succeed, they would be less likely to join those seeking to limit opportunity for them. These are the students for whom required placement and the required freshman course are most valuable, for they are most in need of guidance and support and most unlikely to take writing courses they fear will confirm their inadequacy (if the program is not required).

This chapter focuses specifically on the role of placement testing and instruction for students with the weakest preparation in writing, those low-scoring students most likely to disappear from higher education as we move into what seems to be an elitist twenty-first century. By summarizing two large-scale studies showing their importance for students most likely to drop out of higher education, I intend to add to the evidence that placement and basic writing instruction have a powerful positive influence on the retention of students with weak preparation for college. I am persuaded that we must attempt to preserve and improve these programs if we are concerned about keeping the "new students" in colleges and universities.

This chapter is based on two sets of studies: a series of follow-up studies of fall 1978 first-time freshmen, produced by the Institutional Research Office of The California State University (CSU) from March 1980 to March 1982, and a series of reports analyzing a four-semester overview conducted by the New Jersey Basic Skills Council, fall 1984 to spring 1989. As the data show, the effect of a placement program followed by a careful instructional program is to allow many students who would otherwise leave school to continue successfully in the university.

THE CALIFORNIA STATE UNIVERSITY STUDIES[2]

The last of five studies prepared by the Division of Institutional Research of the CSU Chancellor's Office is dated March 1982; it presents data compiled $2\frac{1}{2}$ years after the study population of fall 1978 freshmen entered the multicampus system. The report notes "that marked differences in continuation exist among groups of students depending upon their participation in the testing program and their resultant test performance" (2). As Table 2.1 shows, of those who did not take the English Placement Test (EPT), despite much urging, only 78.7% remained in school the following spring; the basic writing group, those scoring at or below 150, continued at a 90.0% rate. When the data are compiled in Spring 1981, $2\frac{1}{2}$ years later, this difference increases: EPT nonparticipants continue at only 37.8%, whereas 51.8% of the basic writing group are still at the university. The continuation difference between the basic writing group and those scoring above 150 is much smaller.

There are several ways to interpret these data. We could hypothesize that students who do not participate in the placement program are less motivated and hence more likely to drop out of school than those who do participate.

TABLE 2.1
Continuation by CSU EPT Participation Fall 1978 to Spring 1981

All Students	Nonparticipant	Score < 150	Score > 150	
Fall 1978—N	1412	1156	1203	3771
Percent continuation				
To spring 1979	78.7	90.0	92.9	86.7
To fall 1979	57.0	73.1	78.3	68.7
To spring 1980	50.0	65.7	72.1	61.8
To fall 1980	40.2	55.4	60.7	51.4
To spring 1981	37.8	51.8	57.8	48.5

(Fortunately for this study, though not for the students involved, the compulsions to participate were not as effective as intended.) There are, of course, many reasons for students to leave school besides inadequate writing ability. Nonetheless, it is striking that the basic writing students, those with low EPT scores and hence weak preparation for college writing, continue at only a 6% lower rate than the high-scoring group and at 3.3% above the average of all students. Placement program participation is clearly a significant factor in continuation in college for students with low EPT scores.

Even more startling is the relation between participation in the EPT and participation in a basic writing instructional program. I should note here that until the placement program began, the CSU was not authorized to offer writing courses below the regular freshman level. This did not mean that no help at all was provided to students with writing difficulties; rather, whatever help that was offered informally by a sympathetic and socially aware faculty had to be disguised and bootlegged—and hence tended to be innovative. With the inauguration of the placement program, special funds became available to support such programs. My perception of the curricular results of this historical oddity is that it had strongly positive effects. No entrenched low-quality "remedial" programs were in place, no undertrained and overworked teachers of such courses were on hand, and few bad rumors of "bonehead" courses existed on the student grapevine. Thus, the English faculties of the CSU campuses were in a position to institute a wide variety of enterprising and useful basic writing programs, including intensive coursework, supplemental mini-courses, and computer-assisted tutorials in a newly supportive environment in 1978. One sign of this vigor is that an estimated 146 students of those participating in the program who passed the placement test nonetheless took a basic writing course; this group, represented by 25 in

TABLE 2.2
Continuation of Fall 1978 First-Time Freshmen Who Took a
Remedial Writing Course Fall 1978 to Spring 1981

All Students	Nonparticipant	Score < 150	Score > 150	
Fall 1978—N	82	209	25	316
Percent continuation				
To spring 1979	87.8	93.3	96.0	92.1
To fall 1979	69.5	78.0	92.0	76.9
To spring 1980	59.8	67.9	84.0	67.1
To fall 1980	43.9	54.1	72.0	52.8
To spring 1981	39.0	52.6	64.0	50.0

the 1981 study sample, had the highest persistence rate of all: 96% in spring 1979 and 64% in spring 1981 (Table 2.2).

Campus differences in the data are significant, but difficult to interpret. They relate in part to differences in the quality and efficacy of the basic writing programs, but many other reasons cause students to drop out or transfer from one institution to another (the study does not distinguish between these two different kinds of events). One campus of the CSU showed a decline of over 46 percentage points in the continuation rate of nonparticipants from spring 1979 to spring 1981, whereas a different campus (in a much more attractive geographic location) showed a decline of only 29 percentage points. On four large campuses (Fresno, Long Beach, Pomona, and San Francisco) the five-term continuation rate for the low-scoring group after completing basic writing instruction actually exceeded that of the high-scoring group.

THE NEW JERSEY BASIC SKILLS COUNCIL STUDY[2]

New Jersey began its assessment and remedial/developmental programs about the same time California did and in part modeled its assessment design on the California program. But there are some important differences between the dimensions of the two statewide programs. Whereas the California program was limited to students admitted to one of the (then) 19 CSU campuses (the middle tier of public higher education, bracketed by the University of California and the California Community Colleges), the

New Jersey program encompassed all public colleges and universities and included reading and mathematics as well as writing. Thus, the New Jersey program evaluation considers 115 different programs at 31 different institutions, ranging from small county colleges to the flagship state university.

Despite these differences, the findings of the New Jersey studies are remarkably similar to those of the California studies. The three most recent reports are dated December 1988 ("Effectiveness of Remedial Programs in Public Colleges and Universities: Fall 1984–Spring 1986"), November 1991 ("Effectiveness of Remedial Programs in Public Colleges and Universities: Fall 1987–Spring 1989"), and January 15, 1992 ("Memorandum to Members, Board of Higher Education"). The most recent memorandum states that "the outcomes data indicate that on a system-wide level, remedial instruction is clearly providing the opportunity for thousands of underprepared students to succeed at college level work" (2).

The reports deal with many areas of statewide concern (such as policy administration and placement criteria) that are not directly of concern here. But the researchers also report on what they call "remedial program outcomes" and "subsequent academic performance" at the system level, issues exactly parallel to those of the California studies. The data show a high level of compliance with placement testing and of acceptance of what the report calls "remedial placement": 95% of the designated full-time students were "enrolled in needed remediation by their colleges within two semesters" (1992, 6) and 74% completed all such requirements. Thus, the New Jersey data do not have much to say about nonparticipants in the program but rather compare those defined by testing as "remedial" and "nonremedial"— groups parallel to the low- and high-scoring groups in California.

The four-semester study of the fall 1987 cohort shows that "66 percent of the full-time students who completed remediation were retained compared with 71 percent of the students who did not need remediation" (6)—a 5% difference, very close to the 6% difference in the California data. Again, as in California, the comparison between those who did and did not complete the basic writing program was dramatic, a 43% difference: "For students who did not complete writing remediation, however, the fourth semester retention rate was only 23 percent" (6).

The most complete data on writing placement are contained in the study of over 10,000 fall 1984–spring 1986 students. At the county colleges, 37% of the full-time students (5,700) and 31% of the part-time students (2,055) were identified for "writing remediation" (1988, 178). At the state colleges, 31% of the full-time students (2,226) and 29% of the part-timers (367) were identified for remediation. At the Rutgers colleges, 15% of the full-timers (789) and 13% of the part- timers (14) were so identified. Almost all of these students were enrolled in the basic writing courses provided for them, and about three quarters of them completed the sequence. When the researchers compared the retention rates of the low-scoring group that completed the coursework to the high-scoring group not required to take this coursework, "students who completed remediation exceeded their non-remedial peers by one percentage point (64 percent vs. 63 percent) statewide" (178). As in California, identified students who do not complete the basic writing courses leave school at a much higher rate; their 19% retention rate was more than three times lower than the nonremedial students. The conclusion is compelling: "There is a clear, positive relationship between completing remedial writing and staying in college" (178).

CONCLUSIONS

We must be careful about generalizing from the California and New Jersey programs, both of which have similar well-designed placement instruments and an energetic faculty committed to assisting low-scoring students with their writing. In e-mail conversations on the Writing Program Administrators computer network, informal reports on the subject show that we can expect variation in persistence data depending on variations in campus, testing, and instruction. For example, William Condon (1994) noted that students in a foundational course in composition at Arkansas Tech "persisted at a higher rate (roughly 75 percent as opposed to the norm of 65 percent for other students)." But on the same day, Frank Sullivan wrote about a study at Temple University of the 1978 cohort which found that "placement into basic writing, on average, does not seem to affect student retention" (1994). All placement instruments are not created equal nor are all basic writing programs equally effective. Nonetheless, the California and New Jersey studies provide compelling evidence of what can be done to help low-scoring students remain in college. The remarkable similarity of the persistence findings despite vast differences in scope, geography, and level of institution suggests some stability of data and potential replicability.

At this writing, both of these programs are victims of political and economic attack; the New Jersey program is but a memory and the California program is barely surviving. Expensive placement testing—and good placement is not cheap—is an inviting target for budget-cutting, and expensive basic writing instruction—which requires small class size and trained faculty—has few powerful defenders in the administrative meetings allocating less money for teaching. As in other political settings, the largely unrepresented underprivileged become an easy mark, and the resurging elitism in the faculties would just as soon be rid of the troublesome students that basic writing programs keep in school.

Those of us concerned about preserving the hard-won higher education opportunities for the new students may not be able to stem the elitist tide, at least not immediately. But we can present the data and the arguments for basic writing programs and force those opposing them to confront the social biases they are endorsing. The argument that our programs do not work is baseless, as other studies and the California and New Jersey data show; given adequate support, we can help most low-scoring students succeed.

NOTES

[1]This article appeared in a slightly different form in the *Journal of Basic Writing* 14 (1995): 75–84, published by The City University of New York, 555 West 57th Street, Room 1601, NY, NY 10019.

[2]The divisions and offices that produced the data used in this chapter no longer exist, so it may be difficult for researchers to obtain copies of the reports cited here. For the California reports, one can write to the Office of Analytic Studies, The California State University, 400 Golden Shore, Long Beach, CA 90802-4275 or to the Office of Systemwide Testing, California State University, Fresno, CA 93740-0354. The New Jersey data may possibly be found at the Board of Higher Education, 20 W. State Street–CN 542, Trenton, NJ 08625.

WORKS CITED

Adelman, Clifford. "The Kiss of Death? An Alternative View of College Remediation." *National Crosstalk*. Vol. 6.3. San Jose: National Center for Public Policy and Higher Education, 1998.

Bloom, Lynn Z., Donald A. Daiker, and Edward M. White. *Composition in the 21st Century: Crisis and Change*. Carbondale, IL: Southern Illinois UP, 1996.

California State University Studies. See Note 1.

Condon, William. Qtd. from e-mail (26 Sept. 1994).

Crowley, Sharon. "A Personal Essay on Freshman English." *Pretext* 12.3-4 (1991): 156–76.

———. "Composition's Ethic of Service, the Universal Requirement, and the Discourse of Student Need." *JAC: A Journal of Composition Theory* 15.2 (1995): 227–39.

Haswell, Richard. "Gain in First-Year Composition: The Empirical Record." <ftp://ftp.csd.uwm.edu/pub/sands/gain.doc>. Sept. 30, 1997.

Lavin, David, and David Hyllegard. *Changing the Odds*. New Haven: Yale UP, 1996.

New Jersey Basic Skills Council Study. See Note 1.

Phipps, Ronald, ed. *College Remediation: What It Is, What It Costs, What's at Stake*. The Institute for Higher Education Policy, Washington, DC, 1998.

Sternglass, Marilyn. *Time to Know Them: A Longitudinal Study of Writing and Learning at the College Level*. Mahwah, NJ: Lawrence Erlbaum Associates, 1997.

Sullivan, Frank. Qtd. from e-mail (26 Sept. 1994).

White, Edward M. "The Importance of Placement and Basic Studies: Helping Students Succeed Under the New Elitism." *Journal of Basic Writing* 14.2 (1995): 75–84.

CHAPTER THREE

Errors and Economics: Inequality Breeds Remediation

Ira Shor

Graduate School, City University of New York

It is the vanity of educators that they shape the education system to their preferred image. They may not be without influence but the decisive force is the economic system.

—John Kenneth Galbraith, *The New Industrial State* (238)

English teachers are inclined to exaggerate the seriousness of error. Since the birth of the composition course in American education, the English teacher has been viewed as the custodian of "refined" usage ... This emphasis upon propriety in the interest not of communication but of status has narrowed and debased the teaching of writing ....

—Mina Shaughnessy, *Errors and Expectations* (120)

My daily life as a teacher confronts me with young men and women who have had language and literature used against them, to keep them in their place, to mystify, to bully, to make them feel powerless.

—Adrienne Rich, "Teaching Language in Open Admissions."
On Lies, Secrets, and Silences (63)

Empowerment does not come with language; rather, language reflects power.

—Frank Smith, *Whose Language? What Power?* (1)

Is anyone surprised to learn that first-year college writing has provoked a long "tradition of complaint" as Leonard Greenbaum called it some thirty years back? One early complaint came in 1912 from the first President of the NCTE, Edwin Hopkins. Unhappy with the workloads of writing teachers, Hopkins entitled his lead article in the premier issue of *The English Journal*, "Can Good Composition Teaching Be Done Under Present Conditions?" He answered his own title question with a single word that began his essay: "No." Unfortunately, Hopkins's complaint was never resolved, insofar as "overwork/underpay" still dominate the field, which began in the 1880s with writing teachers "oppressed, badly paid, ill-used, and secretly despised" (Connors "Overwork/Underpay" 108). On this cracked foundation, a formidable empire of writing instruction grew, with Harvard first imposing a written entrance exam in 1874 (failed by half the students who took it), first offering freshman comp in 1885 (which became the only required course there by 1897), and first recording a "literacy crisis" in 1894 (when Harvard student writing was assessed after a decade of comp) (Berlin, *Writing Instruction*; Ohmann, 1995)

In this chapter, I argue that the tradition of complaint emerges from social contradictions undermining the majority of writing students and teachers. My argument takes Galbraith's advice seriously, that the economy drives educational policies, practices, conflicts, and outcomes. To connect writing instruction to economics, I make four claims about the traditional language arts dominating mass education in the past century:

1. Writing instruction's focus on correct usage and academic discourse actually represents a political process where the social construction of people and the larger culture is at stake.
2. Writing instruction's vast and contentious terrain is dominated by practices that primarily serve the needs of an elite and not the majority of students and teachers despite resistance to and innovation against the predominant "refined usage" paradigm.
3. Writing instruction's social function is to help reproduce inequality, which requires mass failure to preserve the hierarchies now in place.
4. Writing instruction's failures are actually it's successes, insofar as mass miseducation maintains the unequal system that originated, finances, and supervises composition, basic writing, and the testing regimes that drive their enrollments.

Consider, first, the vast national immersion in language instruction. As important developmental experiences, language arts are required from elementary grades through college. This long-term instruction in the "correct use" of language helps shape how students and teachers see the world and act in it. In this regard, James A. Berlin ("Contemporary Composition") proposed that writing instruction was actually about socialization though apparently about linguistic skills: "To teach writing is to argue for a version of the world . . . [I]n teaching writing we are tacitly teaching a version of reality and the student's place and mode of operation in it." (766) Berlin (*Composition in Context*) put composition inside the socializing effects of curriculum in general: "A college curriculum is a device for encouraging the production of a certain kind of graduate, in effect a certain kind of person. In directing what courses will be taken and in what order, the curriculum undertakes the creation of consciousness" (46). To Berlin, a writing curriculum connected teachers and students with social forces in the larger culture beyond the classroom. Yet, although every curriculum directs student development, and no pedagogy can be neutral, the outcomes of formal instruction are limited by the degree of student resistance. Some of the resistance operating in classrooms was examined with thick description in two books of mine, *Empowering Education* and *When Students Have Power*. What I focus on here is the social context of basic writing (BW) and regular comp to account for the long tradition of complaint dogging both.

STARTING FROM THE BOTTOM

To begin this account of writing instruction's contradictions, I think of an old Yiddish proverb: "With one *tuchas* [behind], you can't dance at two weddings." Mainstream writing instruction is caught in this dilemma, trying to dance at two weddings (two life stories) at the same time with one *tuchas:* the upbeat story of opportunity and success for all through education and literacy vs. the downbeat story of unequal schooling and lesser outcomes for the majority. Literacy and schooling are officially promoted as ladders to learning and success but are unequally delivered as roads to very different lives depending on a student's race, gender, and social class (Bowles and Gintis; Brint and Karabel). Mass education is miseducation for most students who come from non-elite backgrounds. (Almost 60% of American families live on $50,000 or less each year; half live on less than $42,300, according to the U.S. Bureau of the Census, Tables 745, 746, 748, and 749.) Underachievement is the outcome of underinvestment in the inferior schools and colleges set aside for this majority of students. For example, public schools have a higher teacher–student ratio than do private ones (*Digest of Education Statistics*, Table 64). Public 2-year colleges spend about $13,000/year less on each student than do public 4-year campuses; private 4-year colleges spend about $8,000/year more on each student than do public senior colleges (*Digest of Education Statistics*, Table 336). Further, the lower a student's family income and the darker the skin, the more likely she or he will take more than one remedial course and enroll at an underfunded community college sometimes promoted as a "career palace" or as "democracy's open door," but where academic culture marginalizes student culture, keeping subordinate groups in their place, as Adrienne Rich suggested earlier (see also Cross; Cohen and Brawer; Dougherty).

Put another way, language instruction is one means among many through which inequality reproduces itself. Formal education in general and mainstream writing classes in particular are cultural practices that attempt to fit students and teachers into the status quo, to develop our cooperation with the way things are, to accommodate us to the unequal society already in place. Because "culture" is not "nature," human society must be built daily by human action. Culture and people do not grow by themselves, like trees or weeds, but must be socially constructed through everyday experiences like schooling. This cultural construction is especially contentious in systems with glaring inequities among races, genders, ethnic groups, and social classes. Experienced daily as as a whole way of life, the predominant culture has been referred to as "hegemony" by Antonio Gramsci. Raymond Williams described hegemony as a process whose central dynamic is renewal of the status quo in the face of resistance to it:

> A lived hegemony is always a process. It is not, except analytically, a system or a structure. It is a realized complex of experiences, relationships, and activities, with specific and changing pressures and limits. . . . Moreover (and this is crucial, reminding us of the necessary thrust of the concept), it does not just passively exist as a form of dominance. It has to be continually renewed, recreated, defended, and modified. It is also continually resisted, limited, altered, challenged by pressures not all its own. (112)

In constructing and defending itself every day, the dominant way of life certainly does not start from scratch, but rather from cultural assets and liabilities accumulated by managing the order of things over a long period of time. Writing classes are one of these assets or tools, a technology for human development also called "cultural action" by Paulo Freire. From a Freirean point of view, the issue is "cultural action for domination" vs. "cultural action for freedom." In this chapter, I argue that the field of writing instruction has served primarily as cultural action for domination though student sabotage and counterhegemonic pedagogies have resisted the status quo. That status quo has a political stake in traditional language instruction, a stake which Robert Pattison defined as increasing the authority-dependence of students: "The teaching of correct written form has for the state the collateral advantage that, besides creating a generally intelligible medium of communication free of ambiguity, it inspires in the learner respect for authority" (65). Respect for top-down authority—sometimes called "the hidden curriculum" (Anyon "Social Class")—is an affective goal of writing classes based in correct usage.

Now, all teachers, traditional or critical, face the problem of establishing their authority in class. However, critical teachers try to avoid the hidden curriculum by foregrounding power issues for negotiation rather than by simply assuming unilateral authority. They attempt to share authority to whatever extent possible (Shor, *When Students Have Power*; Tayko and Tassoni). A power-sharing pedagogy is certainly more democratic than one with top-down authority. But, power in every setting is affected by gender, age, and race, among other factors, because inequality means that men, older folks, and White people carry more authority into class than do women, younger instructors, and minorities. On campus, for example, a tenured White male professor will most likely have an easier time asserting authority or distributing it than will a Black female adjunct under 30. With these gender, age, and racial caveats in mind, I agree with Pattison that emphasizing correct usage represents an effort to extend dominant authority, which is neither easily imposed from the top nor simply embraced at the bottom, as Noelle Bisseret noted in her study of class and language:

> Dominant and dominated languages are the inevitable result of the existing social system but also the scene of a power struggle. Pejorative words of popular origin which designate the act of talking ("to rattle on," "to jabber") allow one to suppose that words are suspected by the dominated. They unconsciously know that the dominant impose their own definitions of the world order through the totality of their practices, including verbal practices, and thereby justify their power. (86)

Language practices used to justify authority is one way to understand the spread of testing and remediation since the 1970s. The expansion of official assessment and basic writing in this period has been part of what I call "the conservative restoration" in school and society, a time when the status quo took the offensive to recover its authority after the protest culture of the 1960s diminished it (Shor, *Culture Wars*). While championing traditional values, restoration policies in the past few decades produced a substantial widening of the income and wealth gaps between the top, middle, and bottom sectors of the population (U.S. Bureau of the Census, Table 747). Mass education, too, from kindergarten to college, became a battleground of restoration (Berliner and Biddle), because the egalitarian 1960s challenged the routine inequities producing miseducation for the majority of students.

Mass miseducation, I am arguing here, is an unavoidable outcome of any system based on inequality. Unequal systems cannot produce a mass of high-achieving, critically literate students because too few resources are invested in non-elite development, because too few good jobs exist in the economy, and because a critical citizenry would question the merits of a society built on White supremacy, male supremacy, and corporate supremacy. Without a doubt, mass success in school and college would lead to an even greater output of higher degrees and higher wage expectations among minorities, women, and working students, which cannot be satisfied in a system that distributes limited rewards even though great wealth accumulates at the top (Wolff). From this point of view, then, I propose that the tradition of complaint against college composition's failures has largely missed the point because writing instruction has in fact been working from the top down to protect and to reproduce inequality but not from the bottom up to develop democracy and to level disparities. The dominant writing pedagogy for the last 100 years—refined usage (as Mina Shaughnessy observed previously), basic skills, grammar drills, abstract forms like the five-paragraph essay, literacy assessments like fill-in-the-blank tests and impromptu writing exams—is a curriculum to produce mass failure among students who are then declared "cultural deficits" needing more remediation and more testing. Mass education, then, structures failure into its outcomes and then transfers blame to the students ("blaming the victim").

In the mass miseducation of students, Shaughnessy's early doubts about dominant writing instruction anticipated the critique of "general writing skills instruction" (GWSI) emerging later in the field (Petraglia, *Reconceiving Writing*). Shaughnessy framed some doubts about traditional writing pedagogy in a 1970 City University of New York publication:

> The term "basic writing" implies that there is a place to begin learning to write, a foundation from which the many forms and styles of writing rise, and that a college student must control certain skills that are common to all writing before he takes on the special demands of a biology or literature or engineering class. I am not certain this is so. Some students learn how to write in strange ways. ("Some New Approaches" 103)

At the Harlem campus of the City College of New York in the heyday of Open Admissions, she went on to describe how one "weak" student followed an interest in medicine to do health research which led to a long report on Egyptian mummies. "The paper may not have satisfied a professor of medical history," Shaughnessy wrote, "but it produced more improvement in the student's writing than any assignments I could have devised" (103). Extending Shaughnessy's doubts, I would argue that if high achievement and critical literacy were desired outcomes, then a very different writing enterprise would occupy the center of composition, one not dominated by refined usage and GWSI (the notion that there are general writing skills that can be taught abstractly and then technically applied in other contexts—see

Agnew and McLaughlin for one study how "remediated" students were unable to transfer their skills to other courses). Instead, writing instruction for democracy (*Cultural Action for Freedom*, in Freire's terms) would be built around small classes for all, close mentoring, power-sharing, problem-posing, portfolio assessment, writing in meaningful contexts that connect the students' personal lives with academic and social contexts, interdisciplinary action projects, and inquiry into the gender, race, and class conditions of the students (Shor, *Empowering Education*; Shor and Pari). Finally, traditional writing classes focused on correct usage and general techniques fail to question the big picture they are situated in, that is, the grossly inequitable economy and its hierarchy of schools and campuses where a small number of students get lavish surroundings and lots of attention while the rest get crowded classes and meager facilities, demonstrating why family income is the most important factor determining who is most likely to graduate high school and college (Mortenson).

WHEN INEQUALITY RULES EDUCATION: THE SOCIAL FUNCTIONS OF FAILURE

Human beings generally prefer success over failure and feeling smart over feeling dumb. Given this routine human preference for doing well instead of doing badly, I would agree with Ted Sizer that persistent complaints about educational outcomes must be the fault of the structures we work in, not of the people who do the work (though structures persist only if we collaborate in enacting them every day). For the most part, the policies and operations of educational structures are the engines driving what teachers and students can accomplish, as Sizer suggested. At the root, the conditions for learning are the result of economic policies, according to Galbraith's opening thoughts given at the beginning of this chapter. In an unequal society where the majority experience is hostile to formal schooling, I am arguing, mass underachievement is neither an accurate measure of student competence nor an accidental outcome, but rather a structured result of education functioning to confirm inequality. In making this argument, I am not the first to forward such an analysis but follow a group of "revisionist" scholars whose work during and after the 1960s revaluated education as a product and preserver of an unequal status quo. Even before critical revisionists like Katz, Spring, Greer, and Bowles and Gintis gained attention, sociologist Burton Clark ("The Cooling-Out Function in Higher Education") offered his famous analysis of "cooling-out." Clark examined how an institution cooled-out students it construed as "latent terminals." In the community college he studied, Clark found an elaborate and unacknowledged cooling-out process downwardly managing student goals through testing, counseling, and courses:

> In one junior college, the initial move in a cooling-out process is pre-entrance testing; low scores on achievement tests lead poorly qualified students into remedial classes. Assignment to remedial work casts doubt and slows the student's movement into bona fide transfer courses. The remedial courses are, in effect, a subcollege. The student's achievement scores are made part of a counseling folder that will become increasingly significant to him. An objective record of ability and performance begins to accumulate. (Clark 572)

Note how entry-level assessment initiates cooling-out and how remediation continues the pressure on students to accept lesser options like vocational training or even dropping-out. In his study, Clark described cooling-out as a diversion of non-elite students away from upwardly mobile liberal arts. Later on, Clark ("The Cooling-Out Function Revisited") made peace with the dubious practice of cooling-out because he saw the mass denial of college degrees as necessary for stability in a system that promotes and limits success at the same time. Clark's accomodation to cooling-out was echoed in Brint and Karabel's critical study of mass higher education, *The Diverted Dream*:

> A more democratic community college would not, it should be emphasized, be a place where the "cooling-out" function has been abolished. As long as American society generates more ambition than its economic structure can absorb, the community college will be actively involved in channeling the aspirations of students away from four-year colleges and universities. Yet this said, there is something deeply troubling, especially in a society that prides itself on its openness, about the covertness of the cooling-out process as it now operates. (231)

Brint and Karabel called for "transparency" rather than subterfuge, suggesting that each college publish its attrition, transfer, and graduation rates so students know what to expect. This is a good idea but still too accomodating to the unequal provision for mass literacy, where the standard curriculum rewards the already-privileged and miseducates the majority.

In truth, the deterrent routine of cooling-out was established long before Clark named the practice. By 1900, colleges used first-year writing as a gatekeeper to university degrees. (Crowley "A Personal Essay"; "Composition's Ethic"). First-year courses evolved remedial and regular tracks, testing regimes and textbook protocols, and skill-based approaches to curriculum, producing the mass failure functional to a system that promises more opportunity than it delivers. To make matters only worse, the empire of first-year composition and basic writing not only "work" when they fail masses of students but also have been built through the gross labor inequity mentioned here, that is, the exploitation of adjunct writing teachers whose pay and stature are woefully below those of full-time faculty (Trainor and Godley; Schell) How did this enterprise pile up so much dirty laundry?

THE EMPIRE'S NEW CLOTHES: COLLEGE COMPOSITION AROUND 1885

The social context of writing programs helps explain why cooling-out has been the mass experience of education. Harvard's invention of first-year comp at the end of the nineteenth century fit the needs of the new industrial capitalism, according to Ohmann. Around 1885, when freshman comp was installed at Harvard and spreading nationwide, industrial output began exceeding agricultural production for the first time in the U.S. As factories led the accumulation of wealth, knowledge became essential to production and profit-making. New machines and processes were needed as well as new literacies for management, accounting, marketing, finance, and research. The growing production of college-educated professionals occurred at a time when skilled and unskilled labor were in great demand generally, despite boom and bust cycles, as millions of European immigrants were urged to relocate to the industrializing U.S. Sudden demands for labor and for new literacies are signs of an unstable status quo. As Gramsci (*Selections from the Prison Notebooks*) proposed, when power relations become insecure, questions of language often come to the fore because language protocols can help establish order and authority. Following Gramsci, Harvey Graff put literacy and schooling into the social context of establishing order:

> Especially with the transitions from preindustrial social orders based in rank and deference to the class societies of commercial and then factory capitalism, the integrating and hegemony-creating purposes of literacy provision through formal schooling only increased. Schooling, with its transmission of a morally-leavened and often qualitatively low levels of skills, became more and more a vital aspect of the maintenance of social stability, particularly during times of massive if confusing social and economic transformation.... Many persons, most prominently social and economic leaders and social reformers, grasped the uses of schooling and the vehicle of literacy for promoting the values, attitudes, and habits deemed essential to order.... (251)

Wild economic expansion places great stress on the status quo in many ways, including in production, communication, and labor supply. Just imagine the speed at which public schools and the new commerce-centered

universities were created from coast to coast in the tumultuous period between the Civil War and World War I. Expanding the output of college grads
to meet demands for professional labor, higher education had to admit students who did not fit the profile of previous cohorts, when campuses were
finishing schools for gentlemen and divines. The new question became: from
the nongentlemanly applicants seeking access, who should be allowed in
and how should they be monitored? Just imagine the speed with which
new curricula, admissions criteria, and graduation requirements were composed. In this age of ferocious cultural construction, the modern university
was born along with the modern corporation, scientific management, the
MLA, the AFL, the machine-gun, and mass-circulation magazines. In addition, an army of industrial labor was constructed from European immigrants
arriving year after year, their children absorbed into public schools charged
with Americanizing them. This was also the age in which Native Americans
were confined to impoverished reservations, their children subject to forced
Americanization at Indian Schools like the one in Carlisle, Pennsylvania,
where their long hair was cut off and their use of Indian tongues forbid-
den. In this time of compulsory acculturation, of headlong need to train
countless numbers of schoolteachers and professionals, of runaway industrial expansion and violent labor conflicts, freshman comp based in refined
usage displaced rhetoric based in oral argument as the center of collegiate
language arts. This happened because written forms of literacy became very
important to doing business and to sorting out the students who would be
trained for the new professions.

As Richard Ohmann put it, Harvard's innovation of freshman comp spread
like "kudzu" when universities began admitting more students to produce
a new professional-managerial class. Entrance exams and first-year writing courses became the premier linguistic gatekeepers. Sharon Crowley has
identified the upper-class bias of Harvard's universal comp requirement,
which began "as an attempt to certify that students who enrolled under the
new elective system were suitable 'Harvard men.' In other words, the universal requirement began as an instrument of exclusion" ("Response" 89).
This use of elite language for testing and instruction fortified top-down authority, enhancing the power of those in power to reproduce their power,
by setting the rules, by including some and excluding most. In Foucault's
terms, we could say that writing instruction was discovered then as a useful
regime of control. The regime of "first-year composition in English Departments" controlled the subject matter and the subject students, what would
be studied how and by whom. This story, told magisterially by Susan Miller,
reveals that "English" adopted canonic literature and literary scholarship as
its high-status bodies-of-knowledge, subordinating comp to the low-status
of language cop and "sorting machine." Performing well in writing classes
became the students' behavioral gate to upper-level courses leading to

degrees and professional jobs. I call this language policy "comp for containment, control, and capital growth," a tool that apparently produced the nation's first literacy crisis, at Harvard in 1894, mentioned earlier, when a board of overseers examined the Harvard students' writing (Ohmann, *Politics of Letters*).

ANOTHER CRISIS ERA: THE 1960S AND AFTER

Basic writing, in this story a junior sibling named by Shaughnessy, added an extra gate in front of the comp gate. From its origins as "remediation," BW blossomed into a specialized field during another age of instability, the 1960s and after, when corporate culture was shaken by mass movements against war, poverty, racism, and authoritarian education. After the rebellious 1960s, a key political project from the top down was restoring the power and prestige of shaken institutions—big business and the military, primarily (the "conservative restoration" mentioned previously). The dissident political climate of the 1960s was still circulating when authorities launched a number of initiatives in school and society. For example, around 1975, a national literacy crisis was declared despite the lack of evidence proving such a phenomenon (see chapter 3 of my book *Culture Wars*). Nevertheless, "the literacy crisis" became a media darling in the restoration press and among traditionalists in education (see the 8 Dec. 1975 *Newsweek* cover story, "Why Johnny Can't Write"), followed by an aggressive back-to-basics campaign and a broad expansion of required testing and remediation. In this context, the BW gate that grew beneath the comp gate functioned as an extra layer of management to reassert authority after an insurgent era had rolled back some campus requirements in first-year writing, among other gains.

As I am suggesting, at the time of BW's explosive birth in the 1970s, the status quo was under siege from below by protest movements whereas its job market was unable to absorb the mass of students from the baby boom generation then graduating college cohort by cohort. Short on jobs worthy of college grads, the economy could not deliver the good life that the American Dream promised from higher education. The output of college grads from the postwar baby boom was thus a second political crisis threatening to discredit the American system, on top of the first crisis caused by protest movements against the war in Vietnam and other injustices. While student marchers filled the streets, degreed candidates flooded a job market that began offering lower wages, contingent work, part-time employment, independent contracting, fewer fringe benefits, and irregular hours—not the expected payoff for a college degree. With the corporate economy and higher education developing in opposite directions in the 1970s and after—one downsizing, the other expanding—more "cooling-out" mechanisms were apparently needed to cope with the contradiction of too many educated people chasing too few good jobs. Cooling-out is useful at such moments because it transfers blame from the system to the individual, encouraging students to internalize fault, to blame themselves for their own failures, especially on entry exams and in first-year writing classes where their errors are legion and their usage not refined. Basic writing, the "subcollege" Clark saw emerging from remediation in the late 1950s, became a greatly expanded territory confining a new tribe of *remediants*, students constructed as cultural deficits (the "latent terminals" Clark encountered 20 years earlier) who would be detained in academic limbo, quarantined in a no-credit curricular reservation. At the heart of these complex maneuvers, the simple fact was that the new collegians encamped in BW were the wrong color and the wrong class, too dark and too low-income to get the same access to 4-year campuses and degrees enjoyed by an elite prior to 1970. The lower a student's family income, the more likely he or she is to attend an underfunded community college and/or be enrolled in remedial courses (Dougherty; U.S. Bureau of the Census, Table 319). For the non-elite, BW became a deterrent and a detention, a mechanism that slows progress toward graduation because students pay full tuition for less-than-full-credit courses that do not count toward the degree and stand in the way of taking regular classes.

This curricular deterrent to student success grew in an era characterized by development-in-decline, that is, when certain privileged sectors of society advanced while overall conditions degenerated. Privileged areas like technology, aerospace, the military, telecommunications, finance, ivy league campuses, pro sports, and upper-class life prospered in the conservative restoration after 1970, while the public sector decayed and while the majority experienced a stagnant or declining standard of living. Against the egalitarian 1960s, authorities in the recent conservative restoration pursued policies to enrich the rich and to empower the powerful, compelling average Americans to settle for less and to do more with less. In educational terms, "less" has meant budget cuts (even as the private sector experienced a boom) and bad-mouthing to undermine confidence in public schools (Berliner and Biddle). In the economy, "less" has meant higher taxes on working families thanks to contingent labor, stagnating wages, and corporate tax loopholes (Mishel, Bernstein, and Schmitt). In the family, less has meant less time for parents to spend with kids because of the longer work hours needed to make ends meet (Schor). Part-time jobs are less than full-time jobs, non-union labor is paid less than union work, and independent contracting is less secure than permanent staff positions. In language arts, BW is less than comp, below regular writing courses in the curricular hierarchy, often noncredit. The rise of BW fit an age when the status quo broadly disciplined the population, restoring traditional authority and its ability to generate inequality, with some disturbing consequences. For example, in the 1990s, students from the richest quartile of families were 10 times more likely to graduate college by age 24 than students from the bottom fourth whereas 20 years earlier, the difference was only four times as great, according to Mortenson.

As I mentioned, required remediation helps slow down student progress toward the bachelor's degree that brings higher wages in the job market. But, if BW is a subcomp gate that helps reduce college grads flooding the job market, BW (like comp) also depresses the wage package for teachers because first-year writing courses are typically taught by exploited (largely female) adjuncts, referred to previously. On the whole, then, the political economy of BW vis-a-vis the reproduction of inequality may be summarized like this: students pay rising tuition for required courses lowered in stature and emptied of credit, which delay and deter their progress toward the commercially valuable 4-year degree, thus reducing the output of college grads in a wage-depressing job market and expanding vulnerable contingent academic labor (unorganized writing teachers) who are overworked and underpaid (the infamous arrangement since 1880, according to Connors "Overwork/Underpay"). Such an arrangement simultaneously lowers the output of 4-year college grads and of PhDs (because overworked, underpaid adjuncts are typically graduate students who have too little free time and money to write their dissertations in a timely manner and thus qualify for the limited number of tenure-track jobs available). These economic functions of BW help ease the jobs crisis by holding down domestic wages at a time when teenage girls in Mexico work for about $1/hour (doing jobs for which the domestic rate is $8/hour or higher), when the daily wage in Haiti is about $2.40/day. With corporate America globalizing in search of cheap labor, with the top 1% now controlling a record 40% of the nation's wealth (Boutwell), higher education can destabilize the status quo if it produces too many deserving graduates in an American economy unwilling to pay them what they are worth. Basic writing, along with regular comp and entry-testing helps produce student failure that stabilizes and justifies economic inequality.

Some mainstream authorities themselves have looked through economic lenses and apparently saw alarming possibilities if millions of students graduated college only to end up underemployed. For example, the grave consequences of denying the American Dream to a generation of ambitious, protesting students were urgently on the minds of some top officials 25 years ago, as recorded by President Nixon's Commissioner of Education Sidney Marland (known then as "the father of career education"). At that early moment in the conservative restoration, the President asked Marland to come up with a major initiative in vocational education with no increase in the budget. Marland did so and wrote about it in his memoir and polemic, *Career Education*. In self-reported conversations with his boss at HEW, Secretary Elliot Richardson, Marland discussed his fears that underemployed college grads in the coming years might become even more radical, causing deeper political unrest because they could not get jobs equal to their credentials, a worry also expressed soon after by economist Richard Freeman in *The Overeducated American*. Try to imagine when the status quo was on the defensive, when corporate culture and conservative forces faced compelling need to restore their authority and to restrict activism in school and society (see Sklar on the influential Trilateral Commission of the 1970s, especially Section V on "Making Capitalist Democracy More Governable"). Then, imagine the declaration of a (fake) literacy crisis in the 1970s (when BW expanded), justifying stringent testing regimes, austere back-to-basics, and traditional core curricula imposed from the top down. Imagine a million protesters parading under Nixon's Watergate windows in Washington, and you can see the urgency of the moment for those besieged at the top. This state of siege against the status quo figured prominently in historian Elizabeth Fones-Wolf's account of that time:

> During the late sixties and early seventies, the probusiness environment constructed during the fifties came under siege. Social movements, including civil rights, environmentalism, and consumer and worker protection, arose—all of which threatened to place powerful constraints on business. . . . Beginning in the mid-seventies, threatened by shrinking profits and worried about the loss of public confidence, the business community remobilized in a fashion not seen since the fifties. (288)

The culture wars that followed this mobilization are now matters of record. Basic writing, "the literacy crisis," more testing, and back-to-basics were some results of this conservative offensive at a time of urgent restoration by the status quo.

CULTURE WARS: RESISTANCE FROM THE BOTTOM, RESTORATION FROM THE TOP

The insurgent 1960s focused a bright light on injustice in America, which never invested equally in all its children, not from the moment Horace Mann (Filler, *Horace Mann on the Crisis in Education*), in Massachusetts in the 1840s declared schooling as "the great equalizer (124)." Obviously, the open secret of American education is that children of poor and working families get far fewer resources at school and at home than do rich kids (something criticized more than 80 years ago by John Dewey in *Democracy and Education* and in 1991 by Jonathan Kozol in *Savage Inequalities*). Just compare the conditions of rural and inner-city schools to suburban ones. Just compare facilities in the nation's 1,200 public community colleges to the top 100 4-year campuses. If schools and colleges were in fact equalizers, what might we expect by now? More equality? As I cited earlier, despite rising educational achievement in the population since 1970, the wealth and income gap between rich, poor, and working families actually worsened (Mantsios; Holmes; Henwood). This inequality has racial and gender dimensions because minority families have a median income about $18,000/year less than that of White families (U.S. Bureau of the Census, Table 745); Blacks and Hispanics have nearly twice the unemployment rate of Whites (Bureau of Labor Statistics); twice as many White folks 25–29 hold 4-year degrees than do Blacks (Mortenson); women students are overrepresented in the lowest-paying college majors, professions, and doctoral fields whereas full-time women faculty earn about $10,000/year less than do men, and have a tenure rate about 20% lower than male colleagues (*Digest of Education Statistics*, Tables 235, 240, and 253). Greater access to college for women, minorities, and students from working families has yet to translate into economic equality.

In terms of access vs. inequality, I'm reminded here of an earlier insurgent period followed by another conservative restoration a century before recent events. David Tyack in *Turning Points in American Educational History* tells the story of a Northern woman who went South after the Civil War to teach freed slaves. In the Reconstruction Era until federal troops left the South in 1877, she had a chance to make a difference before White supremacy restored its sway. At that moment, the teacher was scorned by local White respectables for teaching "social equality" instead of sticking to the ABCs preferred by them for the new freedmen, now legally entitled to education. Before the War, it was a crime to teach slaves to read and write; White teachers were fined and literate slaves were beaten or worse (for a dramatization, see the film *Nightjohn*). Then, after the War, the defeat of the slavocracy created a democratic opening. To stop equality, White supremacists turned to lynching, to Jim Crow law enforcement, to sharecropping peonage, and other measures. Postbellum, unable to completely deny Blacks access to education, the Southern conservatives' preferred curriculum was the ABCs, as one way to limit the consequences of losing the Civil War. Apparently, the three Rs was the curriculum least threatening to the old order. Later, another study of Black access to education in the South, Gunnar Myrdal's *An American Dilemma*, examined Southern schools and noticed that Black students were being tracked into agricultural jobs (boys) and domestic service (girls) even though these labor markets were declining. They were being trained for jobs that were dying out. Myrdal noted that the dead-end curriculum for Black students was still very basic in their segregated schools (the three Rs and vocationalism, which Dewey criticized as a mass curriculum fortifying hierarchy and class divisions, in *Democracy and Education*). Some 40 years after Myrdal and 70 years after Dewey, John Goodlad's 8-year study *A Place Called School* found a similar racial inequity in curriculum access. Black and Latino students were overrepresented in training programs for the lowest-paying vocational careers. One of Goodlad's brilliant co-researchers, Jeannie Oakes, focused specifically on tracking. In *Keeping Track*, she described in some detail the basic skills/vocational sorting-out of students, noting the absence of research showing that tracking improves student learning. I have been arguing that research may not support the advantages of tracking (Welner and Oakes), but it remains a pervasive practice for political reasons related to inequality. Writing programs have been one instrument for constructing unequal outcomes through separate tracks for BW and regular comp.

Against my argument that BW tracks and deters students, some earnest colleagues defend BW as a sanctuary to protect students who would be thrown out of college even sooner if not for a sheltered program. Where is the evidence to support this shelter claim? Harvey Wiener, a BW supporter, has also called for research to document this assertion of BW's positive role. Like Wiener, also supporting college-level remediation, The Institute for Higher Education Policy found that even though a big chunk of freshmen (17%) took remedial writing courses in 1995, "Research regarding the effectiveness of remedial education has been sporadic, typically underfunded, and often inconclusive.... [T]here is a dearth of information regarding how well remedial students perform" (10). It should surprise no one that the Institute also found that wherever minority enrollments were high, remediation pass rates were low (4). In one attempt to research BW's effectiveness, Baker and Jolly failed to disaggregate their results for race, avoiding the thorniest issue of remediation, how it particularly targets non-White students for cooling-out, a reality documented by Agnew and McLaughlin in their look at the results of their BW program.

Still, many well-intentioned teachers stand behind this dubious shelter. Do these dedicated teachers conflate their own devotion to students with BW itself being a positive, democratizing force? We can be devoted to students while also criticizing BW (or even eliminating it). For example, consider Mike Rose's patient tutoring of his students at UCLA (*Lives on the Boundary*). His tutorial labor meant a lot to those students, but Mike is not a special advocate for BW, being rather critical of remediation: " ... the curriculum in developmental English breeds a deep social and intellectual isolation from print; it fosters attitudes and beliefs about written language that, more than anything, keeps students from becoming fully, richly literate" (211). Yet, others building the field, like Hunter College's testing-leader Karen Greenberg, stood by the benefits of BW. But, it was not helpful for BW advocates like Greenberg to argue that "36% of the students who graduated from Hunter within the last five years were students who completed basic writing courses.

Moreover, approximately 55% of the students who graduated from Hunter within eight years are basic writing 'graduates' " (69). These figures, unfortunately, do not prove the value of BW. What must be shown is that these Hunter students could not have graduated without BW. Was BW a curricular shelter essential to their graduation or was BW a detour in their progress toward a degree they could have gained sooner without remediation? This same question was not addressed 6 years later in Baker and Jolly's efforts to research BW's success. At the City University of New York, numbers of students are discouraged from continuing in college because they must take low-credit remedial courses taught by underpaid adjuncts (Pereira, Cobb, and Makoulis). Others were deterred by the unvalidated writing exam known as the CUNY Writing Assessment Test (Otheguy). These, it seems to me, are some of the hard issues BW advocates must face to justify the maintenance of a BW track beneath comp, along with the maintenance of costly testing/placement bureaucracies that centralize administrative control and abrogate faculty authority. (Outside testing drives curriculum and transfers power away from classrooms, teachers, and students, an unhealthy outcome if we want education for democracy.)

My questions here draw on Peter Dow Adams's research at his community college about students who evaded BW and succeeded in regular comp at a rate equal to or higher than those who took the remedial course. Mary Soliday and Barbara Gleason (see also Soliday) found similar results when they mainstreamed BW students into comp in an experimental project at City College (the oldest campus of the City University of NY): "An external reader's assessment of student portfolios demonstrates that remedial-placed students were competitive with college-level placed students at the end of the two-semester course.... [A] third of the time, readers judged the remedial-placed writers to have produced very good work; most of the time they judged this group [of mainstreamed BW students] to be good or average..." (64, 72). If most BW-designated students passed their enhanced, credit-bearing regular college writing course without first taking BW, why did they need to be tracked into BW in the first place? In this regard, the Pereira report at CUNY (cited previously) also questioned the tracking of students into BW because of the uncertain relationship between student test scores on entry exams and their subsequent academic performance: "... the data of this study have shown that freshmen are just as likely to pass regular courses as non-regular [remedial] courses. Thus, without supporting evidence (and we have always been without it), we are not in a good position to deny students access to regular courses based upon the assertion that their low scores on the basic skills tests will preclude their satisfactory completion of the regular courses" (Pereira, Cobb, and Makoulis 178). We do have to question the testing regimes that fill up BW classes if testing advocate Ed White joined Brian Huot to report a shocking 48% of colleges using SAT, ACT, or some other nonwriting short-answer test to assess writing (see also Glau for a program using ACT/SAT for placement). Another 49% use the notorious timed, impromptu essay graded on the 1–6 scale (like the CUNY WAT), which Peter Elbow and the late Alan Purves described as an invalid test of writing ability. I am reminded here of Mina Shaughnessy's comments on the anti-writing context of the timed impromptu: "Without strategies for generating real thought, without an audience he cares to write for, the writer must eke out his first sentence by means of redundancy and digression, strategies that inevitably disengage him from his grammatical intuition as well as his thought" (*Errors and Expectations* 82). High-stakes, one-shot writing exams violate the best things we have learned about effective writing processes in the last 30 years. Also, short-answer instruments discriminate against minorities, according to CCCC's "Writing Assessment: A Position Statement," which opposed the isolated conditions of impromptu exams: ". . . standardized tests, usually designed by large testing organizations, tend to be for accountability purposes, and when used to make statements about student learning, misrepresent disproportionately the skills and abilities of students of color" (433). Finally, Thomas L. Hilgers concluded that ". . . bad assessment is what gets most students labeled as 'basic writers.' Bad assessment drives the curriculum and the evaluation of most basic writing courses . . ." (69). I would add that instead of bogus testing and depressant remediation we need programs based in field projects and social contexts, which Lee Odell has argued for in "Basic Writing in Context: Rethinking Academic Literacy."

Can BW exist without bogus assessment? Alexander Astin commented on the arbitrary sorting-out of BW students: "Most remedial students turn out to be simply those who have the lowest scores on some sort of normative measurement—standardized tests, school grades, and the like. But where we draw the line is completely arbitrary: lowest quarter, lowest fifth, lowest 5 percent or what? Nobody knows" (quoted in Institute for Higher Education, *College Remediation Policy* 7). Astin also observed how variable the criteria are from campus to campus. Though arbitrary and inconsistent, such assessment is the cheapest ways to get the greatest control of teachers, students, and curriculum. To sum up, then, the assessment and tracking regimes represented by BW and comp comprise language policy for containing three things: first, the fiscal costs of mass higher education (while lavish funds are spent on elite campuses and affluent students); second, the political costs should non-elite students critically question the status quo, doing what Paulo Freire called critically "writing and reading the world"; and third, the economic and social costs of increasing the output of college grads whose aspiring numbers contradict a job market seeking cheap labor at home and abroad.

Yet, despite this, the Institute for Higher Education Policy still argued for the public benefits of maintaining college remediation. But the Institute based its claims in the general benefits for students of "going to college," not in the specific benefits of remediation itself (for which its own report could not find data) (19). This evasive argument essentially repeats the undocumented "shelter defense" of BW, that ending remediation means ending the special sanctuary of BW that protects weak students from swift exclusion or expulsion from college. Like many well-meaning BW supporters, the Institute cannot imagine college without remediation. Instead of recognizing breakthrough mainstreaming projects like those at City College or South Carolina or Chico State, the Institute falls back on soft avowals that remediation teaches "generalizable skills" (19) like writing and critical thinking, even though Mina Shaughnessy and others have questioned such a foundational notion for language arts (called GWSI earlier—general writing skills instruction).

As nonstop culture wars rage, writing teachers in the trenches have done heroic labor against the odds. I've seen their dedication while teaching BW at the City University of NY for 15 years. I still teach first-year comp at an urban working-class campus of CUNY, the College of Staten Island. My criticism of the history and politics of writing instruction is not a criticism of my colleagues, full-time or adjunct. To make better use of our professional talents and dedication, we could begin with Peter Elbow's ideas for restructuring writing courses (see *Composition in the 21st Century*). Basically, he recommends portfolio assessment to replace the bogus timed impromptu. He also proposes extended writing classes that would graduate students as they complete their course projects, not on a semester timetable. Peter Elbow endorses the mainstreaming experiments underway at South Carolina by Rhonda Grego and Nancy Thompson, who set up writing studios as peer-group tutorials connected to regular writing classes. For further alternatives to the dominant language arts now in place, I also recommend Petraglia's volume on GWSI (*Reconceiving Writing*), Horner and Lu's collected essays on BW (*Representing the "Other"*), John Mayher's award-winning critique of mainstream language arts and current-traditional rhetoric (*Uncommon Sense*), and Bruce Herzberg's report on service-learning at Bentley College ("Community Service and Critical Teaching"). The call to "weave" pedagogy and politics in examining writing instruction has come not only from Horner and Lu but also from Tom Fox ("Standards and Access") and from the collaborative work of Hull, Rose, Fraser, and Castellano.

In addition to setting BW and comp in their social contexts, we also need to revive the Wyoming initiative, to pick up where brave Jim Slevin, Sharon Crowley, and more recently Eileen Schell and Karen Thompson have brought us, in terms of exposing the shameful foundations of "English": the subordination of composition to literature, the denigration of teaching in favor of publication, the academy-wide exploitation of underpaid, overworked part-time instructors, and the higher workloads and lower funding accorded two-year campuses. As one initiative, I propose a "Labor Policy": "All positions in the field are designated full time, to be divided at any program only at the request of instructors themselves should any choose not to work full time. Split positions would carry full-time benefits even if some prefer less-than-full course loads." Regarding the costs of this Labor Policy, some may think that money does not exist to pay for it. Any who wonder where the money is should remember the vast surpluses now being amassed by government at all levels as well as the billions lost each year to corporate welfare and tax loopholes; also, look at the huge military budget in a time when the Cold War is over and no superpower threatens the U.S.; finally, writing teachers on each campus should find out how big a surplus their local BW and comp programs generate each year. First-year writing is a cash cow because full tuition is collected from students whereas part-time wages are paid to most teachers. No costly equipment is needed for writing instruction as is required in engineering labs or in nursing departments. Basic writing and comp are like the former colony of India, the jewel in the crown, a territory generating surplus wealth for the imperial metropoles of literature study, graduate seminars, and desk-potato administrators. In terms of enforcing the Labor Policy, I would suggest that any institution not complying be targeted with a "corporate campaign": high-profile negative publicity informing prospective students, teachers, and parents that this college's labor and language policies interfere with good teaching and learning. The time to take this kind of action is long overdue. Remember Edwin Hopkins's 1912 article in the first issue of the new NCTE *English Journal*, where he gave a decisive "No" to the question, "Can Good Composition Teaching Be Done Under Present Conditions?" That was 90 years ago.

If we are serious about teaching well and about students learning to write passionately and thoughtfully, and if we are serious about democratic education in a just society, then we need a Labor Policy on the one hand and a critical curriculum on the other. Let us promote ethnographic, context-based, socially-oriented, interdisciplinary writing and community literacy (which Howard Tinberg and Linda Flower have advocated). To the extent that any college's Writing Across the Curriculum program discourages bogus assessment and encourages critical perspectives on academic discourses, it is an alternative to build on. We can also invite students to do literacy projects about the college, about conditions in their communities or on their jobs, or about questions in society-at-large. Many teachers have already moved away from skill-and-drill exercises, away from composing without a context. Writing teachers committed to cultural democracy and critical literacy can examine their departmental conditions and decide what strategies for changing curriculum and testing would work best where they are. No one plan for change will work anywhere, everywhere, or all the time. For example, good mainstreaming experiments, like those at South Carolina and at City College, needed structural as well as thematic changes, different course/credit/staffing structures as well as new student-centered subjects and methods, like the literacy narratives deployed by Soliday and Gleason at City (see Soliday's "From the Margins to the Mainstream").

The advance of inequality in recent years has meant cutbacks in public education and social programs, leaving many teachers and students feeling isolated and defensive. This is understandable, given the assault on their standards of learning and living. Feeling vulnerable, many think little or nothing can be done to challenge the status quo and to push for constructive change. The truth is that a lot has been done already. In literacy, the field is rich in material supporting critical-democratic language arts (Auerbach; Berlin and Vivion; Downing; Fitts and France; Brookfield; Brookfield and Preskill; Berlin, *Rhetorics*; Tayko and Tassoni; Nieto). Around the country, critical teachers are testing limits. One such teacher and scholar, Tom Fox ("Basic Writing"), insisted that "The need is not so much to initiate students into the discourse community, to teach them the particular forms of language in the academy. Instead, we need to convince students that this community is theirs, that it will not work against their identity and their interests" (75).

"What to do?," as Elsbeth Stuckey asks in *The Violence of Literacy*. Find local allies and colleagues with whom to study, talk, experiment, and plan campaigns against testing, against tracking, against skills-based teaching, against exploitation of part-time teachers, and against cuts to education and other social services. Remember that "Any decision about language teaching is a moral and political decision," as John Rouse (12) said. Follow Carole Edelsky's sense that "Retheorizing language education to make it serve education for democracy means highlighting the relationship of language and power.... It means figuring out and then spelling out how systems of domination are part of reading and writing, part of classroom interaction, part of texts of all kinds—and doing that as part of our constant and primary, not secondary, enterprise" (255). And, do not confront the lion alone, Paulo Freire warned when he was alive, because transforming society is not a weekend on a tropical beach (Shor and Freire).

Sometimes it is said that we get the history we deserve, which is another way of saying that resistance from the bottom up can limit regimes imposed from the top down. We can know the unequal system in whose arms we come of age; we can learn the history and politics that brought racist and undemocratic arrangements into being at our schools, colleges, and worksites; we can take some risks together to change conditions, against language policies that divide and discourage, in favor of inspired learning and teaching, critical writing and reading, which may yet call into being social justice and a humane democracy.

WORKS CITED

Adams, Peter Dow. "Basic Writing Reconsidered." *Journal of Basic Writing* 12.1 (1993): 22–36.

Agnew, Eleanor, and Margaret McLaughlin. "Basic Writing Class of '93 Five Years Later: How the Academic Paths of Blacks and Whites Diverged." *Journal of Basic Writing* 18.1 (1999): 40–54.

Anyon, Jean. "Social Class and the Hidden Curriculum of Work." *Journal of Education* 162 (1980): 67–92.

———. *Ghetto Schooling: A Political Economy of Urban Educational Reform.* New York: Teachers College Press, 1997.

Auerbach, Elsa. "Literacy and Ideology." *Annual Review of Applied Linguistics* 12 (1992): 71–85.

Baker, Tracy, and Peggy Jolly. "The 'Hard Evidence': Documenting the Effectiveness of a Basic Writing Program." *Journal of Basic Writing* 18.1 (1999): 27–39.

Berlin, James A. "Contemporary Composition: The Major Pedagogical Theories." *College English* 44 (1982): 765–77.

———. "Postmodernism, the College Curriculum, and Composition." *Composition in Context: Essays in Honor of Donald C. Stewart.* Ed. W. Ross Winterowd and Vincent Gillespie. Carbondale, IL: Southern Illinois UP, 1994. 46–61.

———. *Rhetoric and Reality: Writing Instruction in American Colleges, 1900–1985.* Carbondale, IL: Southern Illinois UP, 1987.

———. *Rhetorics, Poetics, and Cultures: Refiguring College English Studies.* Urbana, IL: NCTE, 1996.

———. *Writing Instruction in 19th Century American Colleges.* Carbondale, IL: Southern Illinois UP, 1984.

Berlin, James A., and Michael J. Vivion. *Cultural Studies in the English Classroom.* Portsmouth, NH: Boynton/Cook Heinemann, 1992.

Berliner, David C., and Bruce J. Biddle. *The Manufactured Crisis: Myths, Fraud, and the Attack on America's Public Schools.* Reading, MA: Addison-Wesley, 1995.

Bisseret, Noelle. *Education, Class Language, and Ideology.* London: Routledge, 1979.

Brint, Stephen, and Jerome Karabel. *The Diverted Dream: Community Colleges and the Promise of Educational Opportunity in America, 1900–1985.* New York: Oxford UP, 1989.

Brookfield, Stephen D. *Becoming a Critically Reflective Teacher.* San Francisco: Jossey-Bass, 1995.

Brookfield, Stephen D., and Stephen Preskill. *Discussion as a Way of Teaching: Tools and Techniques for Democratic Classrooms.* San Francisco: Jossey-Bass, 1999.

Boutwell, Clinton E. *Shell Game: Corporate America's Agenda for Schools.* Bloomington, IN: Phi Delta Kappa, 1997.

Bowles, Samuel, and Herbert Gintis. *Schooling in Capitalist America.* New York: Basic, 1976.

Bureau of Labor Statistics. "Employment and Earnings." January 1996: 160–3.

CCCC Commission on Assessment. "Writing Assessment: A Position Statement." *College Composition and Communication* 46 (1995): 430–7.

Clark, Burton. "The Cooling-Out Function in Higher Education." *American Journal of Sociology* 65 (1960): 569–76.

———. "The Cooling-Out Function Revisited," *New Directions for the Community Colleges.* Ed. George Vaughan. San Francisco: Jossey-Bass, 1978, 15–32.

Cohen, Arthur, and Florence Brawer. *The American Community College.* San Francisco: Jossey-Bass, 1982.

Connors, Robert J. "Crisis and Panacea in Composition Studies: A History." *Composition in Context: Essays in Honor of Donald C. Stewart.* Ed. W. Ross Winterowd and Vincent Gillespie. Carbondale, IL: Southern Illinois UP, 1994. 86–105.

———. "Overwork/Underpay: Labor and Status of Composition Teachers Since 1880." *Rhetoric Review* 9 (1990): 108–25.

———. "Rhetoric in the Modern University: The Creation of an Underclass." *The Politics of Writing Instruction: Postsecondary.* Ed. Richard Bullock and John Trimbur. Portsmouth, NH: Boynton/Cook, Heinemann 1991. 55–84.

———. "The New Abolitionism: Towards a Historical Background." *Reconceiving Writing, Rethinking Writing Instruction.* Ed. Joseph Petraglia. Mahwah, NJ: Lawrence Erlbaum Associates, 1995. 3–26.

Cross, K. Patricia. *Beyond the Open Door.* San Francisco: Jossey-Bass, 1971.

Crowley, Sharon. "A Personal Essay on Freshman Composition." *Pretext* 12 (1991): 155–76.

———."Composition's Ethic of Service, the Universal Requirement, and the Discourse of Student Need." *Journal of Advanced Composition* 15 (1995): 227–39.

———. "Response to Edward M. White." *Journal of Basic Writing* 15 (1996): 88–91.

Dewey, John. *Democracy and Education.* New York: Free Press, 1966 (first published 1916).

Digest of Education Statistics. National Center for Education Statistics, Washington, DC, 1997.

Dougherty, Kevin. *The Contradictory College.* Albany, NY: SUNY, 1994.

Downing, David B., ed. *Changing Classroom Practices: Resources for Literary and Cultural Studies.* Urbana, IL: NCTE, 1994.

Edelsky, Carole. "Education for Democracy." *Language Arts* 71 (1994): 252–7.

Elbow, Peter. "Writing Assessment in the 21st Century: A Utopian View." *Composition in the 21st Century.* Ed. L. Bloom, D. Daiker, and E. White. Carbondale, IL: Southern Illinois UP, 1996. 83–100.

Filler, Louis, ed. *Horace Mann on the Crisis in Education,* Yellow Springs, OH: Antioch, 1965, p. 124.

Fitts, Karen, and Alan W. France. eds. *Left Margins: Cultural Studies and Composition Pedagogy.* Albany, NY: SUNY, 1995.

Flower, Linda *Problem-Solving Strategies for Writing in Colleges and Communities,* New York: Harcourt Brace, 1998.

Fones-Wolf, Elizabeth. *Selling Free Enterprise.* Urbana, IL: Illinois UP, 1994.

Foucault, Michel. *Power/Knowledge.* Ed. C. Gordon. New York: Pantheon, 1980. Chaps. 5 and 6, pp. 78–133.

Fox, Tom. "Basic Writing as Cultural Conflict." *Journal of Education* 172 (1990): 65–83.

———. "Standards and Access." *Journal of Basic Writing* 12 (1993): 37–45.

Freeman, Richard. *The Overeducated American.* New York: Academic Press, 1976.

Freire, Paulo. *Cultural Action for Freedom.* Baltimore: Penguin, 1972.

———. *Education for Critical Consciousness.* New York: Seabury, 1973.

Galbraith, John Kenneth. *The New Industrial State.* Boston: Houghton-Mifflin, 1967.

Glau, Gregory. "The 'Stretch Program': Arizona State University's New Model of University-Level Basic Writing Instruction." *Writing Program Administration* 20 (1996): 79–87.

Goodlad, John. *A Place Called School.* New York: McGraw-Hill, 1984.

Graff, Harvey J. *The Labyrinths of Literacy.* Philadelphia: Falmer, 1987.

Gramsci, Antonio. *Selections from Cultural Writings.* Cambridge, MA: Harvard UP, 1991.

———. *Selections from the Prison Notebooks.* New York: International, 1971.

Greenbaum, Leonard. "The Tradition of Complaint." *College English* 31 (1969): 174–87.

Greenberg, Karen. "The Politics of Basic Writing." *Journal of Basic Writing* 12 (1993): 69–71.

Greer, Colin. *The Great School Legend*. New York: Penguin, 1972.

Grego, Rhonda, and Nancy Thompson. "Repositioning Remediation: Renegotiating Composition's Work in the Academy." *College Composition and Communication* 47 (1996): 62–84.

Henwood, Doug. "Talking About Work." *Monthly Review* 49 (1997): 18–30.

———. "Trashonomics." *White Trash: Race and Class in America*. Ed. Matt Wray and Annalee Newitz. New York: Routledge, 1997. 177–89.

Herzberg, Bruce. "Community Service and Critical Teaching." *College Composition and Communication* 45 (1994): 307–19.

Hilgers, Thomas L. "Basic Writing Curricula and Good Assessment Practices: When'er Shall the Twain Meet?" *Journal of Basic Writing* 14 (1995): 68–74.

Holbrook, Sue Ellen. "Women's Work: The Feminizing of Composition Studies." *Rhetoric Review* 9 (1991): 201–29.

Holmes, Steven A. "Income Disparity Between Poorest and Richest Rises." *New York Times* 20 June 1996: A1.

Hopkins, Edwin. "Can Good Composition Teaching Be Done Under Present Conditions?" *The English Journal* 1 (1912): 1–10.

Horner, Bruce, and Min-Zhan Lu. *Representing the "Other": Basic Writers and the Teaching of Basic Writing*. Urbana, IL: NCTE, 1999.

Hull, Glynda, Mike Rose, Kay Losey Fraser, and Marisa Castellano. "Remediation as Social Construct: Perspectives from an Analysis of Classroom Discourse." *College Composition and Communication* 42 (1991): 299–329.

Huot, Brian. "A Survey of College and University Writing Placement Practices." *Writing Program Administration* 17 (1994): 49–65.

Institute for Higher Education Policy. *College Remediation: What It Is, What It Costs, How It Works*. Washington, DC: The Institute, 1998.

Katz, Michael. *The Irony of Early School Reform*. Cambridge, MA: Harvard UP, 1968.

Kozol, Jonathan. *Savage Inequalities: Children in America's Schools*. New York: Crown, 1991.

Mantsios, Gregory. "Class in America: Myths and Realities." *Race, Class, and Gender in the United States*. Ed. Paula Rothenberg. 3rd ed. New York: St. Martin's, 1995. 131–43.

Marland, Sidney Percy. *Career Education: A Proposal for Reform*. New York: McGraw-Hill, 1974.

Mayher, John. *Uncommon Sense*. Portsmouth, NH: Boynton/Cook Heinemann, 1990.

Miller, Susan. *Textual Carnivals: The Politics of Composition*. Carbondale, IL: Southern Illinois UP, 1991.

Mishel, Lawrence, Jared Bernstein, and John Schmitt. *The State of Working America, 1998–1999*. Ithaca, NY: ILR/Cornell UP, 1999.

Mortenson, Thomas. *Postsecondary Education Opportunity*. Iowa City, IA, 1998.

Myrdal, Gunnar. *An American Dilemma: The Negro Problem*. New York: Harper and Row, 1964 (first published 1944).

Nieto, Sonia. *Affirming Diversity: The Sociopolitical Context of Multicultural Education*. 3rd ed. New York: Longman, 1999.

Oakes, Jeannie. *Keeping Track*. New Haven: Yale UP, 1985.

Odell, Lee. "Basic Writing in Context: Rethinking Academic Literacy." *Journal of Basic Writing* 14 (1995): 43–56.

Ohmann, Richard. *English in America*. New York: Oxford UP, 1995 (first published 1976).

———. *Politics of Letters*. Middletown, CT: Wesleyan UP, 1987.

Otheguy, R. *The Conditions of Latinos in the City University of New York*. New York: Board of Higher Education, 1990.

Pattison, Robert. *On Literacy: The Politics of the Word from Homer to the Age of Rock*. New York: Oxford UP, 1982.

Pereira, Joseph, Edward S. Cobb, and Hariclia Makoulis. *The Nature and Extent of the Undergraduate Educational Experience at the Colleges of the City University of New York: A Comparison of Latino and Non-Latino Subgroups*. New York: Lehmanm College, The Latino Urban Policy Initiative, 1993.

Purves, Alan. "Apologia Not Accepted." *College Composition and Communication* 46 (1995): 549–50.

Rich, Adrienne. "Teaching Language in Open Admissions." *On Lies, Secrets, and Silences*. New York: Norton, 1979. 51–68.

Rose, Mike. *Lives on the Boundary*. New York: Penguin, 1990.

Rouse, John. "The Politics of Composition." *College English* 41 (1979): 1–12.

Schell, Eileen. "The Costs of Caring:'Femininism' and Contingent Women Workers in Composition Studies." *Feminism and Composition Studies*. Ed. Susan Jarratt and Lynn Worsham. New York: MLA, 1998. 74–93.

Schor, Juliet. *The Overworked American*. New York: Basic, 1993.

Shaughnessy, Mina. *Errors and Expectations*. New York: Oxford UP, 1977.

———. "Some New Approaches Toward Teaching Writing." *Journal of Basic Writing* 6 (1980): 103–116 (first published 1970).

Shor, Ira. *Critical Teaching and Everyday Life*. Chicago: U of Chicago P, 1987 (first published 1980).

———. *Culture Wars: School and Society in the Conservative Restoration, 1969–1991*. Chicago: U of Chicago P, 1992 (first published 1986).

———. *Empowering Education*. Chicago: U of Chicago P, 1992.

———. *When Students Have Power*. Chicago: U of Chicago P, 1996.

Shor, Ira, and Paulo Freire. *A Pedagogy for Liberation: Dialogues on Transforming Education*. Westport, CT: Greenwood, 1987.

Shor, Ira, and Caroline Pari. *Critical Literacy in Action: Writing Words, Changing Worlds*. Portsmouth, NH: Boynton/Cook Heinemann, 1999.

Petraglia, Joseph, ed., *Reconceiving Writing, Rethinking Writing Instruction*, op. c.t. (on p. 32).

Sizer, Ted. *Horace's Compromise: The Dilemmas of the American High School*. Boston: Houghton-Mifflin, 1984.

Sklar, Holly, ed. *Trilateralism: The Trilateral Commission and Elite Planning for World Management*. Boston: South End, 1980.

Smith, Frank. *Whose Language? What Power? A Universal Conflict in a South African Setting*. New York: Teachers College Press, 1993.

Soliday, Mary. "From the Margins to the Mainstream: Reconceiving Remediation." *College Composition and Communication* 47 (1996): 85–100.

Soliday, Mary, and Barbara Gleason. "From Remediation to Enrichment: Evaluating a Mainstreaming Project." *Journal of Basic Writing* 16 (1997): 64–78.

Spring, Joel. *Education and the Rise of the Corporate State*. Boston: Beacon, 1972.

———. *The Sorting Machine Revisited: National Educational Policy Since 1945*. White Plains, NY: Longman, 1989 (first published 1980).

Stuckey, Elsbeth. *The Violence of Literacy*. Portsmouth, NH: Boynton/Cook Heinemann, 1990.

Tayko, Gail, and John Paul Tassoni. *Sharing Pedagogies: Students and Teachers Write About Dialogic Practices*. Portsmouth, NH: Boynton/Cook Heinemann, 1997.

Tinberg, Howard. "Ethnography in the Writing Classroom," *College Composition and Communication* 40 (1989): 79–82.

Trainor, Jennifer Seibel, and Amanda Godley. "After Wyoming: Labor Practices in Two University Programs." *College Composition and Communication* 50 (1998): 153–81.

Trimmer, Joseph. "Basic Skills, Basic Writing, Basic Research." *Journal of Basic Writing* 6 (1987): 3–9.

Tyack, David B. *Turning Points in American Educational History.* Cambridge, MA: Harvard UP, 1967.

U.S. Bureau of the Census. *Statistical Abstract of the United States: 1998.* Washington, DC.

Welner, Kevin G., and Jeannie Oakes. "(Li)Ability Grouping: The New Susceptibility of School Tracking Systems to Legal Challenges." *Harvard Educational Review* 66 (1996): 451–70.

White, Edward M. "An Apologia for the Timed Impromptu Essay Test." *College Composition and Communication* 46 (1995): 30–45.

Wiener, Harvey. "The Attack on Basic Writing—And After." *Journal of Basic Writing* 17.1 (1998): 96–103.

Williams, Raymond. *Marxism and Literature.* New York: Oxford UP, 1977.

Wolff, Edward N. *Top Heavy: The Increasing Inequality of Wealth in America and What We Can Do About It.* New York: New Press. 1996.

CHAPTER FOUR

Ideologies of Access
and the Politics of Agency

Mary Soliday

English Department, City College of New York

When the mainstreaming debate erupted around 1992, the most significant argument for preserving basic writing intact was that it offers an institutional haven for culturally diverse students. Such programs ensure diversity, writes Edward White: "I believe that we must preserve these programs if we are concerned about keeping the 'new students' in colleges and universities" (78). According to Karen Greenberg, basic writing programs ease underprepared students into the academy: "The instruction provided by basic writing courses enables students to acquire the academic literacy skills, motivation, and self-confidence to persevere and to succeed in college" ("Response" 94; and see "Politics"). If we abandon the programs, Deborah Mutnick fears, we abandon a historical commitment: "If we simply eliminate basic writing courses ... I fear the margin will simply shift, in many cases outside the academy altogether, as we return to a pre-open admissions, whiter, more middle-class university" (46; see Hull et al.).

Basic writing and freshman composition play an important initiatory role for students who are new to college. But such courses bear only a share of the responsibility for ensuring access to college for those students White designates as "new." To explore the relationship between remediation and access to the liberal arts, I want to examine a dominant ideology in which basic writing is equivalent to access in ways that exaggerate, or at least simplify, the agency of programs and teachers. It is important to examine this influential ideology of access because it tends to downplay or even exclude other factors—especially material or institutional ones—which affect

55

students' access to the BA. We tend to assume that the fate of open access depends heavily upon remedial programs. In assuming such a close relationship between access and remediation, we may fix our gaze so narrowly upon the efficacy of one program that we obscure alternative explanations for students' success or failure at college.

The power of a basic writing program to enhance access depends upon how it is embedded within a particular ideology of access. As Terence Collins notes, basic writing is not a monolith: "we all have created Basic Writing from our multiple perspectives in our multiple sites" (100). At the same time, however, basic writing has also been partly "created" by Mina Shaughnessy and her association with the writing program at the City College of New York (CCNY), where I teach. CCNY is the flagship college in the larger urban system, the City University of New York (CUNY), which pioneered a controversial open access policy for the urban working class in the late 1960s. Along with its short-lived open access policy, CUNY also developed a variety of innovative remedial programs in writing, reading, math, and study skills. I want to use CCNY and CUNY as representative examples of one ideology of access which, although unique or "site-specific" in many respects, has also had a national impact upon remediation's status.

A powerful site of remediation, CUNY has had a dominant influence upon professional talk. According to Jeanne Gunner, an "iconic discourse" emerged from CUNY in the 1970s. Tied to Shaughnessy, this discourse "is a repetitive exercise in heritage" that has shaped debate for the past 20 years (28). Repeatedly marked as the founder of the field, "Shaughnessy is perpetually posited as the starting point from which later ideas flow and to whom they are attributed, not necessarily conceptually, but always relationally" (28). More importantly for my discussion, Gunner notes further that Shaughnessy's

> ... name is grounded in a specific era and location as well: Mina Shaughnessy invokes "CUNY," or a particular construction of CUNY, whose geographical-temporal coordinates are political and material. "CUNY" as a discursive element serves to situate Basic Writing discourse in a sociopolitical context of hostility to access and to race-, ethnicity-, and class-based difference. The CUNY open admission struggles of the 1960's and 1970's thus form a multiple context for the struggles of the 1990's, a context that is both site-specific and site-iconic. The institutional site exceeds its own historical facts, and, in Basic Writing discourse, "CUNY" becomes an overdetermined term. (30)

Gunner is speaking of CUNY's professional status, but in tense debates about remediation in the state and city of New York in the 1990s, participants repeatedly locate CUNY's ongoing struggles within the context of the 1960s. Today's arguments are specifically embroiled in a local sociopolitical context;

but these debates over open access and its relationship to remediation also reflect the broader, national sea change within liberals' hearts about the social role and responsibility of public higher education. CUNY's struggles "exceed" its immediate environs because this ongoing conflict reflects—and helps to shape—a national rethinking, and ultimately repudiation of, the liberal middle-class commitments to the urban working classes made in the 1960s.

To make this argument, I will briefly discuss the origins of CUNY's access policy in the context of current debates; I will also focus on one of CUNY's influential liberal critics, James Traub, a journalist for intellectual forums like the *New Yorker* and the *New York Times*. I will then overview longitudinal studies of CUNY students' progress through remedial courses to examine how an ideology of access promotes a politics of agency. This politics, I will conclude, shifts responsibility for CUNY's struggles toward remediation and away from the devastating economic privatization of public higher education that has affected students' educational careers.

ORIGINS AND PROGRESS OF AN AMBIVALENT POLICY

Though first-year writing courses do offer genuine support to new students, they also, as Tom Fox argues, are sometimes established to mediate conflicting institutional goals. This is to say that writing courses—and especially remedial courses—can serve ideological purposes by solving crises generated by the competing desires to expand enrollments while protecting traditional standards and/or mediating between those standards and new curriculums. In Susan Miller's view, composition studies was created in the late 1890s as a compulsory program that, embedded within the newly formed English Department, helped to stabilize and protect the new emphasis upon vernacular literature. More broadly, equated primarily with an entry-level course, composition ". . . began in a political moment that was embedded in ambivalence about how to assimilate unentitled, newly admitted students in the late nineteenth century 'new university,' which was in turn formed to address its era's social, economic, and political changes" (79). At CUNY, basic writing provided excellent instruction for some students, but it also addressed its own era's sociopolitical changes in highly ambivalent ways. In his analysis of the discourse of open admissions at CUNY in the 1970s, Bruce Horner identifies a binary opposition, which aligns nontraditional students with political militancy and a lack of skills, and opposes them against a traditional curriculum, CCNY's constituency of Jewish students, and their alleged desire to assimilate into the mainstream (Horner and Lu). This discursive formation is ideological because it works to resolve the conflict that Miller identifies:

in this case, CUNY's need to admit a new population of students without transforming the traditional college.

The alignment that Horner describes in key documents about CUNY's open admissions policy eventually allowed an institution like City College to detach the remedial project from traditional studies and faculty. Such a detachment occurs because, as both Horner and Mike Rose observe, the ideology assumes that remediation is necessary for students admitted under standards which are revised only for them. The status of "new," which is awarded to particular groups of students, obscures not only their historic, national presence, but also the ongoing revisions of admissions standards and curriculum that also define the history of American higher education.

Since the late nineteenth century, this history is one of relentless expansion and institutional differentiation. Laurence Veysey comments that, between 1890 and 1915, "Everywhere the size of enrollments was tied to admissions standards" (357); as "new institutions" like Cornell, Stanford, and the University of Chicago opened, they gave a "welcome to nearly all comers, no matter how ill prepared" (357). One result was a crisis over standards and remediation, most famously at Harvard College in 1875, but also at Yale and other private eastern colleges in the early 1900s (358). Curriculum changes reflected the growing power of the natural sciences; admissions changes reflected the desire of institutions to expand their research mission and promote the broader exchange value of a college degree. Still, although the majority of the 4% of young Americans who attended college in 1900 were men of Anglo-Saxon origins, the increasing numbers of women, Jews, Catholics, and African-Americans fueled concerns that a "'new and democratic'" element was diluting traditional standards and curriculum (271).

Sixty years later, expanded access to college resulted in another wave of "new students" who seemed to be primarily minorities. But in *Right versus Privilege*, David Lavin, Richard Alba, and Richard Silberstein find that "the majority of students who attended college [nationally] as a result of expanded access were whites" (230). In the case of CUNY, Lavin et al. further note that substantial numbers of open admissions students were Whites. According to one national survey they discuss, by the mid-1970s, 93% of all 4-year colleges offered some type of remediation (230). Again, reflecting these national trends, 44% of all students at CUNY's senior colleges in 1970 required some form of remediation in writing, reading, or math (234). More particularly, although "Regular students [at CUNY] were far less likely than open-admissions students to need remediation," 30% admitted under pre-open admissions criteria did require remediation in one area (234). "Paradoxically," these researchers conclude, "many of those who were not, formally speaking, beneficiaries of open admissions [at CUNY] became eligible for support services that were primarily intended for others"

(237; for more recent figures underscoring the broad scope of remediation, see Boylan; Knopp; Phipps).

Minority students at CUNY required more remediation than Whites, and minority students benefited from CUNY's revised admissions standards, but large numbers of White students also required remediation—both those Whites who took advantage of open access and those who were admitted to CUNY under pre-open access standards (which had been quite selective). Indeed, although minority students at CUNY in the late 90s require more remediation than Whites do, still, a significant 38% of White students admitted to CUNY fail one of the three skills tests all students must take (Staples). This is not an unusual percentage given the historical struggle over the persistent need for college composition at many institutions (e.g., see Brereton). But discussions about access do not address the skills deficiencies of this third of the population because expanded access is more firmly aligned with students of color and students of color with remediation. In CUNY's case, remediation seems singular because it is attached to a foreign body of students, and at CCNY, to working-class people of color—in the 1970s, to inner-city African-Americans, and Puerto Ricans.

Remediation has not only been racialized, it has also been aligned with students' oppositional politics. For example, in the 1990s, conservative retellings of CUNY's decision to revise admissions standards foregrounds a Black and Puerto Rican student takeover of CCNY. "CUNY's transformation began with a violent student strike in April 1969," announces Heather Mac Donald (11). "In the mid-1960's," John Leo opines, "CUNY instituted the nation's first affirmative action program for minority students, but racial disturbances and a violent takeover of one campus by black and Puerto Rican students quickly upped the ante" (20). "The transformation of City College from the 'Harvard of the poor' into a place where most students are incapable of doing genuine college-level work is a consequence of the open-admissions decisions made under duress in the late 1960s," intones the *New York Post* ("CUNY's Opportunity").

Elite private colleges voluntarily pioneered the earliest summer bridge programs for minorities as well as the first affirmative action policies—and some of these were begun in the 1950s (Bowen and Bok 4–7). But CUNY's critics portray open access as the result of political pressure because in this way they can oppose "decisions made under duress" to the meritocratic structures in place before the 1960s. In that decade, as Mac Donald explains, "It was no longer enough for a college merely to educate; universities were called upon to enfranchise minority groups through admissions and curricular change. Few universities were as profoundly affected by this shift in expectations as CUNY" (10). Whites have always benefited from both affirmative action and open access policies, but critics argue that open access exists solely to redress minority grievances. "[C]alled upon to enfranchise minority groups," institutions were forced to develop policies and/or programs that conflict with both traditional standards and "neutral" curriculums that characterized an earlier era.

But as has been the case historically in higher education (e.g., Levine), CUNY's shift in mission reflected demographic changes and the expanded use of a college degree within the city. For instance, demography alone could have affected CUNY's enrollments. The flight of Whites to Westchester and New Jersey, the end of quotas for Jewish students at private colleges, and the 1965 Immigration Act, which opened the doors to non-European immigrants, redefined the urban constituency to which CUNY would have to respond if it wished to expand enrollments—or even to survive in a changing urban landscape. Accompanying these changes, of course, was a shift in the postwar urban economy away from manufacturing and toward the financial and service sectors, which gave a college degree a heightened exchange value within the metropolitan area for larger numbers of students.

CUNY's access policy was highly politicized because it had the complex burden of negotiating the competing interests of multiple groups ranging from business interests to politicians, from private colleges to CUNY alumni. For instance, politicians involved in a mayoral election, small private colleges nervous about their own enrollments, and a faculty riven by the struggles of the 1960s, were all concerned with the impact of open admissions. Mediating these jockeying groups within the city was a famously aggressive media, which included sensationalist tabloids as well as national newspapers and television. Then as now, the media celebrated City College's legendary role as the Harvard of the Jewish proletariat in the 1930s, 1940s, and 1950s. In this tale of the meritocratic, pre-1960s society, immigrant students succeeded because they were eager to assimilate into mainstream intellectual life. Still fondly referred to today in this way by CUNY's Board of Trustees (see Arenson), the Jewish immigrant is ideologically aligned against remedial students of color and their oppositional, inner-city attitudes.

"HAVING IT BOTH WAYS": REMEDIATION'S AGENCY

Ideologies resolve crises; in CUNY's case, ideological alignments served to mediate an urban crisis. Another way of stating the case is that CUNY's basic writing courses satisfied the competing desires and interests of ideologically opposed groups: there never was a consensus about CUNY's open access policy. Out of this overdetermined welter, remediation emerged as the symbolic standard bearer of open admissions and consequently became almost solely responsible for sustaining open access.

The CUNY open access policy emphasized access and excellence; but at CCNY, students were expected to achieve excellence before they could have access to the traditional liberal arts. Mina Shaughnessy often remarked on the tension that resulted from admitting students into a program without devoting substantial resources to it. Such a policy, Shaughnessy suggested to an interviewer in October 1977, narrowed the responsibility for open access to "one cheap course" (Maher 211). "The institutions that want it both ways finally can't have it both ways; they either have to decide that they can [educate the students fully] or they can't," Shaughnessy flatly stated (Maher 211). In 1972, Shaughnessy wrote a 25-page memo to the City College administration that explains what she meant by trying to have it both ways:

> This concern for what came to be called "maintaining standards" pressed most directly on the remedial teachers of the college, who were charged with the task of transforming within a semester or two their "disadvantaged" students into students who behaved, in academic situations at least, like "advantaged" students. This, of course, was impossible. More seriously, it started things off in the wrong direction: *it narrowed the base of responsibility for Open Admissions students to the remedial programs,* [emphasis added] giving "regular" departments an illusion of immunity from change; it channeled most of the Open Admissions money into remedial programs and into counseling that was aimed at helping students adjust to the college world; but it provided no support for research into the learning problems of the new students (significantly, the only research so far to emerge from Open Admissions has been statistical reports on grades and drop-out rates); and it encouraged remedial teachers, under pressure to produce imitations of the model "bright" students as quickly as possible, to go on doing what writing teachers have too often done before—work prescriptively rather than inductively, removing mistakes without trying to understand them. (Maher 121)

It is often argued that remedial programs shelter underprepared students: but Shaughnessy suggests these programs shelter the regular, full-time faculty from the students. Consequently, the policy prevented the growth of disciplinary roots. If remediation was not institutionalized as a discipline, then its role would always be a purely initiatory one, unable to extend into and throughout the regular academic life of the college. As Horner comments, this "strategy of accommodation rendered Open Admissions vulnerable by representing it as additional to and a potential drain on programs assumed to be integral to the university and its 'standards'" (13).

Anne DiPardo's ethnography of an adjunct basic writing program at "Dover Park University" (DPU) further illuminates how other colleges institutionalize ambivalent policies. Two decades after Shaughnessy's memo, DiPardo shows how DPU, a 4-year college located in a rapidly changing Californian urban area, attempted to accommodate conflicting goals and interests through a special access program. DiPardo documents how "patterns of tension" structured the talk about the new students and the programs designed to assimilate them into academic cultures (37). For example, although DPU spoke loftily of expanding access, *"Many faculty and a number of administrators felt torn between their support for educational equity and their desire to maintain acceptable academic standards"* (41, her emphasis). And although the university established policies to welcome culturally diverse students, in actuality, the "adjunct programs" designed to support these students remained segregated from the academic disciplines and their faculty (39–40). Treated as a "cohesive group" rather than as individuals (56), these students provoked conflicting discourses about integration and separatism that the program's ambivalent goals reflected. On the one hand, the program was expected to integrate students into mainstream campus life, whereas on the other, it was expected to prepare students for that life within a separate program.

Through an ambivalent access policy, DPU resolved, however partially, competing ideological tensions on a California campus that serves White, middle-class students but is located in a region soon to be dominated by "minorities": DPU reaches out to new communities, while also protecting its traditional faculty. By developing an "adjunct" program, DPU seems to be committed to a goal of sustaining cultural diversity, even though the special program is largely administered and staffed by graduate students, undergraduate peer tutors, and special programs personnel.

It is no wonder, then, that when institutions participate unevenly in open admissions, remedial or adjunct teachers assume an inflated sense of responsibility over the destinies of their students' educational careers. For example, Gunner notes that one of the key features of CUNY's "iconic discourse" is the "idealized identity for the basic writing teacher" (31). Among other characteristics, this figure "identifies with and champions basic writers" and "enacts a Virgilian role of guide into academic discourse" (31). Less poetically, the basic writing teacher assumes the institutional role of the preserver of access because responsibility is not a collaborative venture between students, liberal arts faculty, professional schools, and special programs. Daniel Royer and Roger Gilles, who have experimented successfully with students' self-placement into remedial courses at Grand Valley State University, argue for this reason that giving students agency is key to reconceiving remediation: "We tell students that their education . . . is their responsibility" (65).

Royer and Gilles advocate self-placement because they believe that when remedial programs assume a singular responsibility, they must necessarily minimize risk-taking and the possibility for failure. At CCNY, an arcane bureaucracy, which evolved between 1970 and 1999, increasingly narrowed responsibility for basic writing students to special programs, while at the same time sharply reducing students' and teachers' abilities to make decisions about placement, grades, or curriculum. New rules were added or old ones newly enforced: remedial courses are compulsory based on test scores; remedial courses do not bear credit; students must complete all their writing requirements, including freshman composition, before enrolling in required liberal arts courses; students must pass three impromptu writing exams to progress through the curriculum; students must fill out their schedules with skills courses to achieve full-time status necessary to gain financial aid, and so forth. Though some of these barriers are unique to CCNY, other programs also deploy similar rules (see Jensen for an interesting case).

JAMES TRAUB AND THE NEOLIBERAL POLITICS OF AGENCY

In the 1990s, rules and tests proliferated at CUNY as right-wing groups attacked the institution as a failed social program, a leftover from the 1960s similar to welfare and affirmative action (see Cooper's summary). However, right-wing criticism is not unexpected: what was new in the 1990s was the national coalition between the right and the neoliberal center. In New York, James Traub, a self-described liberal, announced to the public that he was going to investigate the effect of 1960s social programs on the intractable problem of inner-city poverty. Just as President Clinton was busy ending welfare as we know it, James Traub was similarly reflecting on the excesses of agency that the middle class had exercised in New York through its famous system of urban higher education. Warmly received by the mainstream press, Traub's book about CCNY, *City on a Hill*, was named a New York Times Notable Book of the Year, and its author was accorded the instant status of an "expert" on CUNY (he had already published one chapter in the *New Yorker*). Traub's book is significant for basic writing scholars to consider because, through description and personal impression, it reproduces the powerful ideology of access that Horner deconstructs. Equally important, Traub also articulates the discontent one segment of the aging post-1960s generation clearly is experiencing as it reformulates its sense of responsibility toward the urban working classes.

The basic argument to emerge from Traub's book is that open access does not succeed because remediation fails. Remediation fails because it cannot hope to erase students' cultural, not just academic, deficits. As Traub observes remedial and elective courses, he discovers two distinct institutions, "the college of the remedial *Inferno* and the college of [the] *Paradiso*" (303). Although indeed remedial courses are, as I have argued, not meaningfully connected to elective courses, Traub finds that this is so because two groups of students populate the different courses. Traveling from the "submarine" depths of remedial courses to the "rarefied" atmosphere of the traditional liberal arts, Traub dramatically discovers that the curriculum reflects an "ethnic hierarchy" created by the students' achievements and cultural attitudes (323; 109). Unsurprisingly, these attitudes correlate roughly with the binary oppositions that Horner describes. Apolitical, hard-working White students who desire to assimilate into mainstream culture are aligned against remedial Black students, a slack work ethic, inner-city culture, ethnic studies courses, and remediation.

Ethnic stratification, Traub argues, naturally restores the meritocratic order that the institution's policies deny. Thus, the top of Traub's hierarchy is peopled by the immigrant students, most of whom are foreign-born and/or Asian; the Black students, who represent "the [top of the] hierarchy of Black achievement," are usually Caribbean, and they succeed partly because they are the products of colonial schooling—the "lycee, where students expected to bend beneath the whip" (246; 250). Although the "elite" students bring with them a "solid ... secondary school education," it is their cultural attitudes that ensure their slots in the hierarchy (13). Unlike their forebears, today's immigrants don't value education for education's sake—sadly, they are vocationally oriented—but they do possess "immigrant drive and first-generation values" (13). They are usually "apolitical," "well dressed, respectful, good natured" (17; 181). Above all, like the Jewish "greenhorns" of the past, the good immigrant student of today accepts the "virtues of acculturation and assimilation ... almost without question" (84; see 41).

By contrast, the bottom of Traub's ethnic hierarchy is peopled by an inarticulate mass of students, overwhelmingly African-American and Latino, marred by poverty and native born. They crowd the remedial writing courses, study skills courses, and Black Studies, where, borrowing a metaphor from a teacher to describe the unhygienic nature of the remedial project, "the shit flowed differently" (166). Rather than bending to the whip of colonial education, these students have been "shaped by the inner-city culture" (91) fostered by the notoriously permissive New York City schools. These students lack motivation—several are, Traub judges, seriously depressed—and are "barely socialized to school" (96). "[V]irtually illiterate" (153), they tend to dress exotically, favoring sculpted hair, Afrocentric robes, or bizarrely painted fingernails.

The new students inhabit the bottom of the hierarchy partly because they bring serious "academic handicaps" to college (207). But crucial as these "cognitive deficits" are to their failure, more important is these students' resistance to assimilation in behavior, style, and thought (136). Many of the Latino students but especially the African-American have internalized the "alienation and hostility" (229) and "an ideology of repudiation and resistance" typical of the "intellectual and cultural isolation of the black community" (230). The Afrocentrist professor (Leonard Jeffries) to whom Traub devotes a long chapter is, he claims, representative of the Black remedial student drowning in "the deep currents of anti-intellectualism ... that ran through large parts of the black community" (271). In other words, Black students are at the bottom of the ethnic hierarchy because they have produced a culture that keeps them there: "[T]he street world where ancient grievances and suspicions are perpetually revived—the world, that is, that has reared many City College students" (235). Such students cannot hope to be "liberated" culturally until they reject the Leonard Jeffries "inside themselves" (271). In sum, the students have so deeply internalized street mythology that it is as inescapable as biology.

An ideologically powerful set of alignments, centered on physical descriptions of students' bodies, emerges from Traub's book. The conventional immigrant students of the 1990s resemble the Jewish "greenhorns" of the past—they are aligned with the desire to assimilate, traditional curriculum, rigorous standards, foreign schooling, and neat dress. By contrast, the exotic Black/Latino body is aligned with oppositional politics, ethnic studies, remediation, soft standards, and the New York City public schools.

Traub uses this hierarchy to establish not only that minority cultures created by inner-city poverty are responsible for the failure of open access: he also argues that the public institutions designed to boost individuals out of poverty perpetuate the cycle of failure. For, ultimately, discussions about remediation are arguments about middle-class authority and responsibility. As Traub asks early in the book: "Do the limits lie in the college or in the students? And this, in turn, begs one of the threshold questions of modern liberalism: How powerful are our institutions in the face of the economic and cultural forces that now perpetuate inner-city poverty?" (5). Addressing his middle-class reader, Traub wonders whether "our" institutions can halt these vague "forces" that create poverty. By the book's end, Traub concludes that "we" cannot reverse the effects of poverty because poverty generates anti-intellectual minority cultures. Therefore, because Traub's most effective criticisms fall upon remedial writing courses, the struggles a few students experience during their first college class become representative of the failure of open admissions more generally. A. M. Rosenthal, former executive editor of the *Times* and a CCNY graduate, thought so: "from a reading of Mr. Traub's book," he wrote, "it is clear that continuing remedial classes would be continuing the basic falsehood of open enrollment at City" (9). In the neoliberal view, the failure of open admissions also becomes representative of those social programs—welfare, affirmative action, bilingual education—that are now being reassessed across the country.

PRIVATIZING PUBLIC HIGHER EDUCATION

In the late 1990s, CUNY's critics argued effectively that remediation has eroded enrollments, slowed down students' graduation rates, and damaged CUNY's ability to offer a quality undergraduate education. In other words,

CUNY's critics tie retention rates firmly to remedial programs rather than to working-class students' ability to fund their educations. To understand how remediation is not wholly responsible for sustaining open access, let alone for damaging the university's overall quality, I want to put the evolution of remediation at CUNY between 1970–1999 into the broader context of the privatization of public higher education. In short, I want to shift the responsibility for maintaining open access toward a class commitment to maintain public higher education for the urban working classes.

Longitudinal views of students' educational fates provide a more complex perspective upon remediation's agency in promoting open access. In the Lavin et al. study I mentioned earlier, the researchers concluded that remediation had only a modest effect upon the first cohort of open access students at CUNY (1970–71). Lavin et al. compare those students who completed remedial courses with a group who failed the same tests but who did not take remedial classes: "Placement in remedial courses was sometimes mandatory and sometimes voluntary" (231). Although qualifying the power of their comparison, Lavin et al. generally argue that taking or not taking remedial courses did not affect students' overall success in college (in terms of accumulating credits or GPA). However, failing or succeeding in a remedial course made a difference. Thus, "sheer exposure to remediation did not add to students' achievements in the senior colleges of CUNY, but success or failure in remedial courses did make some difference" (253). For the latter group, the remedial coursework "added slightly to educational attainment" in terms of staying in school (252).

What seems to impact students' progress at a school like CUNY is a constellation of institutional policies and economic factors that David Lavin, this time with David Hyllegard, explored in a later book, a longitudinal study of the fates of CUNY's first open access cohort. In *Changing the Odds*, Lavin and Hyllegard also compare the fate of the 1970 cohort with a cohort from 1980. After controlling for differences between the two groups, Lavin and Hyllegard conclude that the 1980 cohort "achieved considerably less academic success" (238) than the earlier cohort, and they attribute this difference to "the changed academic context created by policy modifications" (239). Such modifications included charging tuition; requiring students to take a battery of standardized tests and to complete sequences of remedial courses; and tightening policies for withdrawing from courses or for transferring between programs and colleges (210–2). Lavin and Hyllegard emphasize the role that working part- or full-time had on the 1980 cohort as students struggled to pay tuition and for mandatory remediation in a city whose rents were spiraling upwards at a dizzying pace. Although socioeconomic background had had a negligible effect upon the 1970 cohort, it became a determining factor in the ability of the 1980 cohort to stay in school.

What Lavin and Hyllegard's study shows is that, although remediation's agency might be limited, open access, when supported economically and institutionally, helped thousands of poor, inner-city Whites and people of color to find and keep white-collar jobs. Open access succeeded in creating an educated, urban class in New York City. From their perspective, providing access to the BA represents a realistic commitment that can be realized given the appropriate resources. Similarly, in her longitudinal study of CCNY students, *Time to Know Them*, Marilyn Sternglass also concludes that offering access to the BA creates new life chances; access to higher education redefined opportunity for many of her case study students.

But in making this claim, Sternglass also offers two critiques of access models that tie remediation to open access. First, Sternglass shows how students' progress was affected by their success in mathematics, science, and other liberal arts courses as well as in their writing courses. For this reason, she puts writing teachers' agency in a fuller educational context:

> Composition instruction cannot be seen in a vacuum. Perhaps that is the greatest lesson that can be learned from examining student writing over an extended period of time. Composition instruction is an important first step in assisting students to formulate their ideas and learn how to express them clearly. But composition instructors should not believe that they are the final influence, or perhaps even the most important influence, in the development of writing abilities. (141)

Second, Sternglass's book sharply underscores how economic and material factors affect the lives of individual students. In this regard, Sternglass focuses especially on Ricardo, whose economic struggle, she says, "encapsulates the feelings and frustrations of many of his classmates" (105). Ricardo felt that his commitment as a student was diminishing: "I've been on the honor roll for three years, but if I can't pay the rent and eat, who cares?" (105). During the mid-1990s—when CUNY was in the throes of cutbacks, tuition hikes, and demonstrations—Ricardo dropped out of school. He returned later and finished a degree in the physician assistant's program, although, as Sternglass notes, he could not, because of economic problems, pursue his lifelong dream to become a doctor, despite high grades in difficult math and science courses.

Ricardo's exhausting struggle "encapsulates" those of other students because CUNY's situation in the 1990s illustrates a broader trend of the privatization of public higher education in the U.S. (Lauter). On one level, privatization involves shifting the burden for funding a public college from the taxpayers to students and their families. The CUNY University Faculty Senate, drawing upon data compiled by the RAND Corporation and PricewaterhouseCoopers, notes that CUNY's tuition increased 93% between 1988 and 1997. Meanwhile, New York State's appropriation to CUNY in constant dollars has decreased 40% since 1980, whereas in 1997, the city's contribution decreased from 19% to 6% (*CUNY Affirmed* 4). To make up this shortfall, CUNY has consistently been forced to raise tuition, increase class size, cut electives and specialized programs, and rely more heavily upon a part-time professoriate.

Privatization takes other forms as well. When CUNY began charging tuition in 1974, the state of New York created the Tuition Assistance Program (TAP) and the Supplemental Tuition Assistance Program (STAP), which could be used to pay for remediation. In 1995, the state legislature abolished STAP and later expanded the definition of remediation to include courses in English as a Second Language. STAP and TAP play a crucial role in students' ability to stay in school over the long term because the federal government's assistance to working-class students has steadily declined. The federal shift away from grants and toward loans along with its cutbacks in direct aid to public higher education began in the mid-1970s (Shor; Callan). As *New York Times* columnist Frank Rich notes, "Ask G.O.P. leaders how universities will replace Federal funding, and the mantra-like answer is 'privatization.'"

Despite this drastic defunding of the largest urban public university in the country, in 1999, the struggle over remediation assumes center stage in public discourse. For example, the Mayor of New York City wishes to "outsource" CUNY's remedial courses by shifting them to private institutions. To gain support for his position, in 1998, the Mayor created an Advisory Task Force on CUNY chaired by Benno Schmidt, President of the Edison Project, which—perhaps not coincidentally—operates for-profit schools. In June 1999, this taskforce published *CUNY: An Institution Adrift*, a 109-page report with lengthy, separate appendices, two of which I referred to previously (RAND and PricewaterhouseCoopers). Rather than analyzing the data contained in its own appendices, however, the Mayor's Task Force focuses in its main report upon remediation as the source of CUNY's allegedly low graduation rates and declining standards. Listing remediation as the first cause of the university's overall decline, the taskforce reproduces in some detail the ideology of access I've been discussing. The CUNY Faculty Senate notices that "the report focuses on remediation to the exclusion of all other academic programs and activities of CUNY" (*CUNY Affirmed* 5). As the report melodramatically puts its case: "the Task Force has been shocked by both the scale and the depth of CUNY students' remediation needs" (Schmidt 21). Not unexpectedly, the taskforce recommends privatizing remediation at CUNY and radically altering admissions standards to create a tiered system like California's (and see Staples).

Tying open access to remediation in this way, the taskforce can argue that CUNY's downsizing is less important than the failure of its remedial programs. Thus, says the *Post*, CUNY should view budget cuts as an "opportunity" to abolish remediation:

> As things stand, CUNY is failing—and not because it doesn't have enough
> funds or top-flight faculty members or first-rate facilities. The problem turns
> on the readiness of CUNY's administrators to accept the bizarre notion that lack
> of preparation for college-level work shouldn't deter students from enrolling
> in the City University's senior colleges or even from receiving a CUNY degree.
> Thus, a huge proportion of the university budget is devoted not to college-level
> teaching but to remediation.

CUNY devotes roughly 2.5% of its budget to remediation, and remediation
has never occupied more than 10% of its whole curriculum. But data do
not always matter in ideological debate. The taskforce, as I mentioned previously, coolly ignored the data produced by the independent accounting
bodies it commissioned. Since 1970, remediation has increasingly assumed
the burden for sustaining access at CUNY, with the result that CUNY's severe
financial deprivation since the mid-1970s cannot assume an equal ideological clout in public debate.

THE PROFESSIONAL POLITICS OF REMEDIATION, 2000

My emphasis upon the politics of agency is important because of these
funding battles, which, at the most abstract level, are battles over redefining
the public sphere. Within the field, however, scholars are also struggling to
clarify their own responsibility in light of a national backlash against remediation. Our sense of professional agency seems to center on our ability to
supply data and to explain to the public what basic writers need. Unfortunately, the repeated calls for data issuing from the pages of the *Journal of
Basic Writing* do not always account for the politics of remediation. In a lead
article in *JBW*, for instance, Susanmarie Harrington and Linda Adler-Kassner
assert that our "collective failure" to discuss the gap between cultural and
cognitive approaches "leaves us, our programs, and most importantly our
students, vulnerable to legislatively-mandated cuts" (16). Harrington and
Adler-Kassner believe we are vulnerable to cuts because we have spent
time analyzing cultural issues rather than examining the "dilemma that still
counts": individual students' errors. "Renewed attention to error," they write,
"will help us to better define and understand what basic writing is, who basic writers are, how we can talk about writers' needs among ourselves, and
how we can represent basic writers and talk about their needs with public
officials" (20).

However, my analysis suggests that many of us are vulnerable now because, in Susan Miller's phrasing, we were institutionalized to be vulnerable.

Mina Shaughnessy showcased individual students' errors in several well-publicized forums, but her program was radically downsized despite her unusual moral status. Her program was downsized not because she lacked data about individual students' errors but because, as Ira Shor documents, the middle-class commitment to open access evaporated, to be followed by a neoliberal redefinition of responsibility perhaps best expressed in Clinton's 1992 campaign slogan "no opportunity without responsibility."

Remediation has been abolished at CUNY's senior colleges and will be eliminated at CCNY in 2001. In the past two decades, numerous scholars and public intellectuals in New York City have testified to the power of remedial education and CUNY to change their own or others' lives. But as the battles were waged around remediation, the inexorable defunding of CUNY continued. Perhaps one useful parallel here is the one Paul Lauter identifies: while public debates focused upon "political correctness" on college campuses in the 1980s, many institutions were in the throes of devastating budget cuts.

Rather than see mainstreaming as the threat to the mission of basic writing instruction or a weakening of access, we need to view remediation's agency within the entire contexts of our institutions. We need to ask how remediation is connected to other remedial programs and prerequisite structures; to placement and exit assessments; to financial aid and to an institution's operating budget. We need also to interpret retention data within the context of students' lives, because retention is so intimately tied to a students' racial and socioeconomic background.

It's surely a mistake to equate a program's presence with the presence of particular students, which—temporarily, as the case of CUNY dramatizes—only partially resolves the contradictions inherent in this dominant ideology of access. The real danger is not that we experiment with new programs, but that we contain our commitment to working-class, culturally diverse students within a single course or program. Perhaps most dangerous of all is that, by focusing so narrowly on the power of a program to change students' lives, we will forget how students' progress through college takes place within a material, socioeconomic reality. As Shaughnessy's former students testify in Maher's biography, significant change can occur in a remedial writing class. However, as Sternglass writes, "most of the students who were placed [at the remedial] levels in my study did not need specific remedial work" (298); they needed rigorous, long-term instruction in reading and writing in several different courses. Conducted over 6 years, Sternglass's case studies reveal that students' growth and change occur within fine-grained sociopolitical contexts to a greater degree than our current arguments about the status of basic writing fully acknowledge. From my perspective, the dilemma that still counts is pervasive racism, the defunding of my institution, and students' ongoing struggles to pay for their education. In rethinking our programs and courses, we need to abandon our sense of exclusive responsibility, complicate our sense of the politics of agency, and look critically at dominant initiatory models and the particular ideologies of access that such models sustain.

WORKS CITED

Arenson, Karen. "Why College Isn't for Everyone." *New York Times* 31 Aug. 1997: 4: 1, 10.

Bowen, William, and Derek Bok. *The Shape of the River*. Princeton: Princeton UP, 1998.

Boylan, Hunter R. "The Scope of Developmental Education: Some Basic Information on the Field." *Research in Developmental Education* 12.4 (1995).

Brereton, John, ed. *The Origins of Composition Studies in the American College, 1875–1925*. Pittsburgh: Pittsburgh UP, 1995.

Callan, Patrick M. "Government and Higher Education." *Higher Learning in America, 1980–2000*. Ed. Arthur Levine. Baltimore: Johns Hopkins UP, 1993.

Collins, Terence. "Response to Ira Shor." *JBW* 16 (1997): 95–100.

Cooper, Sandi. "Remediation's End." *Academe* (1998): 14–20.

CUNY: An Institution Affirmed: Response to the Report of the Mayor's Task Force. University Faculty Senate. http://www.soc. qc.edu/ufs/response.htm (July 1999).

"CUNY's Opportunity." *New York Post* 20 Feb. 1995: 20.

DiPardo, Anne. *A Kind of Passport*. Urbana, IL: NCTE, 1993.

Fox, Tom. *Defending Access*. Portsmouth, NH: Boynton/Cook Heinemann, 1999.

Greenberg, Karen. "The Politics of Basic Writing." *JBW Special Issue* 12 (1993): 64–71.

———. "Response to Ira Shor." *JBW* 16 (1997): 90–4.

Gunner, Jeanne. "Iconic Discourse: The Troubling Legacy of Mina Shaughnessy." *JBW* 17 (1998): 25–42.

Harrington, Susanmarie, and Linda Adler-Kassner. "'The Dilemma that Still Counts': Basic Writing at a Political Crossroads." *JBW* 17 (1998): 3–24.

Horner, Bruce, and Min-Zhan Lu. *Representing the 'Other.'* Urbana, IL: NCTE, 1999.

Hull, Glynda, et al., "Reply to Peter Elbow." *CCC* 44 (1993): 588–9.

Jensen, George. "Bureaucracy and Basic Writing Programs; Or, Fallout from the Jan Kemp Trial." *JBW* 7 (1988): 30–7.

Knopp, Linda. "Remedial Education: An Undergraduate Student Profile." *American Council on Education Research Briefs* 6.8. Washington, DC, 1995.

Lauter, Paul. "'Political Correctness and the Attack on American Colleges." *Higher Education Under Fire*. Ed. Michael Berube and Carl Nelson. New York: Routledge, 1995. 73–90.

Lavin, David, Richard Alba, and Richard Silberstein. *Right versus Privilege*. New York: Free Press, 1981.

Lavin, David, and David Hyllegard. *Changing the Odds*. New Haven: Yale UP, 1996.

Leo, John. "A University's Sad Decline." *U.S. News & World Report* 15 Aug. 1994: 20.

Levine, David. *The American College and the Culture of Aspiration, 1915–1940*. Ithaca: Cornell UP, 1986.

Mac Donald, Heather. "Downward Mobility: The Failure of Open Admissions at City University." *City Journal* Summer 1994: 10–20.

Maher, Jane. *Mina P. Shaughnessy*. Urbana, IL: NCTE, 1997.

Miller, Susan. *Textual Carnivals*. Carbondale, IL: Southern Illinois UP, 1993.

Mutnick, Deborah. *Writing in an Alien World.* Portsmouth, NH: Boynton/Cook Heinemann, 1996.

Phipps, Ronald. *College Remediation.* Washington, DC: Institute for Higher Education Policy, 1998.

Rich, Frank. "The Unkindest Cut." *New York Times* 12 May 1995: 4: 15.

Rose, Mike. "The Language of Exclusion: Writing Instruction at the University." *CE* 47 (1985): 341–59.

Rosenthal, A. M. "An American Promise." *New York Times Book Review* 2 Oct. 1994: 7: 7, 9.

Royer, Daniel, and Roger Gilles. "Directed Self-Placement: An Attitude of Orientation." *CCC* 50.1 (1998): 54–70.

Schmidt, Benno, et al., *CUNY: An Institution Adrift: Report of the Mayor's Advisory Task Force on CUNY.* 7 June 1999.

Shor, Ira. *Culture Wars.* Chicago: Chicago UP, 1986.

Staples, Brent. "Blocking Promising Students from City University." *The New York Times* 26 May 1998: A20.

Sternglass, Marilyn. *Time to Know Them.* Mahwah, NJ: Lawrence Erlbaum Associates, 1997.

Traub, James. *City on a Hill.* Reading, MA: Addison-Wesley, 1994.

———. "Class Struggle." *New Yorker* 19 September 1994: 76–90.

Veysey, Laurence. *The Emergence of the American University.* Chicago: Chicago UP, 1965.

White, Edward. "The Importance of Placement and Basic Studies: Helping Students Succeed Under the New Elitism." *JBW* 14 (1995): 75–84.

CHAPTER FIVE

Mainstreaming? Eddy, Rivulet, Backwater, Site Specificity

Terence G. Collins
University of Minnesota, Twin Cities

Kim Lynch
Cambridge Community College

We want to argue caution in the conversation about mainstreaming basic writing and basic writers. In so arguing, we may provide an unwelcome voice. After all, the mainstreaming moment has produced some impressive curricular transformations in support of students (see, for instance, Grego and Thompson; Soliday and Gleason; Glau), and is built on rationales against some of which, at least, it is difficult to argue. Our purpose is not to be gratuitously reactionary toward a way of thinking that in many instances prompts a revitalization of the basic writing curriculum, and of the institutional standing for that curriculum, in service of students who are most at risk of being excluded from higher education by the reascendant right. Rather, we want to offer a perspective on mainstreaming that argues several points:

- The case for mainstreaming too often has been built on theoretical narratives which posit an overly—sometimes conveniently—homogenized basic writing status quo against which mainstreaming is placed as a universally desirable fix.
- There are competing research bases relevant to the discussion of mainstreaming, and these databases need to play a significant role in our discussion.
- Practice in basic writing and in developmental education at large is varied as a function of the local situation.

- Only local decisions will have power as we search for ways to better serve, in our various writing courses—whether "basic" or "main-streamed"—students whose inexperience with prestige-valorized writing marks them as pariah in specific elitist colleges and universities.
- And finally, we will use the example of the basic writing program at the University of Minnesota-General College, where one of the authors works, to problematize the notion of "mainstreaming."

In all of this, we would point first to Deborah Mutnick's thoughtful caution that in articulating our professional differences on this issue, all of us must be careful about making an argument that might call for the demise of basic writing, lest our own arguments be used to further the regressive denial of access to students whose class and race mark them as targets of those who seek to reinscribe exclusionist policies in higher education. Mutnick points to the regressive imperatives at work in colleges and universities, asserting, "If 'basic writer' disappears as a name, actual students may disappear as well" (12). It would be ironic, indeed, if the mainstreaming moment's argument about the most appropriate location of effective supports for inexperienced writers were to be used by others to further exclude the very students whose social and intellectual well-being is the object of the argument.

We want to begin by examining two powerful articles that might lead one toward an abolitionist or mainstreaming posture. Both articles feature the homogenizing tendency that surfaces in the mainstreaming argument. Because of the respect the authors command among many of us who work in basic writing, we will point at their work as being typical of the way a straw man of abstracted "basic writing" is sometimes constructed to promote main-streaming. The first is David Bartholomae's "The Tidy House: Basic Writing in the American Curriculum." Bartholomae's article, more than any other, can be called seminal in the conversation about mainstreaming. Deriving significant power from the author's long association with basic writing, the piece lays out the shaping terms of the mainstreaming argument. The other is Ira Shor's "Our Apartheid: Writing Instruction and Inequality." Because of his usually thoughtful insistence on critical pedagogy and equity in higher education and because of the alarming trope of apartheid Shor uses to attack basic writing in mustering his appeal for mainstreamed alternatives, the piece defines the urgency of the discussion.

The theme of the "Tidy House" is by now fairly familiar. Bartholomae posits an abstracted entity "basic writing," figured here as a curricular mono-lith of tired liberalism, which is imposed on students willy-nilly in service of cultural replication, as a scam perpetrated to promote the job security and existential comfort of those who work in basic writing, and as an instance of otherizing institutional cynicism derived from our racially categorical culture. With basic writing constructed universally in this way, it is easy for him to spend the first three-quarters of his essay arguing against something so suspicious. Bartholomae asserts:

> I think basic writing programs have become expressions of our desire to produce basic writers, to maintain the course, the argument, and the slot in the university community; to maintain the distinction (basic/normal) we have learned to think through and by. The basic writing program, then, can be seen simultaneously as an attempt to bridge AND preserve cultural difference, to enable students to enter the "normal" curriculum but to insure, at the same time, that there are basic writers. (8)

Bartholomae continues:

> Basic writers may be ready for a different curriculum, for the contact zone and the writing it will produce, but the institution is not. And it is not, I would argue, because of those of us who work in basic writing, who preserve rather than question the existing order of things. (15)

The dismissive assertions grow textually from a confessional posture Bartholomae adopts in the paper's front end. He recounts his surprise and his pain and his guilt in serving as the agent of the memorable "Fuck you" paper he received in an early effort at teaching basic writers. The memory of the "Fuck you" paper, working in tandem with an idiosyncratic appropriation of Shelby Steele (9–10), leads Bartholomae toward his abolitionist intermediate position in the article. In the final quarter of the article, Bartholomae shifts to being coy. He questions whether he really believes his own argument to abolish basic writing, whether his crisis of conscience as a chief perpetrator of a system in which the "Fuck you" paper is writ large for him, is politic. Is it his own tired liberalism, or all of ours, which is in play? Is his critique just another "story" he is spinning, as he says he is so fond of? Is he creating his own "Fuck you" paper here because things in the culture and in universities have gotten complicated and he cannot see his way clear of it all? We are sympathetic. Surely there are basic writing programs constructed out of cynical motives and maintained at least in part by urges which are self-serving. But why are we unconvinced by Bartholomae's musings? Why do we come away thinking he is, in fact, dishonest here?

The passages quoted provide a kind of clue, perhaps, which points us toward what is wrong with Bartholomae's essay in general, and toward what is perhaps wrong with a great deal of the abolitionist or mainstreaming position. Having acknowledged that there is a great deal of diversity in the way basic writing students are taught across the country (8), he slides into a comforting, if mythical, theorized singularity in discoursing basic writing. Within that theorized singularity, Bartholomae posits a degree of homogenization of basic writing which is self-serving, convenient. In the first quoted segment, he slips subtly from a baseline of "*the* [emphasis added] skills course, the course that postponed 'real' reading and writing" (7–8) to "basic writing programs" to "*the* [emphasis added] basic writing program," whereas in the second he refers to "a different curriculum" (not, as one might expect, curricula) and "*the* [emphasis added] institution" (why not "our institutions"?) served by "an existing order of things." Throughout the piece—or at least its first three quarters—he builds his case as if there were a single entity, a "Tidy House of Basic Writing, Inc." operating coast to coast, replicating safe houses for tired liberals who run and teach THE COURSE in the presence of student "Others" the institutional company has manufactured and supplied.

Having played out this neoconservative scenario dressed up like a postcolonial insight, he backs off in the final quarter of the article. He sees that if basic writing disappears, so will the students served by such programs, and his liberal history will not let him do that. More to the point, he changes the locus of his discourse. Having constructed a straw man of conveniently homogenized "basic writing" in the singular, and having attached his argument to the theorized singularity of "basic writing" against which he implies a need for something else, without naming the something else, he propels himself at the end toward local action. He vows to "begin to formally question the status of basic writing at my own institution" (21).

In re-reading the piece some 7 years after it first appeared, we are struck by how passively the profession at large (Karen Greenberg, we note, excepted) has let Bartholomae work both sides of the street in this piece, by how strange it is that we have let him have it both ways as he plays out his angst against the imagined singular entity, and then wises up in the end to the fact that there is no "Tidy House" apart from his own institution.

In "Our Apartheid: Writing Instruction and Inequality," Shor explores the ways in which higher education and Composition can be manipulated to serve entrenched, classist interests. In many respects, Shor's piece is a thrilling synthesis of disparate perspectives on how students get sorted out and ground up in a factory model of higher education. When his attention turns to basic writing, though, he falls into the same homogenizing trap as does Bartholomae. He presents the undifferentiated entity "BW" as the agent of educational apartheid, "a containment track below freshman comp, a gate below the gate" (94), as a "colony" raided to fuel the belletristic metropolis of graduate and professional education. Like Bartholomae, Shor asserts a grandly unified evil entity—"an extra sorting-out gate in front of the comp gate, a curricula [sic] mechanism to secure unequal power relations" (92). He continues that "BW has helped to slow the output of college graduates . . . part of the undemocratic tracking system pervading American mass education, an added layer of linguistic control to help manage some disturbing economic and political conditions on campus and off" (93).

(It is worth noting, we think, that by appropriating the term "apartheid," Shor may also trivialize the profoundly evil, fatally delimiting experience of those who live or have lived under racial apartheid. We are not sure how noting this changes the argument, if at all, but we feel compelled to do so.)

Throughout his piece, Shor conflates uncritically the historical policies of the right and the motivations and local actions of student advocates, access support programs that led to basic writing courses in many sites, and to the place of basic writing in all institutions. Like Bartholomae, Shor constructs a conveniently abstracted singularity of "BW" against which he writes a provocative critique of class conflict in construction of exclusionist patterns in higher education. In so doing, though, he generalizes unforgivingly toward his convenient "BW" abstraction, oddly oblivious to myriad local realities that do not fit the convenient abstraction required by his trope.

Much of the mainstreaming debate is fueled by ideological argument and theory, as in the cases just discussed. These voices echo the earlier "Symposium on Basic Writing" (Laurence et al.) in which the ideological terrain of basic writing courses was explored and in which were bared the anxieties of some basic writing teachers relative to the rhetoric of CUNY's early open admissions advocates and in view of the institutional positions occupied by basic writing teachers and students at many sites. Like some critics of basic writing courses and programs in the "Symposium," Bartholomae and Shor invoke theory and their own version of conscience while ignoring the specific practices of widely varied and institutionally situated courses that serve a broad range of students who have not yet established as their own the ways of writing, which elitist faculty and governing boards use as markers to exclude them.

Less vital to the argument, to date, has been analysis of outcomes derived from various basic writing courses or their mainstreamed successor courses. This inclination away from quantitative study on the question is curious. Is it solely theory that guides our conversation? After all, there are databases available that provide a window on reasons to be cautious about rushing toward an abolitionist mainstream position as well as on local, site-specific approaches toward mainstreaming, which might be useful in informing other local practices. The quantitative studies provide a complicating strand to the mainstreaming conversation, supporting specific local revisions of how the most vulnerable students can succeed in writing courses, while also pointing us toward caution when making sweeping generalizations about how basic writing courses necessarily fail such students.

In some ways, the Fourth National Basic Writing Conference from which key articles in *Journal of Basic Writing* 12.1 are drawn marks the beginning of the current mainstreaming discussion. Among those seminal pieces, just alongside Bartholomae's "Tidy House," was Peter D. Adams' "Basic Writing Reconsidered." Adams makes a case for needed research to answer the question "whether segregated basic writing classrooms are the *best* [emphasis in original] environment for helping basic writers develop into proficient college level writers" (24–25). Troubled by his institution's practice of tracking students into basic writing on the basis of a flawed assessment tool and by the sometimes trivial curriculum that students so tracked encounter in basic writing courses at his institution, Adams examines course enrollment patterns and college success rates of students "placed" into his college's basic writing courses.

Adams finds troubling patterns when he analyzes his institution's data. He notes, for instance, that for students tracked into the lowest level of basic writing, the chances of succeeding in the credit-bearing writing courses at Essex Community College may actually be reduced if they follow the recommended course sequence through basic writing. Those students who avoided preparatory courses to which they were directed by the Essex placement mechanism succeeded in the credit course at a higher rate than they would have had they followed the placement "tracking." Adams discovered, and was rightly troubled by, a pattern that turned on its head the purpose of what was intended to be a supportive curriculum. Adams is careful not to overgeneralize from his data. He acknowledges the local nature of the research, and calls for more systematic analysis of the effects of placement-toward-tracking, noncredit systems of basic writing, and patterns of student success mediated by various forms of writing instruction. Adams provides a nice example of how local data can prompt a local rethinking of practice.

Similarly, Greg Glau, writing about the "stretch" program for ENG 101 at Arizona State University, offers a thoughtful institutional-specific alternative to a noncredit basic writing course. (The course and its rationale are described in "The 'Stretch Program': Arizona State University's New Model of University-level Basic Writing Instruction." Statistics on success rates used here are drawn from "Stretch Program Statistics," an e-mail posting to the Conference on Basic Writing listserv discussion CBW-L@TC.UMN.EDU, 14 Sept. 1997.)

The "stretch program" offers a year-long alternative to noncredit courses preparatory to ASU's one-semester ENG 101 course. Students are placed into the course on the basis of ACT or SAT scores, which identify them as being at risk of failure in writing courses at ASU. The stretch course replaces the noncredit preparatory ENG 071 course. Initial 3-year statistics support the stretch model for ASU students. Retention is improved by 61%; student success in the course and in the next course is remarkably high, better than it is for "regular" ENG 101 students; students evaluate the course as having been of benefit. From any point of view, the course better serves the needs and aspirations of ASU's "high-risk" students than its predecessor did. Although the course still has some of the negative characteristics Shor and others might attribute to basic writing courses (the placement mechanism, for instance), the stretch model "works" as a successor to the noncredit model that it replaces. Glau has been careful to use his data to critique a flawed ASU system and to create, test, and evaluate an alternative for his institution.

Advocates of mainstreaming, such as Shor, point to the FIPSE-funded work of Soliday and Gleason as an example of the virtues of mainstreaming. Soliday and Gleason have created a two-semester, credit-bearing "enrichment" course at CCNY for students who place into the "remedial" track (most typically, a sequence of two "remedial" and one "college-level" course, with reduced and noncredit status). Their results are impressive. Using FIPSE funding to support an ambitious evaluation of their "enrichment" pilot, Soliday and Gleason have been able to document high levels of satisfactory student achievement in credit-bearing courses and significant positive shifts in student attitude toward writing, writing courses, and themselves as writers.

So far as we know, Soliday and Gleason have not made claims about the generalized efficacy of their approach, nor does their published work indicate that they are inclined to do so. That is, they have been careful to describe their project as what it is: an institutionally contextualized project, which helps members of the CCNY community imagine alternatives to the extant placement and curriculum patterns in CCNY.

Perhaps the most ambitious use of institutional data to examine the success of students placed in basic writing courses is Edward M. White's "The Importance of Placement and Basic Studies: Helping Students Succeed Under the New Elitism." White analyzes information from the Division of Institutional Research in the California State University system office and the New Jersey Basic Skills Council Study. He is an interested analyst, to be sure, and is clear in positioning himself as writing against elitist, exclusionist practices among the resurgent right, and also as providing a counterweight to the "new abolitionists" in composition studies who argue for elimination of courses and programs—like basic writing—which support students identified by their institutions as being at highest risk of failing.

White's examination of the California and New Jersey data point toward conclusions that support thoughtful placement and careful instruction in things like basic writing programs. White's analysis suggests that such placement and careful instruction can lead to increased retention of students most at risk of failing. White acknowledges that flawed placement instruments or badly funded or badly designed curricula work against student success. His conclusion is that, based on data from the early 1980s, there is a strong case to be made for special placement into good basic writing courses, and that such placement tends to increase student retention and supports student progress. His analysis complicates the picture, to be sure, indicating that there is indeed something to be gained for students when their entering abilities are assessed carefully and when that assessment is used to place them into well-designed courses outside the so-called mainstream.

There are some apparently conflicting stories here. But there are also some elegant lessons relevant to the way in which the mainstreaming argument has unfolded so far. Adams has done a very credible preliminary critique of his home institution's practices of tracking, the irresponsible use of a testing measure with questionable validity, and the flawed outcomes of his institution's curriculum built on bad information. In view of the analysis he has done, he and his colleagues have begun to change the ways they think about placement and the ways in which they see the segments of their curriculum. Glau makes a strong case supporting change in how his institution works with writers who are thought to be likely to fail in the default writing course, and Soliday and Gleason give yet another alternative for institutional response. Meanwhile, White's analysis of system data suggest that in some instances an informed status quo can be seen to serve the academic progress of vulnerable students very well, tempering the mainstreaming urge.

At another level, the data-based pieces just noted lead us to ask whether, in fact, there is a mainstream or whether there are simply local rivulets that follow specific institutional topographies and reflect local conditions and local cultures. Perhaps oddly, one of the things that key records of the mainstreaming argument make clear is that there are any number of course-by-course and site-by-site variations upon the theme of basic writing. The conveniently asserted singular entity against which Bartholomae and Shor write as proponents of abolitionism or mainstreaming is shown for the straw man it is by the strongest of mainstreaming voices.

This is what we would expect, though, isn't it? In their work on "situated evaluation" of curricular innovation, Bertram C. Bruce and Joy Peyton argue that all local realizations of any innovation are bound to be distortions of that innovation. They argue that in adopting any innovation, we are "typically faced with a challenging task of resolving conflicts between old practices that derive from powerful situational constraints and imperatives of the new [approach]" (10). From site to site, from institution to institution, then, adopters of any curricular idea will shape it in light of local exigencies, local attitudes, and local opportunities. Mainstreaming at any number of sites would thus seem to be a rather predictable step as institutions modify practices in the face of new information, new opportunities, new constraints. As Bruce Horner demonstrates, there is a long history of writing instruction designed to serve the needs of students about whom traditionalist faculty have expressed doubt or hostility, a history that predates the development of Basic Writing in the 1970s at CUNY and has a wider contemporary bandwidth than that imagined by homogenizing critics like Bartholomae and Shor. Research by the National Center for

Developmental Education, for instance, indicates that fully 74% of colleges and universities offer some sort of work in reading, writing, or mathematics for students who are seen as "underprepared," an enterprise involving 3 million students and 100,000 faculty or staff, including a wide range of approaches and status markers. There may have been episodes in our history when curricular uniformity in basic writing might have been observable (after the publication of Wiener's *The Writing Room* or Bartholomae and Petrosky's *Facts, Artifacts, and Counterfacts*, perhaps). But on the whole, the landscape of writing instruction in the service of students at various college and university margins is more varied than we as a profession have acknowledged.

IS IT MAINSTREAMED YET?

We promised to illustrate aspects of this argument using the basic writing program at the University of Minnesota-General College (where co-author Terry Collins works). Our basic writing course is a two-term, credit-bearing sequence, which fully meets our University's lower division writing requirement and traces its roots to the General College Writing Lab courses first offered in the 1930s. The contemporary version of the course is highly supported with technology, class size (=18), and a walk-in reading/writing center where tutors and other resources are available. Graduate students from a variety of disciplines, full-time professionals, and tenured/tenure track faculty all teach our basic writing courses. The basic writing curriculum and its faculty are a key part of the larger developmental general education curriculum for General College students, who are drawn primarily from the lower two quartiles on the University of Minnesota's new student admissions formula [high school rank + (ACT comp × 2)]. Thus, our students are admitted to General College and its programs, including the basic writing sequence, prior to transfer into a degree program. Successful transfer usually takes place in the second year of enrollment. All developmental course credits, with the exception of high-school equivalent mathematics, transfer for eventual degree credit.

Students in General College tend to be economically poorer and more racially diverse (by a factor of three) than are students in the University of Minnesota-Twin Cities at large. They are more likely to be single parents, to be first-generation college students, or to use a language other than English in their homes than are their peers in the University at large. They tend to have academic and socioeconomic histories like those of students served in many basic writing programs, although the social context of basic writing students at large is widely ignored in our professional literature.

A decade ago, faced with information about dismal progress toward degree on the part of our students, we abandoned all noncredit "preparatory" courses and recycled money budgeted for such courses into buying down class size in the credit sequence and building writing classrooms with good technology. The ineffective "preparatory classes" were driven by a faulty, administratively mandated placement mechanism. In decommissioning such courses, we challenged and abandoned all placement subsequent to the initial admission placement into the General College (except for our most inexperienced ESL student, primarily refugees from Southeast Asian and East African countries). Instead, we simply placed all of our incoming students into the enriched, more aggressively supported two-semester "basic writing" sequence. The curriculum in the sequence has been described elsewhere (Sirc, Sirc and Reynolds), and can be accessed via http://www.gen.umn.edu. Quickly stated, we offer writing workshops which are intellectually grounded in critical reading organized by thematic questions and in which student writing is elicited in response to what we hope are real questions with undetermined, complex answers.

Recurring institutional research over the intervening decade tells us that General College students evaluate our basic writing courses very favorably, see them as both challenging and valuable, and, in retrospective assessments, attribute significant power to these courses in accounting for their eventual college success. We know that 100% of the General College students who successfully transfer into degree-granting colleges at Minnesota complete the basic writing sequence (data based on Fall 1996 cohort). And we know that those who find a way to avoid the basic writing courses or who postpone enrolling in them tend to fail to transfer into degree programs, and they drop out at elevated rates. Institutional research tells us that 87% of our virtually open-admissions students are passing the courses and meeting the lower division writing requirement—GED holders to 50+ percentile students at pretty much the same rates. Moreover, when they take the next writing course (an intermediate composition course or an upper division writing course in the college of transfer), they pass it at the same rates as do their competitively admitted peers who satisfied the lower division writing requirement in another unit.

In many ways, I suppose, our experience anticipated that of Soliday and Gleason or Glau. Over the past decade, we jettisoned a very ineffective series of noncredit courses; dumped a useless placement tool; decreased class size to increase instructor–student contact; rewrote the credit-bearing curriculum based on multicultural education principles and the best practices we could locate in the basic writing and composition literature; shifted the pedagogy toward a collaboratively designed workshop format; built sufficient capacity so that all sections meet all the time in networked computer classrooms; and shifted to a collaborative administrative, training, and mentoring model.

We have seen increased, timely student progress toward their stated goals, instituted an aggressive institutional research system to monitor how we are doing, and we have seen all three tenured faculty associated with the program's transformation earn the university's highest teaching awards in recognition of the effort.

But did we "mainstream?" Most emphatically not. There is still a much bigger, much more loosely structured and less well-supported "composition program" in the very selective College of Liberal Arts to which prestige and recognition are awarded in ways our program (because of our pariah status as open admissions) can only imagine. Our students are isolated structurally from the mainstream liberal arts curriculum until they transfer into a degree-granting program. Whereas Liberal Arts students take a single lower division writing course, our students take a two-term sequence of basic writing courses. Is there differential fiscal support for the main composition program vs. the basic writing program, as is sometimes asserted to be the norm? Yes, but the differential runs just counter to the usual claims. On any reasonable measure—class size, ratio of full-time vs. part-time faculty and staff, technology, tenure and promotion credit, administrative support, professional development support, tutorial support—the basic writing courses, located at the center of General College's self-conscious developmental curriculum, are much better supported than are the composition courses in liberal arts. We and our students are much better off in any number of ways precisely because we maintain our separate backwater, as opposed to mainstreamed, position in the university.

If we have not mainstreamed, then perhaps the question ought to be, "Do we run the kind of basic writing program against which the mainstreaming discussion is oriented?" We do not think we do. In fact, many who advocate mainstreaming would insist that what we did was to mainstream our basic writing program. After all, our basic writing courses anticipated characteristics of courses developed by Grego and Thompson, Soliday and Gleason, Glau, and others. But we resist that interpretation of what has happened here. We prefer to assert, rather, that what we have created is a best possible local realization of the kind of writing course that serves a "basic" or developmental student. We would assert further that Grego and Thompson, Soliday and Gleason, Glau, and others have done precisely the same thing. Driven by local exigencies, opportunities, and the desire to serve institutionally marginalized students in the most effective and respectful way possible, we, they, and uncounted colleagues who work in basic writing courses in a variety of institutions have created the best site-specific social and intellectual writing situation possible for our students.

"Mainstreaming" rhetoric too often (and too conveniently) implies that there is a single entity X (bad, essentializing, otherizing, exploitive basic writing) that ought to be transformed into entity Y (good, liberating, mainstreamed composition). Isn't it more complicated than that? And shouldn't we know better?

WORKS CITED

Adams, Peter D. "Basic Writing Reconsidered." *Journal of Basic Writing* 12.1 (1993): 22–36.

Bartholomae, David. "The Tidy House: Basic Writing in the American Curriculum." *Journal of Basic Writing* 12.1 (1993): 4–21.

Bartholomae, David, and Anthony Petrosky. *Facts, Artifacts and Counterfacts: Theory and Method for a Reading and Writing Course.* Upper Montclair, NJ: Boynton/Cook Publishers, Inc., 1986.

Boylan, Hunter, and Barbara S. Bonham. "The Impact of Developmental Education Programs." *Review of Research in Developmental Education* 9.5 (1992): 1–4.

Bruce, Bertram C. "Innovation and Social Change." *Networked-Based Classrooms: Promises and Realities.* Ed. Bertram Bruce, Joy Kreeft Peyton, and Trent Batson. Cambridge: Cambridge UP, 1993. 9–32.

Glau, Greg. "The 'Stretch Program': Arizona State University's New Model of University-Level Basic Writing Instruction." *Writing Program Administration* 20 (1996): 79–91.

Grego, Rhonda, and Nancy Thompson. "Repositioning Remediation: Renegotiating Composition's Work in the Academy." *College Composition and Communication* 47.1 (1996): 62–84.

Horner, Bruce. "Discoursing Basic Writing." *College Composition and Communication* 47.2 (1996): 199–222.

Laurence, Patricia, Peter Rondinone, Barbara Gleason, Thomas J. Farrell, Paul Hunter, and Min-Zhan Lu. "Symposium on Basic Writing, Conflict and Struggle, and the Legacy of Mina Shaughnessy." *College English* 55.8 (1993): 879–903.

Mutnick, Deborah. *Writing in an Alien World.* Portsmouth, NH: Boynton/Cook Heinemann, 1996.

Shor, Ira. "Our Apartheid: Writing Instruction and Inequality." *Journal of Basic Writing* 16.1 (1997): 91–104.

Sirc, Geoffrey. "*The Autobiography of Malcolm X* as a Basic Writing Text." *Journal of Basic Writing* 13.1 (1994): 50–77.

Sirc, Geoffrey, and Thomas Reynolds. "Seeing Students as Writers." *Networked-Based Classrooms: Promises and Realities.* Ed. Bertram Bruce, Joy Kreeft Peyton, and Trent Batson. Cambridge: Cambridge UP, 1993. 138–60.

Soliday, Mary, and Barbara Gleason. "From Remediation to Enrichment: Evaluating a Mainstreaming Project." *Journal of Basic Writing* 16.1 (1997): 64–78.

White, Edward M. "The Importance of Placement and Basic Studies: Helping Students Succeed Under the New Elitism." *Journal of Basic Writing* 14.2 (1995): 75–84.

Wiener, Harvey S. *The Writing Room: A Resource Book for Teachers of English.* New York, NY: Oxford University Press, 1981.

CHAPTER SIX

Those Crazy Gates and How They Swing: Tracking the System That Tracks African-American Students

Eleanor Agnew and Margaret McLaughlin
Georgia Southern University, Statesboro

> I believe myself to be an intelligent person, [but] my reading and writing world took a major hit when I took a college placement examination (CPE). I did not pass and had to take Developmental Studies Writing. I had never felt like such a failure. I felt incompetent, inadequate, and did not know if I was college material.
>
> —Bennie, a student

The controversy over tracking vs. mainstreaming is nothing new. At the 1992 Fourth National Basic Writing Conference in College Park, Maryland, a number of speakers debated the issue. The keynote speaker, David Bartholomae, questioned whether it is the profession or the students who are best served by basic writing programs, programs that maintain a distinction between "basic/normal" writers and attempt to standardize student voices (8). The following spring, the *Journal of Basic Writing* published the plenaries of the conference. Peter Dow Adams presents data from an informal study he conducted at his institution, which suggests that the disadvantages of basic writing classes may outweigh the advantages (33). Jerrie Cobb Scott explores factors that she believes contribute to a "recycling of deficit pedagogy" in many basic writing programs: a narrow definition of literacy as simply the ability to read and write, a definition that results in skills and drills pedagogies (47). Karen Greenberg, however, argues that most basic writing classes provide students with an opportunity to succeed academically, an opportunity they would not have if they were mainstreamed (69).

Ira Shor disagrees, saying that Greenberg's argument means almost nothing without substantiating proof that "these students could not have graduated without BW" (96). This decade-long discussion over whether underprepared writers should be tracked into basic writing or mainstreamed into freshman English classes, however, has not addressed a crucial aspect of the issue: the assessment system being used to determine students' course placement.

During a formal longitudinal study, which we conducted between 1993 and 1998, we found that it was not the basic writing course itself that negatively impacted our students' lives as much as the invalid assessment system that framed the program. We also discovered that an assessment system that lacks conceptual validity and interrater reliability is often most damaging to African-American basic writers whose home speech is African American Vernacular English (AAVE). Our findings suggest that unreliable and invalid writing assessment may contribute to the widely recognized cycle of academic failure and high attrition rates for Black students. Smitherman, in fact, believes, "The speech of blacks, the poor, and other powerless groups is used as a weapon to deny them access to full participation in the society" (*Talkin* 199).

African-Americans, in fact, are placed in college remedial classes at four times the rate of Whites, yet they receive only 6% of all bachelors' degrees granted each year (Gray). Steele presents similar findings: "Throughout the 1990's, the national college dropout rate for African-Americans has been 20 to 25 percent points higher than that for whites" (44). Rickford notes, "...in 1996... African-American students were performing more poorly in school than students from virtually every other ethnicity, particularly in the central areas of reading and writing" (1). Fidler and Godwin also refer to several studies that describe high college attrition rates for African-Americans, as do Feagin, Vera, and Imani. Additionally, after conducting a study of African-American college-level writers, Balester concludes, "School does not always provide an escape from racism but rather serves as a gatekeeping function to keep minorities in place" (10).

Statistics are one thing; real students with real lives and hopes are another. When Shanda came to our office at the end of the 1999 Spring Semester, we regretfully handed her an In Progress slip and told her we were sorry her exit essay had not passed. When we gave her the bad news, only the scoring results had been released, and we had not yet seen what she had written. However, after reading her essay, we thought it was a competent analysis of several complex characters in Ernest Gaines' *A Lesson Before Dying*, a novel her class read during the semester. We also thought that the evaluators' written objections on the score sheet were inconsistent and petty: one evaluator wrote only "comma and word errors, comma splice, awkward;" another "Real problems, especially in the intro., pronouns usually to blame;" a third evaluator wrote, "Good" or "Great" next to five of the eight criteria listed on the score sheet, and added, "lots of high points here, but the first body paragraph doesn't demonstrate 'being a man' " and then failed the essay. Shanda had written in response to the following prompt:

> "A hero is someone who does something for other people. He does something that other men don't and can't do. He is different from other men. He is above other men" (Ernest J. Gaines, *A Lesson Before Dying*, 191). Using Gaines' definition of a hero, write an essay explaining in what way(s) Jefferson and/or Grant Wiggins and/or someone you know is a hero (or heroine).

Nothing in the prompt suggested "being a man" was necessary. In fact, Shanda had illustrated that three of the characters in the novel, one a woman, all met Gaines' definition of a hero. Furthermore, try as we would, we could not find any pronoun problems in the introduction; had we and the graders been reading the same paper? We did note, however, several AAVE features, which, for us, did not interfere with the fluency of the text.

Although there is no appeals process at our university for students who fail the exit essay, we were so troubled by what had happened to Shanda's essay that we took it to an administrator. He read it himself, remarked that the paper was "wonderful," and clearly a passing essay. Ironically, he did not remember that he had been one of the evaluators who had failed the essay 2 days earlier.

THE SYSTEM

The 1995 CCCC Writing Assessment position statement recommends that "assessments of written literacy... should elicit from student writers a variety of pieces, preferably over a period of time" and states that "one piece of writing—even if it is generated under the most desirable conditions—can never serve as an indicator of overall literacy, particularly for high-stakes decisions." Even worse, "[t]ens of thousands of college-bound students are 'placed' into writing classes on the basis of assessment other than writing" (Hilgers 72). Students at our institution are among those tens of thousands: they are placed in basic writing classes on the basis of their high school GPA and SAT verbal scores. After placement, the only writing that counts at many institutions, including our own, as well as the whole University System of Georgia, is the timed, impromptu exit essay—a testing instrument that many assessment theorists consider invalid because it is "designed to reward the person who can come up with an idea fast and throw together some good sentences" (Purves 549), and is "based upon an outdated theory supported by an irrelevant epistemology" (Huot 551–2).

Not only do assessment specialists doubt the validity of impromptu essays as a high stakes testing instrument, but the interrater reliability of holistic scoring can also be questioned. Charney argues that the validity of holistically graded writing samples "has never been convincingly demonstrated" (68), and Lucas and Carlson refer to the need for "some systematic control" of the holistic assessment process, stating that the last stages of assessment should "focus on training readers, scoring the samples resulting from the performances, conducting statistical and qualitative analyses to establish reliability, validity... and to determine the assessments'... social consequences" (quoted in Camp "New Views" 143–4).

Furthermore, Ruth and Murphy state that writing prompts should be tested for the complexity of thought and writing skill required of the student: "The assigned writing task plays a critical role in determining how students perform and whether testers are measuring what they think they are measuring" (12). At our institution, however, students in different sections face a widely varying range of topic complexity because instructors individually create the exit essay prompts for their own classes. In contrast, White describes a "well established" model for essay test development (*Teaching* 60) and reminds us that writing ability fluctuates "according to the mental operation demanded by a particular writing topic"(68). Under this model, essay test topics are pre-tested, revised and pre-tested again before students write the real essay. During the pre-test phase, topics are screened for clarity, reliability, validity, and interest (68). White notes, "The fact that test questions must themselves be tested is not well understood" (64). Davis, Scriven, and Thomas also emphasize the importance of field-testing essay topics (89–90).

In addition, only the most cursory attempt at reader reliability is attempted in our program: before the holistic group scoring begins, a brief 15-minute calibration session is held where instructors defend personal reasons for evaluating sample papers as passes or fails. No attempt is made to train readers, or to establish test validity, or to discuss the social consequences for a student whose essay fails.

Social consequences are extremely high at our institution. If the exit essay is passed by two of three graders, the writer is eligible to enter Freshman English I. If the essay is failed by two of the three graders, the writer must repeat the course. Basic writing students who have not passed the exit essay by the end of their third semester are excluded from the university and must wait 3 years before becoming eligible to apply for re-admission. No appeals process exists.

THE EXIT CRITERIA

The Exit Criteria Score Sheets list eight possible strengths, ranging from "clear communication" to "adequate length," but graders usually write in any sentence-level deficits they find: typically s/v agreement, missing verb and noun endings, pronoun, and punctuation errors. How evaluators mark the criteria sheets clearly reflects the department's focus on grammatical and mechanical correctness above all other considerations. Not until we conducted our longitudinal study, however, did we discover the degree to which such a focus prevents many students whose home language is AAVE from ever entering regular college English classes.

BACKGROUND OF THE STUDY

In 1993, the year we began the longitudinal study, almost half of the entering freshmen were placed in remedial courses at our school, a regional university in southeast Georgia with an enrollment of about 14,000 students. Across the state, the media was focusing a great deal of attention on the large numbers of students in college remedial classes, the low graduation rate of these students, and the high cost of remediation for taxpayers—reportedly, $25.6 million dollars annually in the state of Georgia (Salzer 10-A). Within our own discipline of composition and rhetoric, controversy as to whether at-risk students should be tracked into basic writing courses continued. In 1992, The National Council of Teachers of English approved a resolution "to support curricula, programs, and practices that avoid tracking, a system that limits students' intellectual, linguistic, and/or social development." And in response to the article, "Remediation as Social Construct: Perspectives from an Analysis of Classroom Discourse," in which authors Hull et al. illustrate how prevailing cultural assumptions about remedial students can negatively affect instructors' perceptions of their performance, Elbow notes that "...it was her placement in a *remedial* class which tempted the teacher into seeing a cognitive deficit" (587). He then bluntly asks, "What justification do you see, really, for remedial classes at the college level...?" (588). These varying viewpoints gave us the impetus to examine our own program.

THE STUDY

During the 1993 fall quarter, 6 years before our recent experience with Shanda's exit essay, our administrators and our students gave us permission to conduct a study that would follow the academic progress of the 61 students who were placed in two basic writing classes we were teaching for as long as they remained at the university. As experienced teachers, we recognized that the students in these two classes were representative of basic writers at our university. Virtually all were recent high school graduates, whose SAT verbal scores ranged from a low of 220 to a high of 410. One-third was Caucasion, and two-thirds were African-American. Most were first-generation college students who perceived a college degree as their ticket to economic prosperity; thus, they entered our classes motivated to succeed.

We began the study with one principal research question, "what happens to high-risk writers after basic writing?" Related research questions included: (1) are there correlations between the attrition rate and students' work in the basic writing class?, and (2) will AAVE interfere with students' success in subsequent college courses? For 5 years, we followed the academic progress of the students through personal interviews, interviews with the students' instructors in subsequent English classes, analyses of their academic transcripts, and examination of their writings.

FINDINGS

When the students in our study wrote their first exit essay, we noticed in the pass rates a racial discrepancy that would become more pronounced with each subsequent academic term. At the end of the first quarter, 37 of the 61 students (60.6%) were successful in passing the exit essay.

- Of the 24 students (25%) who were required to repeat the course, six (25%) were White; 18 (75%) were Black.
- All five of the White repeaters (100%) passed the second basic writing course; 10 (55%) of the Black students passed.
- Of the seven Black students who were required to take a third basic writing class, six (85.7%) left the university before the end of their second year.
- Of the 40 Black students in the study, six (15%) were dismissed from the university for failure to exit remedial courses. None of the 21 White subjects was dismissed for failure to exit remedial courses.

When we compared these figures to the 1993 university-wide numbers, we found a similar pattern.

- Of the 828 entering Black freshmen, 398 (48%) were tracked into basic writing classes; 533 of the 1927 entering White freshmen (28%) were placed in basic writing classes.
- At the end of the first quarter, 240 of the 398 (60%) Black basic writers and 238 of the 533 (45%) White basic writers had to repeat the course.
- At the end of the second quarter, 137 of the 398 Black students (34%) and 183 of the 533 White students (34%) had not exited.

- After three quarters, 134 of the 398 Black students (34%) and 97 of the 533 White students (18%) had not exited.
- At the end of the fourth quarter, 124 of 398 Black students (31%) and 95 of the 533 White students (18%) had not exited.

Thus, almost twice the percentage of Black students (124/398 = 31%) as White students (95/533 = 18%) did not have the opportunity to pursue higher education at Georgia public colleges and universities for another 3 years.

THE LARGER PICTURE

The findings of our study and the figures from our institution reflect a nationwide pattern (Gray; Chapman; Presley). To explore the many possible reasons for the wide disparity between the percentages of Black and White students for whom basic writing bars the gates to higher education is clearly beyond the scope of this study, but even a cursory review of the literature suggests that socioeconomic factors, self-imposed cultural obstacles, inadequate educational backgrounds, and Eurocentric faculty and curricula may be a few of the contributing factors (Fidler and Godwin; Steele; Feagin, Vera, and Imani). Our research suggests still another possibility: the inflexible assessment styles of some English instructors can impede the progress of students whose home language is AAVE.

STUDENT WRITINGS

We studied the academic writings of a number Black/White pairs of our subjects with similar SATV scores. Excerpts from the portfolios of one of these pairs and a summary of their individual academic histories illustrate what we found in virtually every case: students whose writings contain AAVE markers had difficulty passing the exit essays.

KYLE AND ROWENA

Kyle, a White male, and Rowena, a Black female, were placed in the same basic writing class when they entered college. They had similar verbal SAT scores, and both knew exactly what majors and careers they wanted. As similar as their academic careers may sound, Rowena's AAVE language greatly hindered her academic progress. Kyle exited basic writing the first quarter, was never on academic probation, and received only one D grade. He stumbled only once in his stride toward graduation: he did not pass the exit essay at the end of the first quarter, but he was eligible to write a second essay, which he did pass. Rowena also did not pass the first exit essay, and she too was eligible to rewrite. Unlike Kyle, however, she did not pass, which made her next two college years very different from his. Rowena had to take two more basic writing classes before she was able to pass the exit essay.

To see if we could find any foreshadowing of what was to come, we studied the autobiographical essays and the exit essays Rowena and Kyle had written during their first basic writing class. The introductory paragraphs for their autobiographical essays follow:

INTRODUCTORY PARAGRAPH—KYLE'S AUTOBIOGRAPHY (OCT. 1993)

Entering my high school years I was surrounded by temptations. I came to Atlanta when I was thirteen. Being a young boy from Indiana, I did not know what to expect. From the age of thirteen to the age of eighteen I encountered many life changing experiences. Three major incidents help result in who I am: Getting my hair cut, quitting smoking, and when Brandi broke up with me.

INTRODUCTORY PARAGRAPH—ROWENA'S AUTOBIOGRAPHY (OCT. 1993)

Coming from a single parent home there are many sacrifices. My family are making sacrifices now to send me to college. I have two sisters, a brother, and a mother. They are giving up a lot of things for me. My mother had planned on retiring from her job this year. She had to put it off, because my father is not around. For a while she has been taking care of us by herself. She is a very independent woman. She has never asked anyone for a handout. In high school I worked and that made things a little easier for her, because she didn't have to worry about me. She told me I didn't need to work the first semester of college, just concentrate on my education. She tries to send me money, on the weeks that she don't have to pay bills. That could be money that she could take the other kids out and get them something nice. I went home last week, because I was broke. Even though she didn't have the cash to spare. We went out shopping for groceries. She bought me more things than I really needed. The kids thought I was getting special treatment, but I wasn't. These were things I deserved for trying to better myself.

What is immediately noticeable is the difference in length and in the desire to communicate. Kyle is very restrained in what he is willing to write about his "life changing" experiences, and what he will tell—getting his hair cut, stopping smoking, and breaking up with a girlfriend—he is forcing into a formula: a brief background statement before a three-pronged thesis. Kyle's voice is impersonal; he is writing in what Taylor and Lee call the "context-independent language style... [a style which] is rigid, controlled and predictable," the same style that Linn calls "formal or frozen" (quoted in Kamusikiri 200). Rowena, on the other hand, is writing a narrative about significant people and events in her personal life. Her writing voice reads like what Chaplin calls "recorded oral language or... a conversation" (quoted in Smitherman, "Blacker" 84). Coleman argues that the narrative style and personal topic lend themselves to the presence of AAVE features that contribute to the student's voice and ownership of the text (493). Ball's research shows that holistic evaluation of student writings may penalize culturally and linguistically diverse students... "for preferring rhetorical patterns that differ from the mainstream academic patterns rewarded in schools" (255).

Similarly, Anokye notes, "The storytelling tradition is strong among African Americans . . . . This is a linguistic style which causes problems with American mainstream speakers who want to get to the point" (48). The same differences between writing styles in the introductory paragraphs Kyle and Rowena wrote for their autobiographies can also be found in the introductory paragraphs to their exit essays:

INTRODUCTORY PARAGRAPH—KYLE'S EXIT ESSAY (DEC. 1993)

TOPIC: Our society is today faced with problems of racial prejudice, unemployment, high crime, drugs, and the formation of teenage gangs. Write an essay telling how any ONE of these problems has affected you or someone you know.

Drugs are a big problem in America's society today. People are arrested or killed by drugs every day. I have been around drugs throughout my teenage years. Not only until last year did drugs have an effect on my life.

ROWENA'S EXIT ESSAY (DEC. 1993)

TOPIC: How do you account for the popularity of one of your favorite entertainers?

Many entertainers are popular for numbers of reasons. They are popularity to me is accounted by their looks, their actions, and their talents. Popularity is very important to an entertainer's life. The entertainer I love the most is

Michael Jackson. Michael Jackson popularity started as a young child, while performing with his older brothers. Michael had a characteristic that made him seem different from his brothers, and other entertainers. He had an innocent attitude that took America by surprise.

Kyle's introduction for the exit essay has the same abbreviated length and toneless voice that we noted in the previous excerpt, and several of his word choices are awkward or inappropriate, but he does not violate standard English usage. Although Rowena chooses to analyze the popularity of an entertainer rather than write a narrative as she did in her autobiography, she retains the strong writing voice and the desire to communicate her feelings, as in the sentence, "The entertainer I love the most is Michael Jackson." Her introduction is unified, focused, and relatively error free, except for "Michael Jackson popularity," an AAVE marker. Writing *they are* for *their* is perhaps a result of hypercorrection, but this type of error so jumps out at anonymous evaluators in large-scale grading sessions that they may overlook Rowena's last sentence in the introduction: "He had an innocent attitude that took America by surprise," which has a clarity and sensitivity not often found in the writings of remedial students. Kyle's essay passed; Rowena's did not, and thus she had to enroll in basic writing for a second time.

When we interviewed Rowena's second basic writing instructor and asked her what she remembered about Rowena, she replied:

ANSWER: She was diligent. She came in with many grammatical problems that tend to go along with the Black English. And she worked hard to clear them up, but it was just not successful. It's hard, you know, to take a student who has grown up with bad speech, and then they put it into the writing, and then they don't recognize that it's incorrect.

QUESTION: What would you say is Rowena's biggest strength as a writer?

ANSWER: She understood what the essay was supposed to be, the argument following through with the support, and everything but it was just the obvious problems.

Despite the extensive work by linguists and researchers who, for the past several decades, have attempted to educate the academic community that AAVE is a "systematic, rule-governed language variety, every bit as complex and sophisticated as Standard English...that draws, in part, upon a distinctive set of stylistic and rhetorical features" (Meier 22–3), this instructor is still calling Rowena's speech "bad" and thus her writing is "bad." Smitherman says that many teachers think that speech of Black English-speaking students is "unsystematic" and "needs constant correction and improvement" even though such beliefs are "linguistically untenable" ("What Go" 50). Baugh agrees, stating, "Linguistic ignorance abounds even among the well-educated. It is not uncommon to hear woefully uninformed comments about language minority students..." (101). What happens to students who work very hard to overcome their "bad" writing is illustrated by the exit essays Rowena wrote at the end of her second and third quarters.

INTRODUCTORY PARAGRAPH—ROWENA'S EXIT ESSAY (MAR. 1994)

TOPIC: What have you found to be the main difference between high school and college teachers? Specific examples are a must to support your reasons and/or beliefs.

The experiences students endure in college are totally different from the experiences in high school. Adjustments are rarely made by students until their second quarter in college. Many students have the idea that the teachers in college and high school teaches the same way, or have the same rules to go by. The main differences between high school and college teachers are their grading system, lack of time to spend on a subject, and the number of students a teacher has to teach.

From this brief excerpt, we see that in the course of 10 more weeks in basic writing, Rowena has learned to use the five-paragraph theme formulaic pattern. She begins with a broad general statement, and with the exception of *endure*, there are no surprising words or images. A subject–verb error persists, but Rowena has learned to fit her ideas into a three-pronged thesis, which many basic writing instructors recommend, not only because it helps an inexperienced writer with an organizational pattern but because it has the added benefit of hastening the evaluation process. Rowena has also learned to distance herself from the topic and to let her voice be subsumed into objective discourse. This essay, however, also was not passed by the exit essay graders; thus, Rowena had to enroll in basic writing for a third time.

Below is the introduction of the exit essay written at the end of the third basic writing course.

INTRODUCTORY PARAGRAPH—ROWENA'S EXIT ESSAY (MAY 1994)

TOPIC: A good attitude helps students succeed in their classes. What are some bad attitudes that students sometimes have?

College students arrive on campus with different attitudes about college.

Attitudes can determine the success of a student. In an academic environment, people should have a positive attitude, but in most cases students do not. Many students have bad attitudes about college that lead to an unsuccessful future. The bad attitudes that some students sometimes have are giving up on themselves, not taking college serious, and blaming others for their failures.

This essay certified Rowena as ready to enroll in Freshman English I. After three basic writing classes, she was finally able to enroll in her first credit-bearing college English class.

Both Kyle and Rowena graduated within 5 years of their college matriculation, but Rowena's path was much rougher than Kyle's. To complete graduation requirements, she had to take basic writing three times, Freshman English I two times, and an Intensive Review Course for the Regents' Writing Exam three times. Rowena also attended summer school three out of four summers to make up for the noncredit courses, but she was still able to graduate in 5 years due to her own extremely high motivation.

DISCUSSION

A poorly designed assessment system is destructive when it determines who should or should not exit noncredit courses. Hilgers states, "It is my belief that bad assessment is what gets most students labeled as 'basic writers'" (69). Once tracked into the system, the burden of proof is on the students to demonstrate that they are not basic writers: regardless of how they perform during the course, they must write a passing essay on an impromptu topic during a timed writing session. Smith describes timed impromptu exit essays as "a strikingly incongruous culmination for [writing] courses" and points out that timed writing tests are "inappropriate (in the worst light, counterproductive) for writing programs informed by current research and theory of composition" (283). Camp agrees, stating "the streamlined performance represented by the single impromptu writing sample, which corresponds to only a small portion of what we now understand to be involved in writing, no longer seems a strong basis for validity" ("Changing" 69). These assessment specialists support our contention that tracking based on invalid and unreliable assessment can be extremely harmful for developing writers.

Black basic writers also face the additional impediment of being evaluated by White graders untrained in composition or linguistic theory, who penalize writing for not conforming to a strict, Eurocentric model. "Concerns about bias in direct essay testing have surfaced only recently," writes Hamp-Lyons. "To students outside the mainstream, essay tests are especially threatening" (51–2). Feagin, Vera, and Imani point out that "the intellectual discourse at traditionally White colleges and universities is for the most part parochial and restricted by subtle or overt Eurocentric interests and biases" (114). That many teachers have little knowledge about the legitimacy of AAVE as a language and thus have negative attitudes about it and those who use it is well-documented (Smitherman; Baugh; Balester; Kamusikiri; Ball and Lardner; McLaughlin and Agnew).

RECOMMENDATIONS

Overlooking the issue of whether tracking in itself is good or bad, we propose that any assessment procedure associated with it would benefit from a closer examination. Too often, breaking out of the basic writing track is more like a game of chance than a measurement of writing skill, particularly when advancement to the next level is determined by one timed, impromptu essay that undergoes capricious evaluation. Many capable writers find themselves going around the track more than once. A study by Otheguy finds that accumulating college credits plays a major role in the retention of minority students (quoted in Soliday 96) and typically, basic writing courses are noncredit courses for which students must pay in time, energy, and money.

Furthermore, if institutions choose to track students into basic writing programs, they need to articulate not only what specific outcomes suggest student readiness for regular English courses, but how they will gauge these outcomes. Belanoff, in "The Myths of Assessment," asks, "Are we grading a piece of writing in any meaningful sense at all? Under what circumstances would a student ever be asked to do this thing we've asked him to do on the test?" (58). Outcomes should be discussed openly by faculty members during frequent calibration sessions where numerous models of student papers are used as bases for discussion. Ideally, faculty should be trained to see the difference between just plain poor, out-of-control writing, and writing that contains AAVE patterns.

The nature of the assessment is critical in a basic writing program because assessment can drive the pedagogy. If a timed exit essay determines "success" or "failure" in the course, basic writing instructors feel obligated to teach toward the test and are not as free to explore nonformulaic types of writing. When the test becomes more important than the course content, students are not necessarily developing as writers, even if they can pass the test. The CCCC Position Statement calls "writing assessment that alienates students from writing . . . counterproductive." Castellano and Smith describe how troubled they are about their institution's timed essay exam: "We end up helping students to write formulaically and superficially and to approach writing as pure performance rather than meaning making" (94).

Most important, we continue to wonder why there is such a rush to judgment of the language patterns of at-risk students, particularly African-Americans, when they are first-semester freshmen who have not even started their credit-bearing English courses. Sternglass' descriptive study vividly illustrates that "even the apparently most educationally disadvantaged students have the potential to achieve academic success if they are given the time and support they need to demonstrate their abilities" (299).

In no way are we suggesting that African-American students should not gain a reasonable mastery of the conventions of written standard English by the time they graduate from college. As Delpit argues, "The language associated with the power structure—'Standard English'—is the language of economic success, and all students have the right to schooling that gives them access to that language" (68). However, our present system contributes to creating a racially-based, two-tier classification of students. We must agree with Jones that, all too often, "racism situates basic writing programs as Jim-Crow way stations for minority students" (73). The psychological impact of the message that they are failures as writers and, ultimately, as students, is extremely damaging.

In "The Importance of Placement and Basic Studies: Helping Students Succeed Under the New Elitism," White illustrates that good assessment can work as a retention instrument, yet he recognizes that "All placement instruments are not created equal, nor are all basic writing programs equally effective" (83). Our research leads us to believe that students such as Shanda and Rowena would have fared better if they had not been tracked into basic writing. Elbow has said it all before: "We've got to be more careful when we place students in remedial tracks or classes" (587). When invalid and unreliable assessment methods invent basic writers who may become trapped in noncredit courses, it is difficult to draw conclusions about how much or how many students benefit from the course.

WORKS CITED

Adams, Peter Dow. "Basic Writing Reconsidered." *Journal of Basic Writing* 12.1 (1993): 22–45.

Anokye, Akua Duku. "Oral Connections to Literacy: the Narrative." *Journal of Basic Writing* 13.2 (1994): 46–60.

Balester, Valerie. *Cultural Divide: A Study of African-American College Level Writers.* Portsmouth, NH: Boynton/Cook Heinemann, 1993.

Ball, Arnetha. "Incorporating Ethnographic-Based Techniques to Enhance Assessments of Culturally Diverse Students' Written Exposition." *Educational Assessment* 1 (1993): 255–81.

Ball, Arnetha, and T. Lardner. "Teacher Constructs of Knowledge and the Ann Arbor Black English Case." *College Composition and Communication* 48 (1997): 469–85.

Bartholomae, David. "The Tidy House: Basic Writing in the American Curriculum." *Journal of Basic Writing* 12.1 (1993): 4–21.

Baugh, John. "The Law, Linguistics, and Education: Educational Reform for African American Language Minority Students." *Linguistics and Education* 7 (1995): 87–105.

Belanoff, Pat. "The Myths of Assessment." *Journal of Basic Writing* 10.1 (1991): 54–66.

Camp, Roberta."Changing the Model for the Direct Assessment of Writing." *Validating Holistic Scoring for Writing Assessment: Theoretical and Empirical Foundations*. Ed. Michael M. Williamson and Brian A. Huot. Cresskill: Hampton, 1993. 45–78.

———. "New Views of Measurement and New Models for Writing Assessment." *Assessment of Writing: Politics, Policies, Practices*. Eds. Edward M. White, William D. Lutz, and Sandra Kamusikiri. New York: MLA,1996. 135–47.

Castellano, Olivia, and Cherryl Smith. "Teaching Through the Looking-Glass: The Ethics of Preparing Students for Timed-Writing Exit Examinations." *Foregrounding Ethical Awareness in Composition and English Studies*. Ed. Sheryl Fontaine and Susan Hunter. Portsmouth, NH: Boynton/Cook Heinemann, 1998. 93–104.

Chapman, Iris T. "Dissin' the Dialetic on Discourse Surface Differences." *Composition Chronicle* 7.7 (1994): 4–7.

Charney, Davida. "The Validity of Using Holistic Scoring to Evaluate Writing: A Critical Overview." *Research in the Teaching of English* 18 (1984): 65–81.

Coleman, Charles F. "Our Students Write With Accents: Oral Paradigms for ESD Students." *College Composition and Communication* 48 (1997): 486–500.

Davis, Barbara, Michael Scriven, and Susan Thomas. *The Evaluation of Composition Instruction*. New York: Teachers College Press, 1987.

Delpit, Lisa. *Other People's Children: Cultural Conflict in the Classroom*. New York: New Press, 1995.

Elbow, Peter. "Response to Glynda Hull, Mike Rose, Kay Losey Fraser, and Marisa Castellano." *College Composition and Communication* 44 (1993): 587–8.

Feagin, Joe R., Hernan Vera, and Nikitah Imani. *The Agony of Education: Black Students at White Colleges and Universities*. New York: Routledge, 1996.

Fidler, Paul, and Margi A. Godwin. "Retaining African-American Students Through the Freshman Seminar." *Journal of Developmental Education* 17 (1994): 34–40.

Gray, Steven. "Study: Blacks Still Lag Behind Whites in College Education." *Savannah Morning News* 27 Feb. 1997: 3A.

Greenberg, Karen. "The Politics of Basic Writing." *Journal of Basic Writing* 12.1 (1993): 64–71.

Hamp-Lyons, Liz. "Exploring Bias in Essay Tests." *Writing in Multicultural Settings*. Ed. Carol Severino et al. New York: MLA, 1997. 51–66.

Hayes, Floyd. "Politics and Education in America's Multicultural Society: An African-American Studies' Response to Allan Bloom." *The Journal of Ethnic Studies* 17.2 (1989): 71–88.

Hilgers, Thomas. "Basic Writing Curricula and Good Assessment Practices: Whene'er Shall the Twain Meet?" *Journal of Basic Writing* 14.2 (1995): 68–74.

Hull, Glynda, et al., "Remediation as Social Construct: Perspectives from an Analysis of Classroom Discourse." *College Composition and Communication* 42 (1991): 299–329.

Huot, Brian."Toward a New Theory of Writing Assessment." *College Composition and Communication* 47 (1996): 549–65.

Jones, William. "Basic Writing: Pushing Against Racism." *Journal of Basic Writing* 12.1 (1993): 72–80.

Kamusikiri, Sandra. "African-American English and Writing Assessment: An Afrocentric Approach." *Assessment of Writing: Politics, Policies, Practices*. Eds. Edward M. White, William D. Lutz, and Sandra Kamusikiri. New York, MLA, 1996. 187–203.

McLaughlin, Margaret, and Eleanor Agnew. "Teacher Attitudes Toward African African American Language Patterns: A Close Look at Attrition Rates." *Attending to the Margins: Writing, Researching, and Teaching on the Front Lines.* Ed. Michelle H. Kells and Valerie Balester. Portsmouth, NH: Boynton/Cook Heineman, 1999. 114–30.

Meier, Terry. "Teaching Teachers About Black Communications. *Rethinking Schools* 12.1 (1997): 22–3.

Presley, John. "Evaluating Developmental English Programs in Georgia." *Writing Program Administration* 8 (1984): 47–56.

Purves, Alan C. "Apologia Not Accepted." *College Composition and Communication* 46 (1995): 549–50.

Rickford, John R. "Language Diversity and Academic Achievement in the Education of African American Students—An Overview of the Issues." *Making the Connection: Language and Academic Achievement Among African American Students.* Eds. Carolyn Temple Adger, Donna Christian, and Orlando Taylor. McHenry, IL: Center for Applied Linguistics and Delta Systems, 1999. 1–30.

Ruth, Leo, and Sandra Murphy. *Designing Writing Tasks for the Assessment of Writing.* Norwood, NJ: Ablex Publishing, 1988.

Salzer, James. "Four of 10 Freshmen Unprepared for College." *Savannah Morning News.* 14 Apr. 1997: 1A, 10A.

Scott, Jerrie Cobb. "Literacies and Deficits Revisited." *Journal of Basic Writing* 12.1 (1993): 46–56.

Shor, Ira. "Our Apartheid: Writing Instruction and Inequality." *Journal of Basic Writing* 16.1 (1997): 91–104.

Smith, Cherryl A. "Writing Without Testing." *Portfolios: Process and Product.* Ed. P. Belanoff et al. Portsmouth, NH: Boynton/Cook Heinemann, 1991. 279–91.

Smitherman, Geneva. *Talkin and Testifyin.* Boston: Houghton-Mifflin, 1977.

———. " 'The Blacker the Berry, the Sweeter the Juice': African American Student Writers." *The Need For Story: Cultural Diversity in Classroom and Community.* Ed. Anne Dyson et al. Urbana, IL: NCTE, 1994, 80–101.

———. "What Go Round Come Round': *King* in Perspective." *Tapping Potential: English and Language Arts for the Black Learner.* Ed. Charlotte K. Brooks et al. Urbana, IL: NCTE, 1985. 41–62.

Soliday, Mary. "From the Margins to the Mainstream: Reconceiving Remediation. *"College Composition and Communication* 47 (1996): 85–100.

Steele, Claude. "Stereotype Threat and Black College Students." *Atlantic Monthly* Aug. 1999: 44–54.

Sternglass, Marilyn. *Time to Know Them: A Longitudinal Study of Writing and Learning at the College Level.* Mahwah, NJ: Lawrence Erlbaum Associates, 1997.

White, Edward M., William D. Lutz, and Sandra Kamusikiri. *Assessment of Writing: Politics, Policies, Practices.* New York: MLA, 1996.

———. *Teaching and Assessing Writing.* San Francisco: Jossey-Bass, 1994.

———. "The Importance of Placement and Basic Studies: Helping Students Succeed Under the New Elitism." *Journal of Basic Writing* 14.1 (1995): 75–83.

CHAPTER SEVEN

Moving the Margins

Marti Singer
Georgia State University, Atlanta

At a recent conference, I met a woman who spoke about the power of narrative in writing. As we discussed briefly the human need to tell our stories, it occurred to me that conferences—all oral and written texts, really—represent a legitimate and formalized vehicle for all of us to tell our stories. Some stories are personal, some professional, some imaginary, but all of them allow for reflection that moves us forward and beyond the events toward insights as we hear ourselves tell them. We need extended and blended stories, sometimes whole new ones, if we are to develop as individuals, as educators, as writers, even as a culture.

The stories shared among basic writing professionals vary in scope and specifics, but they seem to carry common themes: student access to the academic community, student success, teacher's experiences, and the training of writing instructors. During the last 10 years of the twentieth century, many of the stories reflect the politics and programs surrounding issues of mainstreaming remedial writers, creating studio models and stretch models that enhance student success, and generally re-visioning ways to work with and provide access for students designated as "remedial" by the institution (Segall; Soliday; Grego and Thompson; Stygall). Many of these storytellers refer to Mina Shaughnessy's vision and fear for a remedial model that separates students from the mainstream of the college or university, "its potential for ghettoizing programs, for labeling students, and for simplifying views of how adults learn language" (Soliday 85). On the other hand, as Soliday continues, "... because remedial programs usually serve the most socially diverse groups of students within an institution, main-streaming can threaten the educational careers of students who otherwise might not be in college. Remedial programs create sheltered educational pockets for academically marginal writers, and as a result some scholars have argued that mainstreaming could eliminate these writers along with the programs" (85). Such is the case for many of the scenarios shared over recent years.

The need to re-visit and to listen to our stories, whether these stories exhibit successes or generate questions or propose new programs, is essential if we are to understand the political and cultural impact of decisions made around basic writing. We must also recognize that sometimes decisions made by institutions and governing bodies such as Boards of Regents are larger than we are, and may not reflect successes or theory or research within a basic writing program. Financial concerns, image, and reputation are often the driving forces behind decisions that affect what actually takes place in education. Those of us in the "trenches" must share our perceptions of the students we serve and the innovations we create toward their success in the academic community. In doing so, we may discover ways to impact not only the students but also the more distant decision makers.

So this is my story. It is one faculty member's reflections about marginalization. It is about a course created to bridge the isolated remedial courses to the freshman composition program without entirely mainstreaming the students. It is about multiple perceptions of language use, audience, collaboration, developing learning communities, and what it means to belong in the academic community. It is about 20 years of teaching, research, and service in a basic writing program at a large urban university. And it is about the constant moving of the margins.

MOVING IN: THE EARLY YEARS

For over 20 years, colleges and universities have struggled with approaches to teaching composition to those students who come to us as basic writers. As the definition for basic writing changes from Shaughnessey's time to the present, and admission standards in many states continuously rise, meeting the needs of these students year after year feels a bit like "hitting a moving target."

In the mid-1970s, the Board of Regents of the University System in Georgia mandated that each of the 33 colleges and universities in the state provide a program of courses for underprepared students in the areas of English, reading, math, and study skills. These programs were to be housed in free-standing divisions in the institutions. These divisions were to be financially independent and not connected to any particular college or department within the institution. At Georgia State University, an urban institution located in downtown Atlanta, each of the areas of English, reading, math, and study skills was designated as a curricular unit within the Division of Developmental Studies, and each unit strived to develop curricula that provided students with the academic skills needed to fully function in the university.

In 1975, the English/composition unit of the program consisted of one basic writing course. The purpose of this course was to prepare undergraduates for the writing demands of the university. As I understand it, the course focused on sentence and paragraph writing and included a great deal of usage and grammar teaching. In the summer of 1980, when I began teaching in this program as a graduate teaching assistant (GTA), a second course in basic writing was introduced. This second course began at a more "advanced" level where students began with paragraphs and moved to essay length writing by the end of the quarter. Students were placed in the lower or upper level course based on their SAT verbal score, their high school English grades, and a predicted grade point average. Placing students in any writing course based on information other than a writing sample posed a variety of problems, but at that time there were no placement procedures that included writing samples. Students could exit the program only from the upper level course, which included an exit essay holistically scored by three raters (not including the instructor) and a passing score on a basic skills (usage) test.

As a former high school English teacher, I remember feeling overwhelmed and astonished not only with the level of writing of the students in my classes at the university, but also with the diversity, both in skill and in culture, within each group. Students came to us with very little schema for academic writing. They ranged from those who thought the spelling of "essay" was "SA" to those who had written research papers in high school and needed mostly encouragement and practice. Some students who had difficulty putting a whole sentence together on paper could converse intelligently about the experiences they had, about their work, and about the ways they solved problems. And, of course, the reverse was also apparent. Younger students who had a clearer schema for written language sometimes had trouble with logic and critical thinking. They were much more unaware of their thinking processes. And they did not realize that the kind of writing expected from them at the university may differ from what they produced in high school. Teaching developmental composition at an urban research university would be more challenging than I had imagined. In addition, I was very unaware of the politics—for about a year.

MOVING ON: THE MIDDLE YEARS

What I had not anticipated was the moving target. Every year or so, the university raised its admission standards, the Board of Regents changed its bottom line, and the curriculum in developmental composition kept pace. In 1984, I completed my doctoral program and became an assistant professor of composition in the Division of Developmental Studies. During the mid-1980s, the Division hired assistant professors with PhDs, doubled the number of professors across the program, and relied on part-time instructors and graduate teaching assistants as the number of students tripled. In addition, we began serving students who needed extra help to pass the Regents exam, a reading and writing test required by the Board of Regents (but separate from Developmental Studies) to graduate from any state-supported college or university. We taught 5-week courses in Regents reading and writing that focused on passing that exam. Students in these classes were often transfer students and students for whom English is a second language, usually sophomores and juniors in status. By 1988, we had fewer students in both the Regents courses and the developmental composition courses who wrote the way that Mina Shaughnessy described "basic writers" and more students who wrote like David Bartholomae's students as he discussed basic writing at Pittsburgh. By this time, both courses in the developmental composition program focused on whole essays, the lower one developing fluency and the upper course logical development, exposition, and argument.

The Division prided itself on the research and teaching that occurred within each unit. The composition professors focused on cognitive development as it related to writing, looking to the work of Jean Piaget, Jerome Bruner, Lev Vygotsky, and William Perry, while keeping pace with the research of Janet Emig, Linda Flower and John Hays, Sonya Perl, Nancy Sommers, and David Bartholomae. We made clear distinctions among ourselves of the differences between a remedial and a developmental model, and strove to focus on the intellectual growth of our students through a developmental model rather than a medical one. On a practical level, I discovered that when students are clear about their focus and the meaning they want to make in writing, the usage errors tend to dissipate and the whole of their writing is more effective.

In addition, the more students became involved in university life, academic and social, the more models of freshman composition we shared with them, and the more we treated them as part of the academic community, the closer their writing came to the academic tone and thinking expected of college freshmen. Our teaching became less concerned with usage and diction and more focused on the readings in the freshman composition texts we chose and on conventions valued in college writing. It seemed that the more we expected from our students as participants in the academic endeavor, the more success we all experienced. Still, students voiced the feeling of being out of sync with the rest of the university, not fully a part. As faculty, we found ourselves continuously defining and explaining what we did within the university, what our research was about, and why it was worthwhile to provide access to such a large group of students.

In the mid-1980s, several of us in the composition unit called for a written placement procedure to help designate the appropriate course for developmental composition students. We were told that, because of the nature of this urban university, the admission procedures and timing at Georgia State, any kind of writing placement was virtually an impossible task. Three thousand essays would need to be scored, many of these in a 2-week period just before classes began and half of these essays would be written by students who would never actually register for classes. Even if we wanted to attempt it, we would have to set it up ourselves, score the essays ourselves—with no compensation or help from the university. We chose to let it go and set up a system within the curriculum whereby students who entered the lower level course, and who performed well on the diagnostic essay written during the first week of class in the lower level course, could be placed in the upper level course. Secondly, if students in the lower level course earned an A or B in the course, they would choose to take the exit essay, and upon passing this essay, exit the program along with those from the upper level course who passed the exit essay. Students then could exit from either course depending on their success in the course and on the exit essay writing sample. All students still had to pass a test of standard written English with a score designated by the Board of Regents and the university. Our primary goal was providing access through preparation.

Every year, we looked closely at success rates for students who exited our program in terms of their success in the freshman composition course. In the mid-1980s, about 70% of students who exited from the upper level course of our program passed the freshman composition course the first time they took it. This figure compared to approximately 78% of students in freshman composition at that time who passed the first time without courses in basic writing. However, the students who exited from the lower level course fared less well in the freshman composition course. Approximately 56% of those students passed the first time they took the freshman composition course. We asked ourselves several questions: is the difference in percentage between the upper level course students and the lower level course students about curriculum differences in the two courses? Do the SAT verbal scores and admissions requirements make a more profound prediction than we thought? Should we move back to the two-course sequence, exiting students only from the upper level course? Or should we create another avenue for students in the lower level course, some of whom seemed ready for freshman composition? Before we could come up with some conclusions or resolve to these questions, admission standards continued to rise, and we were faced with new issues.

MOVING BEYOND: YEARS OF CONTINUOUS CHANGE

Toward the end of the 1980s, rumors on campus, articles in the media, and conversations in the Division circled the subject of "doing away" with developmental studies at some of the universities in the state, and instead, serving underprepared, at-risk students at the junior colleges and smaller 4-year schools. We were aware of other states—Ohio, Florida, California— where this kind of change was taking place. At the time, most of us felt confident that the Board of Regents would not completely dissolve the programs so well established in the state, but pressure to upgrade standards at the secondary school levels and the shift in affirmative action guidelines and other political activities gave us plenty of concern. In the early 1990s, the Division was "encouraged" to change its name from the Division of Developmental Studies to the Division of Learning Support Programs. Still we were not particularly alarmed. We were a free-standing division with a teaching/research mission.

However, in the mid-1990s, we became the Department of Learning Support Programs, a department within the College of Arts and Sciences. This shift particularly made many of the faculty in our department nervous about the future of learning support for students, not to mention our own positions in the university. This political change challenged us to redefine our mission, our curriculum, perhaps our futures. The Dean of the College encouraged us to think about retention efforts for undergraduates on a larger scale than learning support for unprepared students. We were also encouraged to develop graduate training for graduate students across the college similar to the courses and mentoring we were currently doing for those graduate students who taught with us. The positive piece, as we saw it, was that by becoming a part of the college where the core curriculum occurs, we might change the perceptions of other departments about the value of working with underprepared students, about creating retention efforts through curriculum change, and maybe—just maybe—feel less marginalized in the university.

Over the years, the English Department and the Composition Unit in Developmental Studies had functioned as distant cousins, respecting the other but not fully engaging in common activities. Some English professors had been outwardly verbal about the "lack of skill" on the part of our students as they came into freshman composition. I advised students not to mention that they were previously in our program unless asked directly. But our becoming a department within the same college happened to occur at the same time that the English Department was developing a Composition and Rhetoric program. As the English Department hired new professors well versed in composition, the opportunity to work together seemed timely. We made several attempts at communicating and working with the freshmen composition program. We exchanged professors. I taught freshman composition and a colleague in the English Department taught our upper level basic writing course. Both departments included the other at colloquia, at orientation meetings, and at faculty meetings where composition issues are discussed and presented. This closer connection influenced the curriculum and program procedures for both the English Department and our Composition Unit as well. We became much more aware of the changes in expectations of the freshmen composition courses and adjusted our curriculum so that students were better prepared to enter the freshmen program in writing. The English Department changed their exit procedures to match more closely the way we had been functioning for many years, a 2-day exit essay process that allows for revision and that reduces some of the anxiety caused by 1-hour timed writing situations.

As the admission standards changed, and as the high schools and the nontraditional students changed, so did the writing from students who were placed in the basic writing courses. We realized that many of the students who were accepted to Georgia State provisionally and placed in the Department of Learning Support Programs had profiles much like the students who were admitted as "regular" freshman just a few years ago. No wonder the English Department could not tell which students were ours anymore, and, in fact, some faculty expressed surprise at the level of writing that came from students in our program. Although our upper level students passed freshman composition at about the same rate as regular freshmen not in our program (often at a higher rate), we found that those who exited from the lower level continued to have less success. We revisited the problem for students who exited our program from the lower level course and expanded our composition curriculum to meet the needs of this group of students. Without realizing it consciously, at first, we created a course that would come very close to the heart of the mainstreaming issues.

THE CO-COURSE

In the spring of 1994, we piloted the Department's first co-course, LS (Learning Support) 082, designed to serve as a "course between" the upper level basic writing course and freshman composition. The course was taught in conjunction with freshman composition, English 111. It was neither a stretch model nor a studio model course, but a completely separate course from freshman composition that students took (for no credit, of course) during the same quarter they took freshman composition. Originally, we had hoped to pair the co-course with specific freshmen composition sections, thinking that it would be a tighter course and easier for the co-course instructor in terms of focusing on writing needs and teacher style. The 1994 pilot had eight students enrolled, five of whom dropped the course (and their freshman composition course). The three who remained passed freshman composition. However, we were very discouraged that students chose not to stay in the course. As we reviewed the curriculum carefully, we recognized that we could not teach this section of composition as an entirely different writing course. Students did not appreciate the "extra work" of a second freshman composition class, and did not see the connection to the freshman composition course they were trying to pass from the English Department. They had, after all, exited Learning Support.

In the Winter of 1996, we tried again. This time I offered the course as a "support" for freshman composition, and designed the curriculum around the English Department syllabus for English 111, adding only those aspects of writing instruction and discussion of readings that seemed appropriate for the class at the time. This time, we did not try to pair LS 082 with any particular English 111 section. The registration nightmare of finding entire sections for pairing convinced us to try the course without the one-to-one match. And it worked.

Students from the lower level course who passed the exit essay with two out of three passing scores were required to take the LSP 082 co-course with English 111. Some students questioned this change in exit requirement, but when I explained to them the percentage of success from previous students exiting from the lower level course, they agreed to give the course a try. Students from the upper level course who passed the exit essay with two out of three passing scores were encouraged, but not required, to take the co-course as well. In addition, the Department invited (by announcement and flyers) non-Learning Support students who had failed English 111 or who just wanted the extra support the co-course could provide them. The enrollment jumped from eight in the first pilot to 30 students in the second one. I taught two sections of the co-course.

I often describe teaching this course as "teaching from the seat of my pants" or "dancing my way through the quarter" as most of the content and instruction came from spontaneous discussion and immediate needs of the students enrolled. The simpler I kept it, and the less rigid I was about what I thought students needed, the more we seemed to accomplish. Although I entered each quarter with a syllabus and plan for each day of class, I learned quickly that the actual content of the class would have to come from the needs of the students present. I began each class with the question, "What's going on in your English 111 class?" Most days students had questions of their own, sometimes about a usage issue, sometimes about structure, sometimes about the procedures of their particular section of English 111. If their questions coincided with what I had planned for the day, fine. If not, I asked the group if they wanted to deviate from the syllabus and focus on "this issue." Most of the time, they wanted to work on the problems and immediate concerns of their classmates, concerns they often shared.

During winter quarter 1996, the 30 students enrolled in LS 082 were also enrolled in 15 different freshman composition sections. It became readily apparent to me as the instructor of the co-course that students in these classes would come to understand that the teaching of writing held many conventions and many idiosyncrasies. Within a week or two of class, we began looking consciously for these conventions and individual preferences for writing product, process, and teaching approach. I learned quickly that I was not only supporting students in their writing development, but I was also supporting each freshman composition instructor for her or his approach and perception of the teaching of writing. I sensed that it was important that the students "believe" that their freshman composition instructor and I had the same basic goals and ideals even though our methods and emphases may vary. I found myself coming up with many analogies from the workplace, from home settings, from sports, and from music to convince the students that although writing may seem tremendously subjective at times, there remain certain conventions that most adhere to in order to make sense within a particular setting.

Increasingly, I recognized that I was not only teaching composition, expanding on others' definitions and explanations, conferencing and tutoring, teaching strategy and encouraging persistence, but I was also helping students see ways to look at the world of academia that they might not have otherwise seen this early in their college lives. I was teaching them about thinking critically and about becoming part of the academic community.

Beyond discussion of various readings that would enhance critical thinking and academic voice in writing, our discussions brought out differences within the composition curriculum from one instructor to another. How is it, they wondered, that in one class students were required to read extensively whereas in another class students read very little? One instructor focused on argument through short socially oriented essays, and another instructor focused on argument through literary study with short stories, poems, and an occasional novel. Why were some instructors sticklers for parallel construction, for MLA style, and for verb and pronoun usage, whereas others demanded certain modes for development and organization? The analogies to sports and work experiences were helpful with these questions. I asked them, "Did every coach you had for soccer focus on the same strategy, the same plays, the same skills? If you had a boss who expects you to use company letterhead for certain kinds of communications, what do you do? How do you learn about the different 'rules' or requirements in various situations?" Through this kind of questioning and discussion, we discovered together that they knew a great deal about survival and flexibility in a number of settings, and that learning and mastering the university conventions would be no more difficult for them than their previous experiences.

This questioning, comparing, and contrasting became topics for response papers as well as general discussion. Probably one of the most powerful discussions for me around this topic came the day that one student began talking about his feelings of being "outside" the university when he was taking his Learning Support courses. "I was at the university, but I wasn't a real student." The co-course, however, seemed to give him a sense that he had stepped over the line and had at least one foot "in" whereas the other remained "out." This straddling of the margin was better, from his point of view, than being completely separated.

MEASURING SUCCESS

Because the primary goal of LS 082 was success in freshmen composition, I chose to compare the success in English 111 for students who had not taken LS 082 with success rates in English 111 for those who had taken both courses the same quarter. To pass freshmen composition, a student had to have a grade of C or better and pass the English Department's exit essay with a grade of C or better. If a student had a passing grade in the class but did not have a passing score on the final, that student received a grade of D in the course and had to retake it. The first time the course was offered and the comparisons completed, we knew we had hit on something successful for students. Of the 30 students enrolled in the winter 1996 course, one withdrew on hardship, three failed the final essay and received Ds for the freshmen composition course, and 26 students passed it (86%). Of the 26 who passed, three earned As, ten earned Bs, and 13 earned Cs. Table 7.1 shows how students in LS 082 compared to the group of English 111 students who were not enrolled in a co-course over several quarters. These grades reflect only the English 111 grades for both groups.

Philosophically, the co-course LS 082 represented a shift from a developmental stance in composition to a learning support stance. Many of the students came to the course with a view of academic writing as a very static, rigid, definable product that they just could not do and that somehow others could. With 15 to 17 different freshman composition teachers represented in the LS 082 classes, students began to see academia as multiplistic, complex,

TABLE 7.1

Student Pass Rates for Freshman Composition (English 111) Compared to Freshman Composition With Co-Course (LS 082)

Number of Students

Grades in English 111 for Students Enrolled	Winter 1996		Spring 1996		Fall 1996		Winter 1997		Spring 1997	
	English 111	English 111 w/ LS 082	English 111	English 111 w/ LS 082	English 111	English 111 w/ LS 082	English 111	English 111 w/ LS 082	English 111	English 111 w/ LS 082
	566	30	325	14	1143	28	743	33	398	14
A	12%	10%	10%	13%	11%	11%	10%	0%	15%	14%
B	35%	33%	32%	27%	39%	29%	34%	45%	33%	29%
C	28%	43%	21%	20%	24%	43%	31%	45%	30%	36%
D	1%	10%	1%	27%	1%	11%	1%	1%	1%	7%
F	5%	0%	4%	0%	2%	4%	3%	1%	4%	0%
W	8%	1%	17%	13%	7%	4%	9%	1%	13%	14%
I	1%	0%	1%	7%	1%	0%	0%	0%	1%	0%
Other	11%	0%	16%	0%	14%	0%	12%	0%	5%	0%
Pass rate	75%	86%	63%	60%	74%	83%	75%	90%	78%	79%

and subjective, and were better able understand these within the concepts of varied audience, convention, and idiosyncrasy as these were discussed in the classroom. Although the quantitative data here indicates student success with the co-course, understanding their growth and success as writers and as members of the learning community came not through looking at the quantitative data, but rather through various methods of reflection. Along with student evaluations, I asked them to write several short reflective papers about their writing and their progress.

Student evaluations concerning the course and the teacher were consistent across the sections of the co-course. Many students commented that the course helped them gain confidence in their writing and in themselves for future courses that required writing. Many requested that the course be offered for more contact hours. They wanted more one-on-one time and more class time for brainstorming and discussion. Many even requested that a similar course be offered to help them with the second composition course (English 112) at Georgia State. Several students expressed that they had "reservations" about the course at first. However, they reported that by the end of the quarter, they felt encouraged and confident and were glad that they had taken the co-course. There were very few negative comments or comments that indicated that students thought that the course was not worthwhile or helpful.

As I review my teaching journal, where I recorded daily impressions, concerns, successes, and meanderings, a few patterns among the comments emerge. First, I was often concerned that I was confusing the students with my openness toward varying teaching approaches. As they came to class to share their freshmen composition experiences, they realized more clearly each time that not all composition teachers take the same approach, have the same perceptions about "good" writing, or evaluate writing with exactly the same criteria. How would I ever help students to see that within the variations, some conventions exist for written product and writing process in the academic community? How could I share my own perceptions for writing without undermining those of the classroom teacher whose students I am supporting, when these perceptions differ from mine? Initially, this concern filled many pages of the journal as I wrestled with a way to deal with differences among instructors. About the fourth week of class, I asked the students to help me generate a list of conventions that they saw across most composition courses (including previous ones) and a list of idiosyncratic differences among them as well. We discussed the concept of audience with new understanding. They were able to come to some amount of peace about the differences and some amount of understanding and relief about the commonalities among their instructors. With so many different instructors represented, students in LS 082 received an important lesson on perceptions, individual differences among instructors, and conventions about academic writing. In subsequent quarters, I asked students to write a short reflective piece about these conventions and idiosyncrasies as a starting place for this discussion. These responses revealed varied notions about composing and compositions that students bring to the writing classroom. As in most situations where we are novices or marginalized, our notions change once we gain knowledge, experience, and access. Some of the students' original notions and memories of writing instruction made me smile; others made me wince.

Response paper #1: What are two or three things your high school English teachers told you about writing? Are these the same or different from the conventions for academic writing that you are hearing about from your college teachers?

- *What's a convention?*
- *My English teachers always told me never to write in first person, never use contractions, and that an essay has five paragraphs with five sentences each. In college my papers have to be typed. My thesis statement is the last sentence in the introduction. My essays have to have a title and my essays could not have any mistakes.*
- *While attending high school my English teachers told me the main point of writing was to grab the reader's attention. They said if I could not keep the reader reading that my essay needed work. My high school English teachers also told me to watch my grammar and punctuation mistakes. They told me to make sure I make very few grammatical errors, so that the reader stayed with the flow of my paper. Next to grabbing the readers attention, the other main point that my high school teachers instilled in me was to make my argument clear. I had to be able to let the reader know what point I was making. Pretty much what my high school teachers told me sticks with me while I am in English associated classes. The only thing that became new to me was the arrangement of my essay, like 4 part, 5 part, and 6 part essay arrangement. But the audience, my grammar, and my argument are still #1 in the key to a decent paper.*
- *While attending high school english was one of my most difficult classes. My english teacher was so hard on us about our writing style. Some of the basic rules he drilled in our head was to have five paragraphs, make complete sentences, and watch for spelling and grammar errors. When my high school career was almost over I was able to follow these rules, and end up with a B paper. Now that I am attending college there are more rules being added to the list. My english teachers want more details, and more sentences to a paragraph. By following the rules I learned in high school, and the rules I'm learning in college, I feel I have what it takes to become a great academic writer. I just need to work on details.*

- *I always remember the teachers stressing one, don't write on the back, two, don't hand in a paper with any pen mistakes, and three, I don't want it if it doesn't have a title. That's really all they said before we turned in an essay.*

Most of the comments concerned the use of standard English, organization, format, and the number of paragraphs and sentences required for a "good" essay. Once in a while, students mentioned development (details and examples), but very few mentioned logic or research. Our list of conventions and idiosyncrasies helped all of us to be more conscious of what readers value, what others thought would help to improve writing, and what they "knew" but did not always execute effectively. Eventually, we built a list of conventions and "things about writing" that we valued and tried to achieve. I believe that this conscious effort to expand our notions of "good writing," along with the contrasts and laughter we managed along the way, contributed to their success in freshman composition and to their feelings of belonging in the academic community.

Another pattern within the teaching journal had to do with student confidence and self-perception. I continually recorded that several capable students seemed worried, angry, confused, just plain scared at times, that they would not succeed in freshmen composition. It took several weeks of class to dispel some of the "myths and monsters" that circulate the campus regarding English 111. It seemed to me that the sources of many of these myths about "everybody flunks freshman composition" are fuzzy and unfounded. Students did not really know where the myths came from and could only cite two or three people who they knew had flunked or had trouble in freshmen composition. As we looked into this issue, and as I brought "hard" data to show them that more than 70% of students who take the course pass it, they spoke less often of this fear. In addition, as their own writing improved during the quarter, many reported that they began to feel like they "understood what was expected" of them, and that they could "do it." At the mid-point of the quarter, I asked students to write a note to me about how they viewed their own progress. These are some of their responses:

- *If I had to give myself a grade today, I would give myself a C+. I try hard to be hard on myself so I won't get too comfortable with the way I write. I'm glad I took this course. You explained to me what I did not understand in English 111. I was so confused last Thursday when we talked about passive voice, but when I left here I felt so much better. I like my English 111 course but I just need more preparation time in writing my papers. I get nervous when I feel rushed. I'd just like for you to keep giving in class essays to write so I can be prepared when I go to my English 111 course.*

- *I am very greatful to be in LS 082 English Composition class. By being in this class I have learned many methods or ways to correct my grammatical mistakes. I don't feel that my first essay was done to the best of my ability due to the topic. Although I was disappointed in my grade on my first essay, after looking over my portfolio I feel that I have about a B average. I truly appreciate the help and time that is put forth to help me correct my essays.*

- *In English 111, I feel that I can write excellent essays, but my problem is that I don't take the time to write a rough draft that is a good bases for the final draft (meaning my rough draft = brainstorm and getting the ideas down; my final draft = my rough draft; my revision = my final draft). I feel I need to take more time preparing myself for the rough draft so that I will be a step ahead instead of a step behind. My average in English 111 class is about a C.*

Other responses included statements like: *"Sometimes I don't understand what she wants on a paper in English 111." "I just found out I need more details in my writing!" "To be honest with you, I still don't see the reason for me to be taking 082. I have B's on all of my essays in English 111."* Not all students sang the praises of the course, but most agreed that it was a valuable experience. When I had asked students early in the term what they had been told about composition, their responses were concerned primarily with the written product. By the midpoint, however, as I asked them to reflect on their progress, the responses indicated an awareness of their own writing processes as well as the product.

A third pattern from my classroom notes had to do with language. Many of the questions and confusions students brought to LS 082 had to do with what instructors meant by "parallelism," "claim," and "refute the opposition." As they began to understand the language of the academy and the conventions and logical structures behind the language, not for its own sake but for the purpose of functioning fully in the community, their participation in the conversation of composing grew. Students tried writing in ways new to them.

Overall, the co-course proved to be highly successful, quantitatively and qualitatively. However, the nature of LS 082 required a teaching style that is flexible and comfortable with a fluid syllabus. Not all of those who taught this course enjoyed the spontaneity and the "coaching" that seemed necessary for successful support of both students and the English 111 instructors. Although the challenge and excitement of meeting students "where they are" on a daily basis were energizing for me, other instructors found teaching this co-course stressful and too "loose." Unfortunately, we did not have enough time before the next moving of the margins to study the aspect of teacher-effect for the co-course. What I saw us moving toward then was something similar to the "studio" model that Grego and Thompson described in their 1996 CCC's article, "Repositioning Remediation." I was hoping to expand the LS 082 concept to the upper level course entirely. With the constant changes in admission standards, I thought we should teach the upper level curriculum to the entry level students, drop the lower level course entirely, and "mainstream" the upper level students into English 111 with the Learning Support co-course. I think it would have worked.

EXPANDING THE MISSION

About the same time our Department was working on the co-course and increased communication with the English Department, the Board of Regents passed a motion to reduce the size of Learning Support Programs at the major research universities in the state. By the year 2001, these schools would serve no more than 1% of the freshman class in Learning Support. Admission standards continued to rise, and SAT scores were reset nationally. In addition, the university system in Georgia shifted from a quarter system to a semester system in the fall of 1998, which added to the tension and changes within the Department. We were encouraged to change our Department name once again, this time to the Department of Academic Foundations, shift our mission from teaching and research in developmental education to larger retention issues, train GTAs for the professorate, and work with at-risk students in different ways.

As a result of this movement, I found my own professional margins shifting as well. In 1998, I became the Director of the Learning Center, a comprehensive learning lab sponsored by our department. I worked toward broadening the scope of that Center from serving primarily Learning Support students to serving all students who found their way to this facility. The Learning Center continued to focus on math, reading, and test-taking, along with composition, but added an ESL component, increased the number of supplemental instruction sections in political science and biology (and graduate students as leaders), added training for writing across the curriculum graduate assistants, and developed online tutoring for writing and math through our web site. I developed and taught graduate courses for postsecondary teaching across the College of Arts and Sciences as well as in the Center for our own tutors and graduate assistants. At the same time, I was joint-appointed in English and taught an American literature sophomore survey course in addition to teaching the graduate courses, directing the Center, and teaching an occasional section of Regents Writing or Learning Support composition. Needless to say, co-courses and issues of mainstreaming basic writers were no longer at the forefront of discussions in the Department.

All of us in the Department were reinventing ourselves and trying out new programs and courses, while maintaining the few Learning Support students still coming our way. As the numbers of students enrolled in Learning Support composition dwindled, we discontinued the lower level composition course and the co-course. Within the last 6 years, the numbers of students served in our Department, across all units, dropped from over 1,200 to under 400. By the fall of 1999, only 18 students were enrolled in Learning Support composition. In addition, since 1996, the number of faculty was reduced from 23 full-time members in our department to seven.

MOVING IN CIRCLES

In September 1999, the Board of Regents passed the motion to dissolve the Department of Academic Foundations on the Georgia State campus. The tenured faculty and staff still on campus were dispersed on January 1, 2000 to many different departments. Most of us were asked where we would like to go. A colleague and I chose the English Department, and others went to the College of Education and the Counseling Center. What was left of learning support for composition was placed within the English Department. While each faculty and staff member saw this movement coming, there is always the jolt that comes with the reality.

Personally, and professionally, I am a bit exhausted. But in my resilience I also find myself open to the opportunities. The English Department at this particular university is a dynamic, thriving environment that encourages its members to do what they do best. Although the Comprehensive Learning Center is now a center for math and ESL tutoring only, and the graduate courses I developed have been discontinued, I am working with graduate students in the English Department through the Writing Across the Curriculum Program, the Regents' Test writing courses, and the Learning Support courses. I am also teaching graduate and undergraduate courses in composition theory, freshman composition and American literature. And of course, my research and service are on going, though these may shift in focus. Yet, even with my Pollyanna, "it'll all be OK" basic attitude toward life, I know we were heading in the right direction with the co-courses for those students who need an alternative method for learning to write in an academic setting and who need survival skills for becoming a viable part of the community.

As for the margins, they will continue to move, particularly for basic writers, however these are defined, who enter this university. In fact, not long ago, while talking with the Director of Undergraduate Composition about the university assessment project, we discussed the need for a writing sample to place students in appropriate sections of freshman composition. It sounded to me that the writing sample my colleagues and I called for 15 years ago might finally come to fruition. In addition, many colleagues in the English Department's Rhetoric and Composition program are interested in mainstreaming all Learning Support students who come our way into the co-course model or some kind of studio model. A studio model or co-course may also serve many non-Learning Support students that the writing sample helps identify as needing support as well. All of these discussions sound familiar. We agree that one of the outcomes of the placement procedures might be that we grow a basic writing program. I have to smile.

As my father used to say, "And so the worm turns."

WORKS CITED

Bartholomae, David. "Inventing the University." *Journal of Basic Writing* 5.1 (1986): 4–23.

Bruner, Jerome. "Language as an Instrument of Thought." *Problems in Language and Learning.* Ed. A. Davies. New York: Heineman, 1975. 162–234.

Emig, Janet. "Writing as a Mode of Learning." *College Composition and Communication* 28.2 (1977): 122–8.

Flower, Linda, and John Hays. "A Cognitive Process Theory of Writing." *College Composition and Communication* 32.4 (1981): 365–87.

Grego, Ronda, and Nancy Thompson. "Repositioning Remediation: Renegotiating Composition's Work in the Academy." *College Composition and Communication* 47 (1996): 62–84.

Perl, Sonya. "Understanding Composition." *College Composition and Communication* 31.4 (1980): 363–9.

Perry, William. *Forms of Intellectual and Ethical Development in the College Years: A Scheme.* New York: Holt, Reinhart, and Winston, 1970.

Piaget, Jean. *Six Psychological Studies.* New York: Random House, 1977.

Segall, Mary T. "Embracing the Porcupine: Redesigning a Writing Program." *Journal of Basic Writing* 14.2 (1995): 38–47.

Shaughnessy, Mina. *Errors and Expectations: A Guide for the Teacher of Basic Writing.* New York: Oxford University Press, 1977.

Soliday, Mary. "From the Margins to the Mainstream: Reconceiving Remediation." *College Composition and Communication* 47 (1996): 85–99.

Sommers, Nancy. "Revision Strategies of Student Writers and Experienced Adult Writers." *College Composition and Communication* 31.4 (1980): 378–88.

Stygall, Gail. "Resisting Privilege: Basic Writing and Foucault's Author Function." *College Composition and Communication* 45 (1994): 320–41.

Vygotsky, Lev. *Thought and Language.* Trans. Eugenia Hanfmann and Gertrude Vakar. Ed. Alex Kozulin. Cambridge: MIT, 1986.

II

Alternative Configurations for Basic Writing

Returning Adults to the Mainstream: Toward a Curriculum for Diverse Student Writers

Barbara Gleason
City College of New York, CUNY

The phenomenon of working adults returning to college has generated a great deal of interest and curricular experimentation since the 1970s. In *Second Shift: Teaching Writing to Working Adults*, Kelly Belanger and Linda Strom describe innovative approaches to writing instruction in five worker education programs affiliated with colleges or universities. Issues associated with remediation must inevitably be confronted by such programs, where the prevailing view is that noncredit remedial courses are inappropriate for mature adults returning to college. At Youngstown State University and Swingshift College, for example, Kelly Belanger and Linda Strom developed a mixed ability writing course addressing the needs of the working students who belong to a steelworkers' union (72–84).

I endorse the position that remediation is inappropriate for adults who are returning to college after a 5-, 10-, or even 20-year hiatus. Far preferable are courses that have been designed to meet the specific needs of working adults, needs that are best understood not by analyzing placement test scores but by understanding these students' diversity in areas such as age, gender, family, educational history, culture, social class, sexual orientation, and employment. By reading students' personal narratives and autoethnographies of home, neighborhood, and work communities, teachers can learn about their students to better assist them in entering the culture of college. Similarly, students' analyses of their own home and community languages can help pave the way for their acquisition of academic literacies (Groden, Kutz, and Zamel; Kutz, Groden, and Zamel). As Terry Dean argues in "Multicultural

Classrooms," composition courses offer a valuable and much-needed space in which students can focus on learning academic culture and, in many cases, "mainstream" culture as well.[1]

For the past 3 years, I have been teaching "remedial" and "college-level" returning adult students in one introductory writing course offered by a worker education bachelor's degree program within the City College of New York (CCNY).[2] Since its inception in 1981, this program—The Center for Worker Education (CWE)—has offered only full-credit college courses in its regular curriculum: the program's founders believed that all CWE students should enroll in full-credit bearing courses, regardless of placement test scores. As a teacher of writing in this program, I have been learning about how the particular needs and interests of these students can dovetail with a curriculum for a mainstreamed writing course.

UNDERSTANDING THE "DIVERSITY" OF RETURNING ADULTS

To encourage students to become acquainted, I ask that they introduce themselves to one other student during the first class meeting. The homework assignment for that week is for each student to write a letter to a peer about the challenges, joys, and fears of returning to college. By following up on initial introductions in class with an exchange of letters, each student learns about the cultural background, educational history, and special concerns of one other person in the class. As they develop friendships, these older adult students often form support networks and encourage each other academically. In addition, this initial assignment enables me to begin to know my students, for I read these letters as well.

I also ask my students to complete a questionnaire about their educational, language, and cultural backgrounds. By learning about my students' educational histories, I am far better equipped to assist them in entering an academic community with specialized forms of communication. I view my role as one of intervening in a lifelong process of literacy development, a conceptual frame for writing instruction best articulated by Louise Wetherbee Phelps:

> But what is it, then, that teaching teaches? Not literally writing as a discursive practice.... *Teaching teaches writing to developing persons within concrete life situations* [emphasis added]. Thus it teaches the development of literacy, addressing itself not simply to particular discourse events and texts but to the whole life process by which literacy—and reflection—become habitual, skilled, mature, and subject to self-understanding.... (71)

With each passing semester, I learn more about the "concrete life situations" of these students and, as a result, more fully appreciate the issues that are likely to concern them. For example, I only recently realized that earning a General Equivalency Diploma (rather than completing high school) may represent an important accomplishment or a sense of educational failure—or both. Reading students' commentaries on their literacies and educational histories allows me to begin assisting them individually early in the semester.

The completed questionnaires of the 24 students who had registered for my spring 1999 CWE writing class reveal the high level of diversity common to introductory CWE classes. As has been true of all my CWE classes, this group was highly heterogeneous in every way except for one: gender. Twenty-one students (86%) were women and three were men—a proportion that has remained constant throughout the six semesters that I have taught in this program. In all other respects, this class was notable for its diversity. Students' ages ranged from 20 to 50, with an average age of 36. Ten of these 24 students were immigrants, all but one coming from countries in the Carribean, Central America, or South America. English was the primary language of 16 students, six were bilingual in Spanish and English, and two were actively learning English as a second language. Eight of the 14 U.S.-born students were African-American women.

These students were just as diverse academically as they were culturally. Ten had earned a General Equivalency Diploma and 14, a high school diploma. Of these 14, five had earned a high school diploma in a country outside the U.S.; that means that only nine in a class of 24 students had earned a high school diploma within the U.S.[3] This variability in high school backgrounds is matched by these students' City University of New York (CUNY) skills test scores and their college grade point averages. Of the 22 students who completed the course, 12 had no test scores listed in the CCNY student database, either because they had not taken the tests or because their scores had not yet been recorded. Of the ten students whose test scores were recorded, four had failed either the reading or the writing test, and six had passed both the reading and the writing test. As for their grade point averages, four students' transcripts indicate that they had GPAs below 2.0 and seven students had GPAs of 3.0 or higher.

From the standpoint of curriculum, there are two ways in which these students' cultural and educational diversity is important. First, these students have a great deal to teach me and each other about their social and cultural worlds; and second, nearly all of these students are struggling at some level to enter into an unfamiliar world of expectations, attitudes, ways of knowing, and styles of communicating. This is even more likely to be true for students enrolled in an elective writing class due to educational insecurities, low grades, or failing test scores. Unlike many middle class, native English-speaking people, these students do not usually experience college as a natural extension of their home communities or even of high school.

Jacqueline Jones Royster refers to this home–school culture gap in an analysis of her own experiences as an African-American woman who routinely crosses discourse boundaries: "Like DuBois, I've accepted the idea that what I call my 'home place' is a cultural community that exists still quite significantly beyond the confines of a well-insulated community that we call the 'mainstream' " (34). One important consequence of this gap, Royster goes on to explain, is that it "narrows the ability [of educators] to recognize human potential" (34). Those of us who function as gatekeepers, however reluctantly, by virtue of teaching entry-level writing courses understand that academic styles of communicating are generally only partially familiar—if familiar at all—to "nonmainstream" students (Bartholomae; Bizzell).

The older adult students who enter CWE have often been observed by their teachers to be remarkably capable conversationalists and oral presentors whose writing skills frequently belie their intellectual and verbal capacities. These students—most of them women—are likely to have raised families and held full-time jobs while maintaining close ties to extended families, which is to say that they have been negotiating complex verbal exchanges for many years. However, many of these students begin learning in college classes before having acquired "essayist literacy"—the generalized academic style of communicating that is characterized by "straightforward, objective, specially organized representations of reality rather than personally authored, socially embedded discourse" (Farr 9). Despite this, many of these students are expert communicators in the oral traditions of their home cultures, a phenomenon that presents special opportunities for teachers in multicultural classrooms.

A CURRICULUM FOR MAINSTREAMING

My CWE writing curriculum comprises a sequence of four assignments that move students from an initially inward focus on their own literacies and languages to a progessively outward focus on the literacies and communication practices of others.[4] The four assignments are (1) a language/literacy autobiography, (2) a storytelling and story writing multitask project, (3) a student interview report, and (4) an ethnographic research writing project. All of these assignments involve students in practicing academic forms of knowing, persuading, and communicating while reflecting on their own literacy experiences and examining the languages and literacies of other people.

The first formal essay assignment is a language/literacy autobiography, which students prepare for by writing a letter to a classmate about combining work with school and returning to college at a mature age. These letters are followed by a more formal autobiographical essay assignment that invites students to examine their formal and informal literacy learning as children, adolescents, and younger adults. Very often, recalling these memories and recording them in writing is painful, for the very events being remembered may account for students' having decided not to pursue higher education earlier. On the other hand, most have successful work histories that bolster their self-esteem and provide the self-discipline and everyday habits necessary to succeed in college. These positive aspects of students' lives can be usefully examined in self-reflective, autobiographical writing.

The second assignment involves a sequence of four successive tasks. Students begin by telling each other brief conversational stories during class and then writing down these same stories. They later transcribe their audiotaped recordings, producing a transcript of an oral story that can then be compared to the written story. In the final phase of the project, students write a comparative analysis of the oral story and the written story, examining differences in story structure, content, and language. At the end of the project, students generally report that they prefer their written stories, and that these stories benefited from the absence of pressure associated with conversational situations and from the opportunity to revise. With this finding comes a new respect for their own writing and a resolve on the part of most students to improve their speaking and storytelling competencies (Gleason "Something of Great Constancy").

Students then move on to writing reports on interviews they conduct with one another about writing. This interview assignment, which I explain more fully below, functions to prepare students for the ethnographic research project—which I view as the capstone assignment of this course. A key value of the ethnographic writing project is its multitask feature: it offers such a wide array of reading, speaking, research, and writing activities that every student can experience some forms of success while stronger writers are always challenged by the analytical and rhetorical demands of writing an ethnographic essay.

In the remainder of this chapter, I will describe the interview assignment and the ethnographic research project, and establish a rationale for their use in a mainstreamed writing course for returning adults.

CAPITALIZING ON CONVERSATIONAL COMPETENCIES

To introduce students to ethnographic research strategies, I begin with a student–student interview on the subject of writing outlined by Peter Elbow and Pat Belanoff in *A Community of Writers* (153–65). The two stated purposes of this interview are (1) for students to learn about writing and writers in a general sense, and (2) for each student to inquire about the specific experiences, attitudes, and aspirations of one writer. An unstated goal of this assignment is for students to get to know each other and form mutually supportive bonds that are sorely needed by commuter students who work full time while attending college. Well over one half of these students reported to me later in the semester that they have formed new friendships during the course of their initial and follow-up interviews (on the phone and in class).

To prepare students for interviewing, I distribute a short written explanation of the importance of scripting a list of questions beforehand, remaining flexible during the interview, audiotaping, and note-taking. We talk in class about the value of ice-breaker questions, being sensitive to privacy issues, and staying focused as an interviewer.[5] For nearly all students, this is the first interview they have ever conducted, it is anticipated with some trepidation, and it turns out to be a surprisingly pleasurable and memorable learning experience. One fall 1999 student succinctly sums up her perception of this assignment's value: "My best work is my interview with Maria. This is the exercise that taught me the most new skills. I interviewed, recorded, transcribed, summarized, and analyzed. I was very pleased with the final draft." Others report listening, asking questions, and incorporating quotes into their writing as particularly important skills that they practiced while interviewing and writing the interview report.

Most students say they value the relationships formed with their peers as well as the research and writing skills they practiced, often for the first time, while working on their interview projects. As much as I value these two dimensions of this project, I prize even more its use of conversational expertise as a resource for developing writers. Many of these students' communication styles differ from the topic-centered, "get-to-the-point" styles common to mainstream American speakers, and their language (oral and written) may therefore be subject to negative evaluation by teachers; nonetheless, these students' communication styles tend to serve them well in conversational situations. Moreover, as Peter Elbow reminds us, we teach to strength by "capitalizing on the oral language skills students already possess and helping students apply those skills immediately and effortlessly to writing" ("The Shifting Relationships" 290).

By inviting them to conduct interviews with one another during class, I encourage students to use their existing language forms as a bridge to acquiring academic styles of thinking, talking, and writing. Students may, for example, speak to one another in both Spanish and English; or they may use a narrative style that seems to "meander from the point and take on episodic frames"—suggested by Akua Duku Anokye as the preferred narrative style of some African Americans (48); others make particularly effective use of humor and joke-telling while conversing with each other. These culturally and personally preferred communication styles are then folded into the student interviewer's written report to illustrate an interviewee's particular style of speaking and as evidence for the student writer's claims. Two features central to academic writing are "the giving of reasons and evidence rather than just opinions, feelings, [and] experience" and the ability to "step outside one's own narrow vision" (Elbow "Reflections on Academic Discourse" 140). Reporting on an interview requires a writer to consider and represent an interviewee's point of view by means of summary, paraphrase, and quotes in a prose style that blends narrative and exposition as well as personal and public forms of writing.

PRESENTING ETHNOGRAPHIC RESEARCH STRATEGIES TO STUDENT WRITERS

In *The Professional Stranger*, Michael H. Agar explains that ethnography refers to both a research process and a written product (1–2). Agar describes ethnographic research as a process that "involves long-term association with some group, to some extent in their own territory, with the purpose of learning from them their ways of doing things and viewing reality" (6). With this general definition in mind, I present ethnography to students as a process that initially entails gaining entry to a community of people and then observing that group's daily routines, rituals, traditional customs, and communicative practices. I go on to explain that an ethnographer records these observations by writing descriptive "fieldnotes" and soon begins searching for recurring themes or topics that will form the basis of an analysis. To further introduce ethnography to students, I rely on *Fieldworking*, an innovative textbook that builds an entire curriculum on the foundation of reading and writing strategies commonly employed by ethnographers (Chiseri-Strater and Sunstein).

To illustrate the forms of writing that I am assigning, I distribute samples of former students' ethnographic essays along with excerpts from a professionally written ethnography. By reading good examples of ethnographic writing, students gain substantial insight into the task they are now being asked to undertake. When we discuss these writing samples in class, I elicit their explanations for why these texts exemplify successful writing: not surprisingly, there are some in every group who already know "what makes writing good" (Coles and Vopat). Such discussions also allow me to demystify the approach I take to evaluating and grading students' final products.

I frequently hand out in class copies of a student's ethnographic essay entitled "You Wanna Play with Me?" The author, Marthe, created a title that gives voice to the children in the Head Start progam she was studying and at the same time alludes to her thesis: that children learn through playing.[6] This thesis appears in her introduction, is developed with examples of children's behaviors all through her essay, and reappears quite persuasively in Marthe's conclusion. After describing the classrooms, the teachers, and the children in this Head Start program, Marthe begins building her argument by presenting and commenting on children playing:

> Everything young children do is a learning experience. In one of my observations of this classroom, I observed how Jade, a happy, confident, assertive little girl took some building blocks and asked me "you wanna play with me?" I explained to her that I came to watch the children play and I asked her if she mind. She answered, "No, but you gonna play with me after?" I answered, "Maybe, if I had time." She then said, "Can you make me a box?" I asked her to try. "I can't try," she whined. As I continued my observation she began to stack the blocks and join them together. After a while she said, "Look, I made a box." From this one attempt Jade did not only strengthen her problem solving skills and develop language, but she also learned how to make a box which in turn helped her develop her self esteem and made her confident in her abilities. Since Jade is very verbal, she also developed her reasoning skills and her social interaction with adults.

A major strength of Marthe's essay is her successful use of narrative and descriptive writing to construct an argument. Her essay exemplifies two points made by Donna Dunbar-Odom: ethnographic research methods offer students the opportunity (1) to " 'own' their research," and (2) to learn that constructing an argument is far more complex than "merely taking and supporting one side of a binary argument" (20).

Because of her enthusiasm for working with small children, Marthe was highly motivated by her research, as she explains in her portfolio cover letter:

> The one assignment I enjoyed the most was my ethnographic research, "You Wanna Play with Me?" I enjoyed this the most because I studied and observed a group of individuals I hold dear to my heart, *children*. Not only are children unique and remarkable individuals, but they are also the group of individuals that society has put at the end of their list.

Marthe's testimonial on her engagement as a writer aligns closely with the feelings of many other student ethnographers: selecting a community for their research generally allows students to spend time with people they want to know better or to study a place of special interest to them. A woman with an emerging awareness of animal rights produced a remarkably fine report on an animal shelter; another woman interviewed several co-workers in her office and analyzed the reasons for a pervasive morale problem; and an immigrant from the Dominican Republic wrote about one of the family-owned stores, or *botanicas*, that sells products associated with *Santeria*, which she describes as a "system of common belief among Dominican and other Carribean people" that "mixes African and Catholic religions." As their teacher, I am continuously learning about the special interests, workplaces, and cultural communities that my students report on, just as they learn from one another by reading their work-in-progress and discussing these research projects with each other in class.

In addition to distributing samples of other students' ethnographic writing, I usually invite students to read an excerpt from Barbara Myerhoff's *Number Our Days*, after which we view her 30-minute film by the same name. Through her descriptive and narrative writing about a community of elderly Jewish immigrants, Myerhoff develops an argument that agism is a pervasive problem in contemporary U.S. society. An unusual feature of her writing is her hybrid style: literary language is combined with a social scientist's purpose. Developing a writing style is not a prominent feature of most introductory writing classes; however, more advanced students often take pleasure in noticing and imitating other writers' styles. In every writing course I have taught, there are some students, usually the more proficient writers, who want to focus on stylistic issues. By closely reading the prose of authors such as Barbara Myerhoff, these students can pursue their interests in developing their own prose styles.

To illustrate the potential that this project holds for diverse student writers, I will describe the cases of two returning adults—one classified as "remedial" and the other as "college-level" by their scores on the City University of New York (CUNY) Writing Assessment Test. I have chosen to underscore the mainstreaming challenge to teachers by selecting two extreme examples of students who are enrolled in the same class. The two students whose cases I cite are "Joan" (age 33) and "Liam" (age 36).

Joan and Liam both withdrew from high school without graduating and later earned their GEDs. Not surprisingly, these two students recall early school failures in the literacy autobiographies that they wrote at the beginning of our course. Educational insecurities and writing anxieties had led both Joan and Liam to register for my elective introductory writing course. But here is where their similarities end. Joan's writing efforts are significantly burdened by a complex learning disorder—a diagnosis she received while enrolled in my writing class. Liam, on the other hand, brings to his college education 19 years of avid reading and a substantial history of political activism that includes crafting political messages for publication in the broadcast and print media.

JOAN

Having left her Brooklyn high school without graduating, Joan had had "to go on public assistance" to support her infant daughter. While her daughter was still very young, Joan worked as a waitress and then as a file clerk in a car wash company. Reflecting back on that period of her life, Joan recalled that she enjoyed working as a file clerk because there was "little reading and no writing" required of her.

At the age of 18, Joan first attempted to earn her General Equivalency Dimploma. She was to fail the exam four times before passing on her fifth attempt 6 years later. Knowing that many others would have given up after failing one, two, or possibly three times, I asked Joan what had induced her to persist in taking and retaking her GED exam until she finally passed. "I wanted to go to college," she explained. "I wanted to better myself," she continued, going on to say that being on public assistance had motivated her to consider attending college. Joan married at 22 and gave birth to a second daughter 2 years later. Childcare responsibilities would further delay Joan's pursuit of a college education.

At 32, Joan began her college career at the Center for Worker Education. One semester later, she enrolled in the mainstreamed college writing course that I was teaching. When Joan was casting about for a community to focus on for her field research project, I asked her what she particularly wanted to learn about. Joan replied that she was interested in college and in learning about being a college student. I suggested that she focus her research on her own college environment. For Joan, this interest in college was no small matter; it represented her struggle to overcome substantial obstacles to learning, literacy, and formal education.

Despite the obvious difficulties Joan experienced with reading and writing on her GED exams and in a chef's school that she attended for 18 months, and despite her deliberate avoidance of jobs that required reading and writing, Joan did not believe that she had problems with reading and writing. Thus, when she failed her CUNY writing assessment test, Joan attributed her poor performance to "test-taking anxiety."

In August of 1998, Joan passed the CUNY reading assessment test but failed the math and writing tests. Had she registered at our college's main campus, or at any of CUNY's other 16 colleges, Joan would have been placed into remedial writing—which in most colleges would have prevented her from being eligible for college composition or for core curriculum courses. However, Joan chose to enter the City College Center for Worker Education, where there are no remedial courses.

JOAN'S WRITING

I first encountered Joan's writing when she responded to a questionnaire that I distributed during the second week of class. Here are four of the questions and her written answers:

- **Why did you enroll in this writing course?**
  So I can learn how to ~~right~~ better   ^writing
  How to use better words. I Drop out of H.S.

- **What concerns do you have about your writing?**
  That Sometime I loose my train of thought.
  What I want to say does not come out on papper.

- **Do you feel comfortable speaking during class discussions? Please explain your answer.**
  Sometime I do and sometime I don't. depends on what is discuss.

- **Do you have any concerns about your language use (speaking or writing)?**
  My *Fear* is when people see my writing they may not understand what I am talking about

These four written responses, as well as the other comments Joan wrote on this questionnaire, portray a student with a history of difficulties in school as well as severe frustrations with writing. Joan's difficulties as a writer were expressed both by the content of her messages and by the forms of her language: sentence fragments, misspelled words, and punctuation errors appeared in nearly every statement she wrote, diminishing only slightly after she acquired some proofreading strategies. However, unlike the writing of most "basic writers" I have encountered, Joan frequently embeds metaphors in her prose, as she does in this passage from her literacy autobiography: "Diaries, stories, letters and poems: I have them all. I enjoy writing, because it lets me be me. I enjoy free writing a lot more. It is like letting the pen and paper do their dance." All through the semester, Joan continued to employ metaphorical language in her expository prose, exhibiting a verbal competency that seemed oddly out of sync with her other competencies as a writer.

While enrolled in her humanities course the previous semester, Joan had learned from her instructor that she would have to improve her writing significantly to remain in college. In an interview conducted after our writing class had ended, she talked about her experiences in that humanities course:

> My first professor...pulled me aside the second week of class and told me to drop out before 'cause...she thought I had PROBLEMS and she wanted me to get tested [for dyslexia]...she came up to me and said "your work is the last work I read out of everybody in all my classes" and I asked her why and she said "I dread reading your work—It's really painful"—and I asked her why—she goes "your fragments your sentence structure" um she says "your writing is atrocious" and those were her exact words and it was like a dagger in my heart and in my pride and I held them back and I bit my lip and I said "ok—I'm still not dropping your class—I'm going to do my best."

Joan did complete her humanities class, earning a passing grade at the end of the term. She also took her instructor's advice to heart and enrolled in my elective college writing course the following semester. As for the passing grade she had earned for the humanities course, Joan believed it to be a "sympathy grade"—a gift from her teacher because her mother had passed away that semester.

The number of spelling errors that I observed in Joan's writing was unusually high, even in the context of a basic writing class. In fact, Joan's unedited writing closely resembles that of a person who is "dysgraphic," that is, a person who has a great deal of trouble producing written language (McAlexander et al. 25–6). A high frequency of errors and unusual errors are two indications of dysgraphia (McAlexander et al. 26). A third signal is writing in which letters are frequently missing/dropped from words, a condition that suggests an "inability to relate sounds to spelling" (28). All three of these conditions apply to Joan's writing. As it turned out, I was the fourth CWE teacher to recommend that Joan be tested for dyslexia. This she did arrange to do.

At midsemester, Joan learned for the first time, at the age of 33, that she had a learning disorder. It is described in her evaluation report as "a combination of inattentiveness, auditory processing, organizational delays and emotional factors"—all of which are "contributing to Joan's short-term memory deficits and delays in language processing."[7] Almost as soon as she learned of this herself, Joan called me at home to inform me of the diagnosis. From this point on, I read and evaluated Joan's writing with this newly diagnosed learning disorder in mind.

JOAN'S ETHNOGRAPHIC RESEARCH WRITING

In the seventh week of our 15-week semester, Joan began her ethnographic research project. She had decided to study her own college community to further her goal of becoming a successful college student. The first assignment Joan completed for this project was a short research proposal.

In a one-page essay, Joan describes the community she will study and several questions she plans to use to frame her observations and interviews. An early draft (labeled "second draft") that she turned in to me begins with the following paragraph:

> As a student at CWE I got the change to observe the students, professors and the receptionists. How the students and professors inter act with the receptionists. How the receptionists get any work done? What is there a different between the day shift and the night shift? Do they realized that the students and Staffs depend on them for the information and services. How do they feel about their job?

In this draft, Joan conveyed the direction her research would take and posed several useful questions. I encouraged Joan to begin proofreading. With the assistance of writing tutors and her computer's software program toolbox, Joan was able to produce a third draft that more closely aligns with the expectations of college teachers. Here is her revision of the paragraph cited above:

> As a student at Center for Worker Education I have the chance to observe the students, professors, the receptionists. I will observe how the students and professors deal with the receptionists. How the receptionists interact with the high demand of students and professors. I wonder if the receptionists get any work done? Is there a different between the day shift and the night shift? How do they do their job? These are some of the questions that I seek answers for as I observed the desk for several weeks.

In this proposal essay, Joan succeeds in identifying the place and the people that she will investigate while posing several questions that she will use to guide her observations. Joan had developed these questions during a conference in which she and I discussed her research plans.

By learning to revise, to proofread, and to request responses from readers, Joan made substantial progress in overcoming her writing anxieties and began to function far more effectively as a student writer. Her newly acquired writing process allowed Joan to stay afloat in class and to manage an intensive 6-week project that entailed writing a research proposal, writing descriptive fieldnotes, interviewing at least one person, and writing a final research report. In addition to talking to me about her learning and her writing, Joan talked to CWE writing tutors, sometimes two or three times per week.

Joan wrote her descriptive fieldnotes during the course of 3 days. She focused her observations on the reception desk, where students, advisors, administrators, and faculty all approach CWE receptionists to request assistance. Once she got home, Joan wrote out and typed her notes, producing ten double-spaced pages of writing—in itself a substantial accomplishment for an insecure and inexperienced writer. Here is an excerpt from the notes Joan wrote on her second day of observing:

> Friday, April 16, 1999
> 4:30pm
> Wow! They must be at least 50 students here this is too much for me. Z, Mr. O, Mr. L, Mr. H, and J W working for their pay to day. So many student. Some look good and some are wearing jean and dress and suits. Some of the students have the hair done nice. I wonder what they are all here for. I can not hear to much anymore., because all the student are talking to each other and my bench is now filled with people sitting on it. There is so much happening around here today

4:45pm
There is a student talking to Z not so nice, but Z is smiling and been nice to
her. Z is now telling student to put there name on the list and they will be call
next. Wow! She control all those students and put them in there place. . . .

Her observations on this day, in conjunction with interviews she conducted
with receptionists and a program administrator, led Joan to conclude that
these receptionists respond very effectively to the many requests that come
their way. In addition, Joan began noticing the heavy demands placed on
CWE receptionists, particularly during evening hours when classes are in
session. In her ethnographic essay, Joan concluded that the CWE receptionists play a centrally important though sometimes underrecognized role
in maintaining a smooth flow of communications among students, teachers,
advisors, and administrators. By reading Joan's report and fieldnotes, I found
myself developing a new respect for these receptionists and for their roles
in this college community.

When writing her ethnographic essay, Joan successfully narrowed the
focus of her research to these CWE workers' experiences and the reception desk as a central gathering place for students and staff. Although the
five-page essay that Joan ultimately wrote would not be considered a good
example of successful college writing by most of my colleagues, I concluded that, for Joan, the act of completing a five-page written report of her
own research was a highly significant achievement in her development as
a writer. Moreover, this essay clearly documents Joan's learning about academic culture generally and, more specifically, about the Center for Worker
Education receptionists and the reception area as a central meeting place.
Equally important, Joan's essay demonstrates her newly acquired abilities
to segment discourse into paragraphs, to ask and answer research questions, to write an essay introduction, and to use quotes to support general
assertions and observations. Joan's collected ethnographic writing includes
a total of 16 (typed) final draft pages: a one-page research proposal, ten
pages of fieldnotes, and a five-page ethnographic essay. The sheer volume
of writing that Joan produced during the 6 weeks that she worked on this
project represented a milestone in her writing life.

LIAM

Liam grew up in a rural Irish farming community that lacked electricity
and television in his early years. On winter nights, Liam and his family
would visit neighbors, playing cards and telling stories for entertainment.
In his literacy autobiography, Liam describes his father as a man with a
"a flare for stortytelling" and his mother as an avid letter writer. Liam's

mother corresponded regularly with relatives overseas, reading the letters she received to her family "aided by only a single gaslight hanging from the ceiling." When he wasn't farming, Liam's father wrote local news for community publications.

Liam recalls learning to read both English and Gaelic in a "small two-room country school." Between the ages of 8 and 12, he often missed classes to help his aging father with farmwork. When Liam entered secondary school at the age of 12, he left a class of only three students for a class of 60. He learned right away that his primary school education had not prepared him to compete academically: "It hit me that I was indeed in at the deep end. I did not recognize many of the subjects the teachers were talking about, nor did I have any knowledge of them." After 3 years of lagging behind his contemporaries and earning low exam grades, Liam left high school without graduating. Today, he looks back on his secondary school experience as a "bad dream."

When he emigrated to England as a young man, Liam hungrily read the *Irish Post*, a newspaper that reported the news from Ireland and addressed topics of interest to Irish immigrants. It was then that Liam developed a keen interest in learning about Ireland and, perhaps as a consequence, he became a voracious reader. A political awakening accompanied Liam's newly acquired reading habit. But writing was another matter. Liam continued to feel deeply insecure about his writing abilities.

In November of 1997, Liam took and passed the three CUNY skills tests in reading, writing, and math. During his first semester at CWE, Liam enrolled in an introductory humanities course that I happened to be teaching. Liam's performance in the class was impressive: in addition to earning an A for his coursework, he ultimately published a literacy autobiography entitled "A Reading Road: From Mayo to Manhattan" in a CWE student journal, *City at the Center*. However, Liam felt extremely anxious about writing and believed himself underprepared as a college writer. I advised Liam to address his concerns by enrolling in a college composition course, but instead he chose to enroll in a remedial writing course at another college. Liam believed that the low stress and low stakes of a remedial course would best serve his needs. After completing this remedial writing class, Liam expressed to me his satisfaction with his progress. He then enrolled in the mainstreamed writing course that I was teaching.

LIAM'S WRITING

I had first seen Liam's writing in the humanities course he had enrolled in 1 year earlier. I knew Liam to be a proficient student writer who could one day publish his essays or stories. In addition to being an avid reader, Liam is an easy conversationalist and a good listener. And, like his father, Liam is a good storyteller. Having tried many different lines of work, Liam had discovered bartending to best suit his temperament and his talents. Bartending has allowed Liam to meet a wide range of people, from compulsive gamblers to "the Romeos, who conquered Beauty Queens from Manhattan to Miami but end up looking for an invitation to someone's house for Christmas or Thanksgiving." Liam is also a sharp observer of people.

When asked to complete a questionnaire at the beginning of his writing class, Liam expressed confidence about his oral communication skills but insecurities about his writing:

- **What concerns do you have about your writing?**
  Writers Block, Critical Writing, Essays, Grammar
- **Do you feel comfortable speaking during class discussions? Please explain your answer.**
  Yes Very Comfortable, Lots of Encouragement from my Professor
- **Do you have any concerns about your language use (speaking or writing)?**
  Not any about Speaking. Writing—(Grammar is a task)

Unlike Joan, who reported being told by a former teacher that her writing was "atrocious" and "painful" for her teacher to read, Liam recalls being encouraged and cites that encouragement as a reason for enrolling in this writing course. In fact, I had found Liam an easy student to encourage; and he had received similarly positive responses from the three teachers who had selected his writing for publication in the CWE student journal.

LIAM'S ETHNOGRAPHIC RESEARCH WRITING

As an immigrant from Ireland, Liam takes a particularly strong interest in Irish-American organizations and publications. At the conclusion of our humanities course, Liam had given me a gift subscription to a magazine called *Irish America* and a book on the recent Irish peace accords. It came as no surprise, then, that Liam would want to focus his research on the Union Students of Ireland Travel, an organization that provides services for Irish and U.S. students who are traveling back and forth between these two countries.

In the opening of his research proposal, Liam asserts his view that Ireland should create a "national service of sorts": a program that would bring Ireland's youth to the United States to "broaden their horizons." He goes on to describe an organization that facilitates travel between the U.S. and

Ireland for college students of both countries. Here is the second half of that proposal:

> The U.S. work and travel program which is sponsored by USIT has been in operation for over thirty years. Every year, students from third level colleges in Ireland travel to the U.S. to be part of this program. USIT helps Irish students to spend up to four months living, working, and traveling throughout the United States. For those students who come here, if only for a short summer stay, it gives them an opportunity to learn about the American way of life.
>
> The staff at the USIT office has already given me the approval to visit one day and monitor their office procedures. The following is information that I would like to find out. How do USIT select what students are accepted into their program, and what students are rejected? How much does it cost a participant? Must all participants be currently in the third level education? How is the program administered here, and in Ireland? How many students come to the U.S. each year? Is employment pre arranged, is this a major task? Is there a support network on the ground here for the students when they arrive, and for the summer? What are the student's opinion of USIT, and the U.S.A.?
>
> I am looking forward to this research assignment, not just because I am Irish immigrant. I was always interested in Irish immigration issues, and I successfully campaigned for a change in the 1965 Immigration Act, as it had unfairly discriminated against Immigrants from Western Europe. I will see first hand how USIT prepares Irish students for America.

A clear strength of Liam's writing is his ability to inform and also persuade his readers with an ethical appeal. In this proposal, Liam establishes his credibility as a writer by making three claims: (1) that he himself is an Irish immigrant, which means he can draw on personal experiences as a source of knowledge; (2) that he strongly advocates travel by Irish youth to the U.S., indicating a sincere interest in an organization that provides services to U.S.-Irish travelers; and (3) that he already understands international travel and immigrants' experiences well enough to ask informed questions. Finally, Liam asserts a type of moral authority by referring to his successful efforts at participating in a campaign against unjust laws affecting immigrants.

Liam conducted his research during the week of his spring break, spending several days at the American Youth Hostel in Manhattan—where the USIT offices are housed. In the course of his research, Liam recorded his observations of people's movements and communications, he interviewed employees and student travelers, and he collected the brochures and pamphlets that USIT provides. By interviewing employees, Liam gained access to the results of a survey questionnaire designed to guage student travelers' satisfaction with USIT's services. USIT employees also shared with Liam the unsolicited letters that they had received from Irish students.

At the end of the semester, Liam reported on the pleasure he had taken from his observations of the people who worked at USIT and of those passing through the offices of this Irish-American organization. I had distributed a list of questions about field research experiences and asked students to respond in writing. Here is Liam's response to one question:

Question: How easy or difficult was this assignment for you?

Liam: This assignment was not as difficult as it seemed to be, when first I read the assignment. I enjoyed observing and writing the field notes. Spending mornings and afternoons at the American Youth Hostel (AYH) was exciting. Interviewing was easy for me as the students were in New York during my research. I felt the notes were very helpful when I was writing my report. My notes were essential to my report.

At the conclusion of his fieldwork experience, Liam had gathered enough specific information to write a substantive ethnographic essay. As is often true of more and less proficient writers, Liam produced a ten-page essay, twice the length of Joan's.

The report that Liam completed portrays the USIT offices, the USIT workers, and the student travelers who come looking for assistance. Embedded in Liam's descriptions are telling details that are informative but also suggestive of more than has been told:

A three-foot high black gridiron rail separates the general public from the American Youth Hostel (AYH) property. Between the gridiron and the AYH building there are a number of benches, round tables and chairs. The tables have umbrellas to provide shade from the morning sun. Most of the seats are occupied by people in their late teens or early 20's, who are sitting around smoking cigarettes, drinking coffee, and bottles of water. It is a scene reminiscent of a Paris sidewalk café. These young people are speaking foreign languages, with the occasional American voice rising above the others. The luggage they have with them tells a geographic story of its own. One tall young man with his hair down to his shoulders, has a travel bag that promotes Argentina, while a young lady, with a punk style hair do and some tattoos, has Norway stamped in bold lettering on her backpack. The T-shirts being worn by these travelers tell a story of where they have been traveling, from the Hard Rock Café in Los Angeles to Miami Beach Florida.

In this passage, Liam uses his descriptions to portray people and also to imply questions about where they have come from and where they are going. One of the more challenging aspects of ethnographic writing is to learn how to use descriptive writing purposefully—to communicate an idea or present an argument. It is usually the stronger student writers who manage to use description for a rhetorical purpose.

On the sixth page of his essay, Liam sums up an experience common to many of the young Irish travelers: "Homesickness and loneliness are two of the most frequent problems the students suffer from when they are in the U.S." With this general assertion, Liam introduces the contents of many thank-you letters that Irish students have mailed to the USIT employees after returning home. Liam cites the volume of this mail and quotes from one such letter as evidence of the positive response of Irish students to USIT and the importance of the services it provides:

> It is obvious from the amount of thank you mail that the staff at the USIT office receive each year from students when they return to Ireland, that their support role means a lot to the visiting students. One of the many letters Maire has on file is from a student who went through a period of loneliness while in New York last year. The thank you letter, which is almost two pages in length, states "Your concern and help took a massive weight off my shoulders. The time taken by you and the manner in which you dealt with me will not be forgotten." So wrote Mary Walsh from County Kerry in Ireland.

Liam's use of textual sources sets him apart from the majority of these student ethnographers. Using printed documents as primary or secondary sources involves transcending the fundamental requirements of the ethnographic writing assignment that I have conceived for an introductory writing class. For more advanced writers, however, citing sources is often a desirable challenge. Marthe, whose work I use to model a student's ethnographic writing, had integrated a secondary source into her text and appended a bibliography to her report.

The ethnographic essay that Liam completed bears many of the hallmarks of "good writing" noted by contributors to Coles and Vopat's *What Makes Writing Good*. Liam's text is a narrative that has a sense of being complete (143); his writing exhibits his commitment to his writing task, and his willingness to share his values with his readers (137). Liam creates an interplay between the particular and the general, reaching from concrete details toward abstract ideas (137); he knows how to create artful beginnings and how to use "attention-getting introductory tactics" (131); he uses a conversational tone that he knows how to translate into writing, avoiding a dull, institutional voice (126). In short, Liam's ethnographic essay exhibits many of the qualities that well-known writing teachers value.

CONCLUSION

Conventional college writing assignments generally fall under one of four categories: (1) personal narrative, (2) expository essay, (3) textual analysis, and (4) library research. For assignments that involve textual analysis and library research, students must first engage in critically reading new and unfamiliar types of texts and then write in a style that relies on logical reasoning and the use of evidence. For inexperienced or "basic" writers, this entire process involves a sudden immersion in academic forms of knowing and communicating and therefore a daunting challenge. As Marilyn Sternglass points out in *Time to Know Them*, these students will acquire academic language forms and writing abilities over time, especially when provided with appropriate instruction. However, they are unlikely to experience success as college writers when they begin by writing textual analyses and library research reports. Instead, they may fail to complete their assignments adequately or, when they do complete them, receive negative evaluations of their writing from teachers. This happened to Joan, who enrolled in Humanities 1 (an introductory literature course) during her first semester of college, and learned from her teacher that her writing was "atrocious" and "painful" to read.

The curriculum that I have outlined here offers one primary advantage to inexperienced writers: it enables them use "the oral [to] sustain the literate" (Brandt 7). Students begin their interviewing and ethnographic projects by using oral language in conversational situations to create two types of primary sources: transcripts of spoken language and fieldnotes. These are forms of writing that the most inexperienced and hesitant writer can dive into without fear of failure or negative evaluation from teachers: although I do comment on the content of these texts—and, very occasionally, make suggestions on how to improve them, I do not grade students' transcripts or fieldnotes. They function primarily as resources for more formal writing assignments.

More experienced student writers, such as Liam—who had passed a placement test prior to entering my writing class, still need to practice analytical thinking, research writing, and many other cognitive and rhetorical skills. All of the assignments in this curriculum require students to go beyond descriptive and narrative writing toward interpretation, inferencing, and analysis. When writing the ethnographic essay, students may choose to cite sources with in-text referencing and a bibliography. This is an appropriate challenge for the more proficient writers and one they frequently accept.

There are many possible avenues toward successful curricula for mainstreamed writing courses. The one I have been experimenting with relies on assignments with two key features: (1) the use of oral language and conversational competencies as resources for developing writers, and (2) sequenced multitask assignments comprising more and less difficult tasks. In addition to well-constructed assignments, there are still many other issues that must be addressed for mainstreamed writing classes: grading practices, support for teachers (for example, workshops and meetings), and support for students (for example, classroom tutors and class size).

In worker education classes, successfully mainstreamed writing courses take on a special significance. Slowing down student progress with non-credit remedial courses runs counter to a primary aim of these programs: they generally accelerate students' academic progress with classes conveniently scheduled in the evenings and on weekends, long class meetings that are held once a week, full-credit bearing courses, and the offer of college credits for life experiences. At the Center for Worker Education, students' academic progress is even further accelerated by four-credit courses in place of the three-credit courses commonly offered in the regular City College curriculum.

Most of the working adult students I have met in my classes are highly motivated to learn and to perform well in their college classes. They bring with them many resources that strengthen their chances of academic success, for example, workplace literacies, conversational competencies, bilingualism, self-discipline, determination, and the confidence so often born of maturity. They nevertheless enter college filled with the anxiety of this being their "last chance saloon."

Returning adult students can increase their odds for success in college by using their existing languages and literacies to negotiate their learning of new discourses and literacies. However, "students in basic writing classes . . . should not be treated differently from students in so-called regular composition courses" (Sternglass 296–7). All students entering college, regardless of writing placement test scores, benefit from immediate engagement with assignments that foster critical reasoning, interpretive reading, analytical as well as narrative writing, and persuasion. A well-designed writing course curriculum for students of highly mixed abilities will meet the dual challenge of allowing underprepared students to experience success while encouraging stronger students to expand the limits of their existing literacies.

ACKNOWLEDGMENTS

I would like to thank Edward Quinn for many useful responses to several drafts of this essay, Karl Malkoff and Barbara Comen for their suggestions and support, and Gerri McNenny for her insightful editing.

NOTES

[1]As Terry Dean points out in "Multicultural Classrooms, Monocultural Teachers," various different theoretical models explain how students can mediate home and school cultures. Shirley Brice Heath is particularly

well-known for advocating ethnography as a venue for classroom learning about home and school cultures. This interactive, reciprocal approach to pedagogy allows for developing shared understanding and negotiation of the various languages and literacies that appear in a classroom community. In contrast to Heath's negotiation model, Paulo Freire calls for students from nonmainstream cultural enclaves to transform mainstream culture rather than being absorbed into it (*Pedagogy* 28). These issues are also addressed extensively in *Writing in Multicultural Settings* (Severino, Guerra, and Butler).

[2]The City College of New York (CCNY) is one of 17 junior and senior colleges that comprise the City University of New York (CUNY).

[3]For a useful discussion of the issues faced by immigrants who are attending college, see Hirvela.

[4]This writing curriculum is one I first used as a teacher in a mainstreamed writing course for younger adult students on City College's main campus. The course formed the heart of a pilot projected supported by the Fund for Improvement in Post-Secondary Education. For overviews of this program's curriculum and its evaluation, see Soliday and Gleason, and see Gleason, "Evaluating Writing Programs in Real Time."

[5]Two useful resources for learning about interviewing are *People Studying People* by Robert A. Georges and Michael O. Jones and "Ch. 7: Interviewing," in *Fieldworking* by Bruce Jackson.

[6]The names of all students whose writing appears in this essay have been changed. Their writing is presented here with their permission and in the form in which I received it as their teacher.

[7]Joan included her evaluation report in her writing portfolio and has granted permission for its use here.

WORKS CITED

Agar, Michael H. *The Professional Stranger: An Informal Introduction to Ethnography*. New York: Academic Press, 1980.

Anokye, Akua Duku. "Oral Connections to Literacy: The Narrative." *Journal of Basic Writing* 13.2 (1994): 46–60.

Bartholomae, David. "Inventing the University." *When a Writer Can't Write*. Ed. Mike Rose. New York: Guilford, 1985. 134–65.

Belanger, Kelly, and Linda Strom. *Second Shift: Teaching Writing to Working Adults*. Portsmouth, NH: Boynton/Cook Heinemann, 1999.

Bizzell, Patricia. "What Happens When Basic Writers Come to College?" *College Composition and Communication* 37 (1986): 294–301.

Brandt, Deborah. *Literacy as Involvement: The Acts of Readers, Writers, and Texts*. Carbondale: Southern Illinois UP, 1990.

Chiseri-Strater, Elizabeth, and Bonnie Stone Sunstein. *Fieldworking: Reading and Writing Research*. Upper Saddle River, NJ: Prentice Hall, 1997.

Coles, William E., Jr., and James Vopat. *What Makes Writing Good: A Multiperspective*. Lexington, MA: D.C. Heath and Co., 1985.

Dean, Terry. "Multicultural Classrooms, Monocultural Teachers." *College Composition and Communication* 40 (1989): 23–37.

Dunbar-Odom, Donna. "Speaking Back with Authority: Students as Ethnographers in the Research Writing Class." *Attending to the Margins: Writing, Researching, and Teaching on the Front Lines*. Ed. Michelle Hall Kells and Valerie Balester. Portsmouth, NH: Boynton/Cook Heinemann, 1999. 7–22.

Elbow, Peter. "Reflections on Academic Discourse: How It Relates to Freshmen and Colleagues." *College English* 53.2 (1991): 135–56.

——. "The Shifting Relationships Between Speech and Writing." *College Composition and Communication* 36.3 (1985): 283–303.

Elbow, Peter, and Pat Belanoff. *A Community of Writers: A Workshop Course in Writing*. 2nd ed. New York: McGraw-Hill, 1995.

Farr, Marcia. "Essayist Literacy and Other Verbal Performances." *Written Communication* 10 (1993): 4–38.

Freire, Paulo. *Pedagogy of the Oppressed*. New York: Continuum, 1982.

Georges, Robert A., and Michael O. Jones. *People Studying People: The Human Element in Fieldwork*. Berkeley: U of California P, 1980.

Gleason, Barbara. "Evaluating Writing Programs in Real Time: The Politics of Remediation." *College Composition and Communication* 51.4 (2000): 560–588.

——. "Something of Great Constancy: Storytelling, Story Writing, and Academic Literacy." *Attending to the Margins: Writing, Researching, and Teaching on the Front Lines*. Ed. Michelle Hall Kells and Valerie Balester. Portsmouth, NH: Boynton/Cook Heinemann, 1999. 97–113.

Groden, Suzy, Eleanor Kutz, and Vivian Zamel. "Students as Ethnographers: Investigating Language Use as a Way to Learn Language." *The Writing Instructor* 6 (1987): 132–40.

Heath, Shirley Brice. *Ways with Words: Language, Life, and Work in Communities and Classrooms*. New York: Cambridge UP, 1983.

Hirvela, Alan. "Teaching Immigrant Students in the College Writing Classroom." *Attending to the Margins: Writing, Researching, and Teaching on the Front Lines*. Portsmouth, NH: Boynton/Cook Heinemann, 1999. 150–64.

Jackson, Bruce. "Ch. 7: Interviewing." *Fieldworking*. Urbana: U of Illinois P, 1987. 79–102.

Kutz, Eleanor, Suzy Q. Groden, and Vivian Zamel. *The Discovery of Competence: Teaching and Learning with Diverse Student Writers*. Portsmouth, NH: Boynton/Cook Heinemann, 1993.

McAlexander, Patricia J., Ann B. Dobie, and Noel Gregg. *Beyond the "SP" Label: Improving the Spelling of Learning Disabled and Basic Writers*. Urbana: NCTE, 1992.

Myerhoff, Barbara. *Number Our Days*. New York: Simon and Schuster, 1978.

Phelps, Louise Wetherbee. *Composition as a Human Science: Contributions to the Self-Understanding of a Discipline*. New York: Oxford UP, 1988.

Royster, Jacqueline Jones. "When the First Voice You Hear Is Not Your Own." *College Composition and Communication* 47 (1996): 29–40.

Severino, Carol, Juan C. Guerra, and Johnnella E. Butler, eds. *Writing in Multicultural Settings*. New York: MLA, 1997.

Soliday, Mary, and Barbara Gleason. "From Remediation to Enrichment: Evaluating a Mainstreaming Project." *Journal of Basic Writing* 16.1 (1997): 64–78.

Sternglass, Marilyn S. *Time to Know Them: A Longitudinal Study of Writing and Learning at the College Level*. Mahwah, NJ: Lawrence Erlbaum, 1997.

CHAPTER NINE

Rethinking At-Risk Students' Knowledge and Needs: Heroes' Decisions and Students' Quests for Identity and Meaning in a Content Composition Course

Rosemary Winslow and Monica Mische
The Catholic University of America, Washington, DC

I fear me this—is loneliness—
The maker of the soul—
Its caverns and its Corridors
Illuminate—or seal—

—Emily Dickinson, #318

Alone is how I start . . .
Alone is how I became,
When one parent went one way
and another went another way,
my sister and myself were split up.
Being alone was me . . . .
The incompleteness in me is searching FOR:
    My self.
    My heart.
    My soul.
    And my family.

—Rachela, responding to Emily D.

We direct and teach in the writing program at a private university in the District of Columbia with an enrollment of 6,500 students, of which undergraduates comprise slightly less than half. At present, at-risk writers are mainstreamed into the first-year composition course in a format similar to the Writing Studio described by Rhonda Grego and Nancy Thompson. We place students in separate sections of the course, which have a weekly small group revision workshop attached, led by a second instructor who also tutors students as needed. This configuration grew out of an experimental content composition course we taught for two summers and two semesters for a heterogeneous group of writers who were all identified as at-risk of making a successful transition to college. Although our current program permits our at-risk writers to complete the required course in rhetoric and composition in the usual one semester, in our experimental program, student success in college coursework and in writing development was evaluated as superior. Despite the high level of difficulty and the clear success in terms of student learning, the experimental course retained the labeling of an at-risk program. The label could not be entirely countered by our efforts, and the program was eliminated as a result.

As in other mainstreaming efforts, an important impetus for us was the opportunity to experiment with eliminating the precollege writing course, which did not seem to help students do well in the college course and which did not carry college credit in all of the schools of the university. In contrast to mainstreaming efforts on other campuses, our student population was identified as at-risk of making a successful transition to college. Only two thirds were underprepared in writing. Thus, our ultimate goal was to increase the chances of success at college through the immediate learning goals of growth in writing skills and using writing to assist students in the ways of thinking, reading, studying, managing time, engaging in discussions, listening, and note-taking needed in various college instructional settings—from tutorial to large-group lecture. By focusing more broadly than on writing development and by considering our first task to be moving past the damaging remedial label, we worked inside the classroom to leave basic/normal categories aside in our thinking and planning. Specifically, we considered social and cultural factors that might require change, especially student and teacher identity, in an effort to turn around student and faculty perceptions of these students and their abilities. Our instruction moved from a fuller range of action than literacy. Where teacher researchers dealing primarily with writing (Glau; Grego and Thompson; Soliday) had students write literacy narratives, we offered a curriculum based on the hero journey, which focused on identity quests made by strong individuals.

We have chosen to report at length on the experimental course because it was there that we rethought and worked out how to teach writing in the same classroom to students of varying preparation while altering their perceptions of their desires and competencies. The category of basic writing represents a damaged and damaging basis for teaching, and it remains entrenched in discussions of mainstreaming, as in the larger field of composition. Can heterogeneous classes work? We think so, if a wider range of writing is practiced for a wider range of purposes, if learning to write is opened up and used as a means of developing thought and communication from a variety of perspectives, if a content-based curriculum is used to assist all students in using their existing knowledge to bring to individual and collaborative inquiry—if, that is, we rethink what students know, can do, and need beyond current boundaries. Writing instruction must include and be done for life purposes, as Shirley Brice Heath asserts must and will happen not too far into the twenty-first century. In this chapter, we give a brief overview of the theoretical framework behind the course we taught; describe the curriculum; demonstrate specific effects with qualitative evaluation of student writing, chiefly by one young woman; summarize our quantitative evaluation of all end-of-term writing over two semesters for all students; and conclude with recommendations and cautions for designing and implementing experimental programs. Although these measures show something of how students benefited from the program, they are insufficient to justify large-scale program changes. We argue here that the need to continue experimenting with program design is crucial so that programs will fit the particular students, teachers, and resources in local situations. Exploring ways to leave at-risk distinctions aside is critical to program design.

LOCAL SITUATION IN SOCIAL/CULTURAL CONTEXTS

Our students were all traditional age, identified as at-risk of making a successful transition to college, but not all were underprepared in writing. Students' backgrounds spanned a very wide range in terms of standardized test scores, kind and quality of secondary education, socioeconomic status, and ethnicity. Therefore, we had to learn to teach a group that was heterogeneous in more ways than writing preparation and background. Teaching a version of our usual precollege writing course to this group one summer enabled us to see that (1) our precollege course did not work,[1] and (2) our students' hurdles were compounded by being labeled "at-risk." Like Grego and Thompson's students, ours also wanted to succeed, but alongside their desire they exhibited anger and frustration, more at their at-risk situation than at the difficulty of learning. Despite wanting to learn, they were reacting instead of choosing a direction in which to proceed toward academic success. Often they did harm to themselves by undercutting their own efforts in various ways when anger was directed against a parent, an administrator, an instructor, or the course. Often, motivation levels fluctuated, but a high level was most often accompanied by anxious talk about getting good enough grades as opposed to a genuine interest in learning. These students seemed to us confused, adrift amid a sea of images and pressures that typically face emerging adults in U.S. society, but our students seemed less able than their peers to lay conflicting messages, pressures, and desires aside to concentrate on learning. Many had difficulties at home that added significant conflict to their lives. Frequently, directions of pressure from peer group, family, church, school, society, and culture were in sharp conflict over values. The at-risk label with its attendant damaged and damaging perceptions confronted them with yet another conflict—their provisional status at the university. When we viewed students' situations through a wider lens than preparedness for academic writing, we saw individuals immersed in a mix of institutions in culture and society who did not know which way to turn to respond to daily and multiple conflicts.

We determined that these needs were foremost for our students: to learn to read and write more complex material and to do so with sufficient speed to keep up in coursework; to decide on their educational goals and act, with energy and motivation, to advance their goals; and to lay aside conflicts that impeded the directions they had chosen to pursue. To minimize impediments to the core tasks of learning to improve language skills, we recognized we had to assist students in building the crucial groundwork of motivation and action centered in students' desires to learn and in their decisions to pursue academic success. Grego and Thompson remark that their at-risk writers expressed "anger, frustration, the desire for success," and they see these emotions standing in the way of learning (71). In our experience, this complex of responses is true of students labeled at-risk for any reason, and it is the label itself that is most damaging. Whereas Grego and Thompson regard student reactive behaviors as "psychic" relations between teacher and student that have become institutionalized (72), we view the behaviors, as the labeling, as resulting from the interconnected relations of culture, society, and individual, which the individual teachers and students have some power and responsibility to change.

THROUGH A WIDE LENS: REFRAMING PERCEPTIONS, RESPONSIBILITIES, AND RESOURCES

To think from new perspectives about who our students were and what they needed, we found that it was helpful to turn to Jurgen Habermas's discussion of identity in *The Theory of Communicative Action*. As with other theorists and researchers on identity, Habermas sees narrative as the main construct for viewing and forming a sense of self. He theorizes identity as formed in narrative embedded in an ordinary understanding of the lifeworld, which is a set of three interconnected domains: the individual, the social, and the cultural. The individual acquires identity in the group via socialization into traditions, which both restrict and provide resources for development. For the individual, "[a]ction, or mastery of situations, presents itself as a circular process in which the actor is at once the *initiator* of his accountable actions and the *product* of the traditions in which he stands, of the solidarity groups to which he belongs, or socialization and learning processes to which he is exposed [emphasis in original]" (135). He both makes and is made by tradition through remaking the narratives available to him. In forming identity narratives, people locate themselves in time and across time with respect to traditions in social space (136). As individuals communicate with each other using narration, they develop a sense of self-understanding that "serves the formation of personal identities" (136–7). Personal identity narrations draw from the resources of tradition, but to form new, coherent ones, students need a rich and deep study of these resources as well as strategies for examining, critiquing, and deciding among them.

Given that narrative give-and-take serves identity formation, as teachers of language and literature we tacitly encourage and support either the unchanging reproduction of the student's identity or its renewal. We chose the hero as the subject at the center of study to allow students to make a parallel journey in which they actively participate in communicative action toward renewal of lifeworld connections. Habermas's exploration of what happens when the lifeworld is disturbed and is not renewed speaks to our at-risk students' difficulties, and suggests that learning cannot be limited to an artificial segmenting of literacy from life needs. Disturbances in the cultural reproduction of the lifeworld, as has happened through massive changes that modern society has undergone, "get manifested in a loss of meaning and lead to corresponding legitimation and orientation crises" (140). Three areas of disturbance correspond to the three domains of lifeworld reproduction processes: "loss of meaning" to the cultural reproduction domain, "legitimation" of the order of interpersonal relationships to the domain of social integration, and "orientation crises" to the domain of the socialized personality. Habermas contends that "*each* of these reproduction processes contributes in maintaining *all* the components of the lifeworld" [emphasis in original] (142). For example, when there is loss of meaning in the cultural domain, there is a loss in cultural identity, social identity, and individual identity. The result is a set of responses that we found in our at-risk students: "withdrawal of motivation," "anomie," loss of "personal responsibility," "alienation," and "crisis in orientation and education" (143). These problems result from responses to the fragmentation of meaning, and its repair cannot be accomplished by individuals alone because fragmentation proceeds from disconnections within and among the domains, and renewal from interaction of social participants.

Habermas's ultimate concern is with how participants in communicative action can arrive at a democratic consensus on normative value through reason. But as our task was to understand the needs of our students, we turned to Charles Taylor's analysis of ethics in modern democratic culture. Taylor traces the negative effects of the three domains to the modern conception of individualism, which forgets the full dimensionality of the person's being in the world. With modern freedom for the individual came the loss of the "heroic dimension," the web of significance in which people were linked meaningfully and purposefully to others and to the natural world:

> People were often locked into a given place, a role and station that was properly theirs and from which it was almost unthinkable to deviate. Modern freedom came about by the discrediting of such orders.

> But at the same time as they restricted us, these orders gave meaning to the world and to the activities of social life. The things that surround us were not just raw materials or instruments for our projects, but they had the significance given them by their place in the chain of being. The eagle was not just another bird, but the king of a whole domain of animal life. By the same token, the rituals and norms of society had more than merely instrumental significance....

> The worry has been repeatedly expressed that the individual lost something important along with the larger social and cosmic horizons of action. Some have written of this as the loss of the heroic dimension to life. People no longer have a sense of a higher purpose, of something worth dying for. (3–4)

Taylor sees the ascendancy of instrumental reason arising in the vacuum of higher purpose beyond the individual as the cause of a restricted sense of "resonance, depth, and richness in our human surroundings" (6); without a higher purpose, people become segregated in their own private concerns and satisfactions, including the "heart"—to the detriment of political and moral action (7–8).

If students have no clear higher purpose, no set identity and meaning already made of the world and their role in it, they have the freedom of choice, including the burdens that go with choice. The paths of heroes making their way through societal and personal change toward renewal can model choice as well as limitation, and the fact that choice exists. In part, a person makes her or his path and who she or he is on that path. To assist students in choosing their directions, and thus their educational routes, with a greater measure of awareness, we designed a challenging, college-level course focused on the hero quest as seen from a range of social and cultural perspectives across time. Students were opened to a study of the individual and society from a cross-cultural, historical perspective in which making choices about identity and meaning dovetailed with making choices as a writer. We thought that students could use, if they wished, their study of the hero quest for its implicit lessons for their own lives, especially that they had a good deal to say about who they choose to be and what they choose to do. Like them, heroes must grapple with conflict about their roles in society and find identity and meaning in experiences as they go through time—our course, and other college courses, for example. Like them, heroes have a good deal of say in who they choose to be and what they choose to do. Like them, heroes must become strong decision makers and agents at the center of personal and, often, social change.

But not only can the hero journey inform, guide, and support students dealing with marginal academic status; it also parallels the development of what David Bartholomae has called the two most salient features of college writing: authoritative voice and stylistic inventiveness. For these to develop, students must travel beyond what they already know into new discourses and perspectives, and they must learn also how to choose a central perspective from which to see and write as individuals amid the discourses. Our curriculum was built from a wide range of literary and nonliterary, visual and verbal, academic and nonacademic reading and writing. All students can learn much, regardless of their kinds and degrees of writing skill. As important, all students bring a great deal of knowledge of social and cultural life to contribute to the study of the subject, so that the distinctions in writing skill are not central to students' contributions to the class.

Students' journeys through our course proceed from the past, encountering various discourses of tradition and focusing on ways a selection of heroes met, grappled with, and responded to a wide range of discourses. The responses of heroes, together with the responses of authors and visual artists, paralleled students' learning responses: they are negotiations through discourses, often critiques, a traveling and tracking of their course. As thinkers, readers, and writers, students engage in a quest to discover, encounter, and perhaps renew their various identities. From these identity positions, they have many perspectives to choose for seeing, interpreting, and writing. To offer rich possibilities for encounter, we juxtapose materials, concepts, and strategies usually kept separate—visual and verbal texts, several humanities subjects, literary and academic modes, school, and rest-of-the world. We go on "city quests" to museums, monuments, and transportation centers, because in these places the past is figured in the present and extends into the future.

From Taylor, we also learned to pay attention to engaging all the dimensions of the person if identity and meaning were to be renewed. We attended to the ways matters of the heart affected learning and redirected the energy invested in anger toward interest in the subject. During the first summer, it became clear that the city quests were the pivotal learning intersections, where classroom and library study met with the experience of knowledge as relevant to life. The intersection of several areas of society and culture in these quests initiated student responses in a fuller dimensionality of humanness that many students claimed was of key value to their intellectual and personal development (Winslow and Mische 90–2). When we saw the powerful effects of the emotional response at these sites powering intellectual learning, we drew from a number of other resources to support and deepen our understanding and use of the interconnections among emotional, physical, intellectual, moral, and spiritual dimensions. Mikhail Bakhtin's writings on the chronotope furthered our understanding of the hero's development at learning intersections (see Winslow and Mische for discussion). Wolfgang Iser's new work, *The Fictive and the Imaginary: Charting Literary Anthropology* extended many of Bakhtin's key ideas and provided strategies for reading and writing assignments geared to developing voice as a creative center engaged in border-crossing activity. Martha Nussbaum's essays on literature and ethics collected in *Love's Knowledge* helped us understand emotion as a necessary consideration in ethical reasoning. Research being conducted on our campus on adolescent moral development by James Youniss and Miranda Yates indicated that high school students who chose to write about their emotional experiences in a social justice class were the ones who went on to show growth in moral reasoning. Youniss and Yates contend that students need to find a perspective on the various values and philosophies inside and outside of the academy and that doing this in a responsible way requires moral thinking and development. They confirm what the ancients knew: moral development undergirds making wise decisions.

After broadening our framework, we looked at our students' writing and listened to what they were saying for the meaning they were making as people with many roles, with various strengths and knowledge, including literary knowledge. This analysis helped us to attend to our students and their writing in terms of the knowledge they brought to the class that could be used as resources to build toward what they needed to learn to succeed in college. For example, Rachela's poem, featured in the epigraph, illustrates several points about her knowledge and needs: (1) she understands and has a preference for literary modes, evidenced by the poetic form and the linguistic play; (2) she employs a mode of reading literature that requires response in the same mode as opposed to an expository analytic response; (3) she is burdened with heavy and multiple demands in her personal life that might impede learning by diverting energy and focus from studies; and (4) the experience of isolation she expresses in the areas of family and faith and her desire for reconnection is a central concern, guiding her interpretation. Elsewhere in the paper containing this poem, she states her academic goals thus: "to raise my family as high as I can" and "to be a Dancer or a Doctor." Throughout the semester, her high goals clashed with her frustration over the difficulty of her studies, her continuing distress about her family, her racial marginalization in U.S. society, and her provisional academic status, with the result that she felt even more isolated. These concerns were so prominent in her life, and consequently in her mind, that she could not separate them from her reading and writing tasks. She could, however, and did, use knowledge she had gained through experience as a way of understanding texts, and she used her preferred mode of creative writing to work her way further into an understanding of academic materials and conventions. Looked at through a sociocultural lens that counts her mode and style of response as competent, her response to Dickinson's poem demonstrates deep understanding, and it is hers, not a mime of teacher talk.

LEARNING INTERSECTIONS: MATERIALS, STRATEGIES, CONNECTIONS

If students are to discredit their at-risk identities, they need to succeed in difficult learning tasks. And if they succeed in a learning environment where they failed previously, then it becomes clear that the responsibility for student success is at least partly institutional. We speculated that using topics and materials that indirectly support sorting through a dialectical movement of critical questioning and wisely choosing a position for the self simultaneously assists the student to enter and transcend sites of conflict while developing a strong center from which to read, think, and write critically. Students are introduced to several humanities disciplines and taxonomies of the hero so that they can begin to see how disciplines operate. Our course is challenging, but students are able to achieve because we start from what they know, we support the learning continually and in several ways, we approach learning as taking perspectives and thinking creatively about how facts are interpreted and knowledge formed.[2] We structure learning tasks in small pieces designed to build skill in noticing details, using conceptual frameworks, and forming generalizations and then we move these aside to build another view of generalizations.[3] A growing repertoire of thinking strategies crucial to college work results, accompanied by an expanding voice and style repertoire as writing activities provides a place to explore creative versions of expression in tandem with academic discourse. We find the creative work nourishes thought and voice, so that academic writing skill advances more quickly than we have seen in our traditional teaching of academic discourse only. Literary texts provide the base for building the knowledge of concepts and the stylistic and rhetorical repertoires. Their modeling of strong prose in various dialects and their examination of strong individuals in moments of cultural and societal transition provide a wealth of resources for thought, discussion, and writing. From the literary base, we range into conceptual texts (psychology, mythography, history, religious studies, semeiotics, film studies, art history, politics); visual texts (painting, sculpture, film, architecture, monuments, museum exhibits); several modes of discourses for reading and writing assignments; and several learning environments (seminar, instructor-led peer workshops twice weekly, tutorials, large group lectures, library, city). Daily contact among the staff and weekly staff meetings assure that learning is coordinated and developed out of students' developing progress and needs.

We find our students live in a mix of excitement and fear as they adjust to a newly independent life, grapple with conflicting cultural values and systems of belief, or face an uncertain future. They often express a heady sense of urgency and possibility as they encounter new worlds and ideas found in historical and literary texts. Our small seminar class size (15 students), frequent conferences, small group writing workshops (four to five students led by a second instructor), and collaborative writing activities seem to help make students comfortable with and find assurance in examining the instructional materials in ways that make sense within the contexts of their lives and their new status at college. Many students are unable to understand the material without connecting personal knowledge to it. About half our at-risk students choose, like Rachela, to focus explicitly on connecting their personal life journeys as an opening to understanding the subject and to deciding whether and how college study could be meaningful for them. Rachela was aware that she began the course amid a complex knot of family, academic, and spiritual crises. A sense of fragmentation and loss of identity had interfered with her connecting in a meaningful way to academia and written texts. Though she desperately desired a college education, she could not envision in any concrete manner her future and the path that might take her there. Her father's abandonment of the family and the resulting forced separation of her siblings intensified feelings of academic and racial marginalization, causing her to question the value and moral teachings of her faith community. Encouraged to encounter literary texts from multiple perspectives, to engage with characters and themes from both a personal and social/critical stance, Rachela discovered that the theme of "family"—the hero's desire to create bonds of love, to integrate self with other—could become a lens through which she could scrutinize literary texts, which to her seemed otherwise impenetrable. In literary texts, she could recognize archetypal patterns and inherent heroism in her own life struggles. Rachela came to realize that although her quest and her pain were ultimately her own, her quest for love, wholeness, and community was part of a larger human striving—and that determination to love self and other (to see, to care, to act) in the face of cultural and institutional forces that threaten to destroy human sanctity and connectedness may be, in fact, the greatest act of heroism.

Like the journey toward self and social understanding, academic discourse begins in asking questions. We begin with studying how traditional peoples asked questions and answered them in myths. We compare and contrast core elements of Greek, Roman, Native American, Jewish, and Christian versions of creation stories and ask students to respond to or revise these as well as write their own. Rachela reworked the expulsion from paradise in *Genesis* from the perspective of Eve, expressing first anger, then profound sorrow in her exile and separation from God. She dedicated an original creation myth to her brother, detailing the mysteries of the universe so as to instill wonder and awe. In her early writings, a thread of themes she would continue to explore surfaced: pain of abandonment, love of family, yearning for a sense of the divine and for a meaningful place in community.

We carry learning about mythic structures into academic discourse by presenting several taxonomies of the hero. This work enables students to see that academic disciplines ask questions, construct various frames through which to view the part of the world they study, and use the knowledge gained to organize and understand what had not been known. Then we read and examine excerpts from Exodus and Milton's *Paradise Lost*, and students frame their findings with a study of archetypes, using either Carol Pearson's feminist revision of Jung's theory of hero archetypes, which traces the inward, spiral journey through six images on three levels; or Joseph Campbell's account of cross-cultural monomythic patterning of separation, initiation, and return, wherein the hero's new knowledge elevates and re-vitalizes his community. They also begin a concurrent reading of Homer's *Odyssey*. This work prepares students for the first large group lecture and city quest on the topic of aesthetics and changes in the hero paradigm through the centuries. To teach the paradigm in historical context, we give a 2-hour interactive slide presentation on art and architecture from ancient Greece through the beginning of Modernism. The presentation does double duty: we examine continuity and change in representations of hero images and we apply conceptual thought to factual details so that learning strategies for reading visual texts carry over directly to verbal texts.

We begin with a slide of one of Paulo Uccello's "St. George and the Dragon" paintings (fifteenth century Italy), depicting a familiar triad: a fierce, fire-breathing dragon, a beautiful maiden, and an armored knight on horseback—the hero-villain-victim paradigm. We ask students to "read" the picture by having them note the use of color, line, composition, lighting, el-ements of foreground and background, body positions, facial expressions, and narrative events depicted inside and outside (before and after) the scene. Then we ask them to use the concepts from Pearson or Campbell to in-quire into the stages of the hero, male/female roles, motivations, and the artist's conception of the cultural and social roles the figures seem to em-body. Students share and negotiate their findings, discovering and justifying interpretations with factual details from the painting. After a sometimes heated discussion, we introduce a modern British poem based on the painting, U. A. Fanthorpe's "Not My Best Side," and stage a dramatic reading so that students can hear all three characters' voices—dragon, hero, and damsel-in-distress. Students immediately recognize and name the irony in the feminist perspectives. They consider specific ways the paradigm is still current today, but note that the contents have shifted into stereotypes that are ironic takes on both medieval and contemporary images the self takes for its identity. Through the archetypal theory they have studied, they see that each individual can embody or suppress one or more of these perspectives but that a full view incorporates all of them in one person. In this way, we pull the personal dimensions into relation with the cultural and social domains as students need these to distinguish and practice interpretive and analytic thinking. In the second hour, slides with images of the hero in Western culture from Ancient Greece through 1910 in sculpture, architecture, and painting inform students about historical material while giving practice "reading" visual forms of cultural expression and interpreting from the evidence of textual details.

Several writing assignments derived from this work. One is a creative piece in which students select a painting and create a narrative, lyric, or dramatic work from the point of view of a character depicted in the painting. Most students (Rachela included) love this because the visual material and the literary forms are more accessible for them. The colors and compositional elements invite them to enter the sometimes beautiful, sometimes startling world of the painting and to encounter imaginatively the hearts, minds, and souls of the characters. Students speculate about characters' past deeds or family histories, detail inward emotional traumas, physical exertions, or spiritual unrest, or they dramatically retell or renew mythic or historical events. Rachela enjoyed this assignment so much that she created dramatic monologues for three artworks: a bronze-cast warrior, a fourteenth century icon of Christ on a cross, an Impressionist mother and child (Mary Cassatt's secularized madonna and child). Entering into and attempting to understand the world of another in its complexity became Rachela's mode of inquiry throughout the course. The approach has wide-reaching benefits: (1) it heightens sensitivity to visual detail and to language, (2) it pushes students to contemplate a realm beyond the self, (3) it expands and deepens the student's understanding of and ability to choose point of view, (4) it gives practice in writing with a strong, sustained voice from a chosen point of view, and (5) it shows writers that fictional and nonfictional texts alike present an idea or argument with proofs built from items of evidence.

For a second assignment, students write a longer thesis-driven paper with supporting arguments and specific visual and verbal textual evidence.

During a trip to the National Gallery of Art, they view more hero images and choose an artwork that embodies one or more hero archetypes. In their essays, students first provide a working definition of the archetype, including a discussion of the fears, goals, values, actions, and beliefs central to that particular archetypal mode of being. They then describe the artwork in concrete detail, using their newly-acquired sensitivity to formal elements to explain their theses about the archetype. If they wish, students can also include their aesthetic and emotional responses to the artwork and their sense of what the artwork, and the artist behind it, seem to be saying—what theme, message, or insights are revealed about human nature, heroic action, or stages of the life journey. For this work, our aim is to improve and make conscious strategies for (1) interpreting from details within a given conceptual framework, (2) forming and supporting a thesis, and (3) organizing ideas—all as necessary tools for pursuing inquiry into a topic and writing about one's findings.

The gallery visit also provides the basis for a third piece of writing that combines formal and aesthetic analyses and emotional response. Students take notes comparing and contrasting the two buildings of the gallery, one built around 1940 on modern classical Greco-Roman principles of design (architect John Russell Pope), as derived from Greek temples in the slide lecture, and the other contemporary in design (architect I. M. Pei). They note the structural and stylistic elements of design as well as the mood or feeling evoked. Throughout the course, students draw on this new knowledge of architectural spaces, choices, and ramifications (a subunit named "hero as architect") in subsequent visits to war memorials, churches, and the U.S. Holocaust Memorial Museum.

These assignments are drafted and taken to writing workshops for one or two revisions. During this first set of assignments, writing improves markedly from first to last draft. Descriptive powers are enhanced, language becomes more concrete, and length usually doubles. Their papers do not always display a standard academic "thesis statement" on this first assignment, but there is at least an implicit focus or organizing principle. More important at this stage, students manage to incorporate and "flesh out" an author's theory without losing their own voices or subordinating their own interpretations and ideas. We encounter few of the labored, near-plagiarized summaries or paraphrases we found so often in students' work before we implemented this course. Students learn quickly to take an interpretive position and support it with a wealth of textual—verbal and visual—evidence, and this helps them make the transition from visual interpretation to close readings of literary texts, a task many students desperately feared.

Here is an example paragraph from the middle of one student's paper in which the task was to interpret a figure in a painting using visual details as evidence to support an interpretation in light of a conceptual scheme,

Pearson's taxonomy of archetypes:

> The jacket does not quite hang right on the Wanderer. The shoulders are worn
> out and stretched. They sag down his arms a bit, making the jacket look like
> it is too big for the man wearing it. The sleeves are meant to puff out, but the
> jacket has been leaned on and squashed that the puffs are sort of wilted and
> wrinkly. He very much looks the part of the vagrant wanderer.

This student has learned to (1) notice a wealth of particular detail, and (2) to
use it to support her view of what archetype the figure in the painting expresses. Because she knows how to notice and talk about visual detail, she
can do so readily and well, and then she can easily transfer this knowledge
to noticing detail in written texts and using it to classify. She has also begun
to learn to cite the conceptual work used as a lens for the data. Yet, because
of the imaginative elements we asked for, she develops her own view of
the character beyond the conceptual framework in the textbook. She imag-
ines what the man must be thinking, and she devotes the remainder of the
paper to an extensive analysis of this type of person, demonstrating her
sharp knowledge of human beings, at least this sort of person. Nearly all
students demonstrate some deep knowledge of human nature; we find that
life experience is a strength many at-risk students bring to class discussions
during literary study. Note too that the student is also learning to use and
cite ideas from others' texts to support her ideas. A cut-and-paste of others'
ideas would be impossible in this assignment.

Before the end of the semester, most students develop academic conventional voices, evident in key aspects of form and style. Here are the opening
paragraphs of two papers that demonstrate a clear sense of a voice knowing
what it means to say. Yet both writers have learned to write clear, concise
thesis statements and to forecast the routes they take to support them. Both
excerpts exemplify a newly-learned grasp of conventions of formal style and
of organizing proof for a significant point.

1. Coming of age is a long process which takes a great deal of time for a
child to blossom into an adult. The child has to go through many experiences
and journeys that will take him from childhood to adulthood. Through out
these journeys he will encounter difficult situations that will test his maturity,
or aid in his moral development. Usually these journeys are inward journeys
to find oneself. Two specific people who went on such journeys of self-
discovery are John Grady Cole in *All the Pretty Horses* and Siddhartha in
Siddhartha. John Grady Cole learned about love and how to deal with
losing love, how to value things, how precious life is, and even though
he was the same age when he returned to the U.S. he had matured into an

adult. Siddhartha successfully found his true self; he learned about love with Kamala and his son, and through his whole life experience he grew as an individual.

2. The significance of family life and home is by far the most compelling theme in *Night* (1960) and *Kindred* (1979). Weisel and Butler attempt to portray an ideal family and home that's not so different from the norm. After they establish that, they plunge their story into a horrible place that contrasts to their first idea of home. The second kind of home that the authors describe is a place that the characters would desert in no time if they had a *choice*. In either case, the characters were forced against their will to leave a place that was a source of comfort to them and be dragged off to the cruel world of inhumanity, while being torn away from their families.

Although there remains some diction in these passages that may not appear in the best writing, the mix of diction shows that the writers are acquiring a more formal vocabulary while unafraid to use their habitual, conversational language; we find that the best, most vivid language increases in proportion throughout the semester if we focus on pointing out strengths and use benign neglect on the less fresh writing. What we like in these paragraphs is the clear thought and organization and the strong, sure voices that come through. This writing represents remarkable progress in the span of 3 months.

In this next example, which is the second paragraph of the paper by writer 2, we noted the good use of textual quotation as evidence of these students' growing ability to make an interpretive point. This was an entirely new skill to these students and one we began to develop in the paper on archetypes in a painting. Similar to the paragraph on the painting (given previously), this paragraph adheres closely to the task of offering relevant and sufficient textual detail as evidence for the comparison the writer is making.

> In the quote, "They went by ... dragging their lives, deserting their homes, the years of their childhood, cringing like beaten dogs," (Weisel 15) Weisel is describing the torture of the Jews in leaving their home. "Like beaten dogs," explains the inhumane treatment that was forced upon these people as they "dragged" their lives away. The way the Jews were driven out is similar to the story of how Adam and Eve were driven away from paradise to a hostile world. Weisel's home was a place that was sanctuary to him, where he "spent so many years in search for God." (15) He describes his home's (community) "atmosphere as peaceful and reassuring." (20)

The strong prose this student's writing attained later in the paper can be seen in the transition from the first part of the paper, on *Night*, to the second part, on *Kindred*:

> Weisel described his home as a place where he sought sanctity. There, people
> were ripped away from their homes never to return. But in *Kindred*, home
> was where "refuge" was found. The character, Dana, unlike the Jews, still had
> the privilege of returning home even if it was on a conditional basis where she
> has to feel that her life was in danger. Since Kevin was Dana's only connection
> at the plantation to her real home in California, Kevin's room was her "place
> of refuge." It was the only place she found comfort from the troubles she
> experienced in that time and place. Home in *Kindred* implies that it's where
> you and your loved ones are supposed to remain. This is clearly seen with
> Carry and Nigel. As soon as Tom Weylin allowed Nigel to build a home for
> Carry and their children, Weylin knew that Nigel wouldn't try to run away. Even
> with Rufus, he loves Dana and he considers her a part of his household. In one
> conversation he tells her, "You'll be all right here. You're home." (Butler 143)
> For Dana, there was also a moment when she was convinced of that, as she
> said, "Home at last." (127) Then she remembered how hostile it really was.

After establishing the points of contrast in the first three sentences, the writer
goes on to elaborate a definition of "home" that is necessary to developing
a complex idea: a "home" that is not to be desired—the task she set out
in the first paragraph. This writer is learning the basic features of academic
writing while keeping a clear and interesting voice.

PERSONAL VOICE AND SELF AND SOCIAL POSITIONING: RACHELA'S JOURNEY

How did students journey through texts using their own orientations and
knowledge to advance into academic territory? At first, Rachela and others found the first full-length text, the *Odyssey*, difficult and unappealing.
Despite multiple lengthy attempts, many students could not find an in-
road: for example, Rachela highlighted twice, with yellow and blue markers, every line of the first two books. Examining the scope and beauty of
Homer's descriptive powers and identifying him as a poet helped Rachela
and others cross the threshold. Applying Pearson's framework, through
which students discovered that Odysseus experiences, at various points,
all of Pearson's types, granted further access, as did applying Campbell's
categories. Through Pearson and Campbell, the "Father Quest" emerged as
a favored theme—Telemachus's search for Odysseus, his initiation into the
heroic world and its values, and his inner growth and outward transformation. Rachela immediately felt for Telemachus, an orphan, abandoned,

without guidance and protection. She felt too the pain and loneliness that Penelope endured and that caused Odysseus' mother to slowly pine away. She felt for Odysseus, trapped and isolated on Calypso's island, mourning the loss of his crew. Homer's text, Rachela came to realize, was a moving portrait of the deep pain of families torn apart by war and domestic upheaval, and a commentary on how we are to treat strangers in our midst.

In a companion field trip assignment, Rachela visited Maya Lin's Vietnam Veteran's Memorial and was moved to tears. She wrote a paper linking Odysseus' homecoming to the return of the veterans, in which the pain experienced by Odysseus' family mirrored the agony felt by the families of men killed in Vietnam. Rachela understood the book and the monument in the triple theme of family, community, and the divine that had early on attracted her deep interest. Beginning and ending this essay with an original poem, she incorporated academic prose, personal writing, and literary writing into the same text. Freedom to mix genres and levels of style enabled her to try out an academic style in her own voice. Here is part of the opening poem and the first two paragraphs of the first draft of the *Odyssey*/Vietnam Memorial paper.

Oh say can you see
that the Veterans are coming
through the war that they fought
through the rockets they died . . .
America, America
God sends his praise on thee
through the families that were hurt
through the land that they held . . .
The Veterans are home.

America will always remember the men and the women who went to Vietnam to fight for the rights of their country. The Veterans will never be forgotten; that is why the Vietnam Veterans Memorial is there today for the heroes to be acknowledged, and receive their praise for having died and suffered during the war. The Veterans lives continue beyond the wall of the memorial; they also remain in the hearts of their families and in the hearts of the shiny sea, America.

My first impression of the Vietnam Veterans Memorial was unimpressive, I asked myself "Where is it? Is that all?" Without knowing the true meaning of the wall, the flagpole, the men's statue, or the women's statue. I was very closed minded. I just wanted to get my work done, and leave. Until I saw people showing emotional feelings as if the Veterans were actually there touching them back. I saw flowers, hats, pictures, and wreaths. Then I started to feel something, nothing big, but a little bit. So I went to the police guard. That he could explain to me the true meaning of each sculpture, the value it hold for the outside world, and the people that it surrounds.

Noticing the pain of families at the memorial, Rachela connects the monument to her reading of Odysseus' story. Both texts had been impenetrable until a way in to meaning and value through personal experience was found; in both, her coming to meaning, value, and identity with characters or other real people in shared experiences enabled the learning process she details in paragraph two—moving slowly from hints of feeling into seeking information. The learning process of searching for and making meaning relevant to herself comprise the substance of the paper. The more formal and objective modes are used throughout the remainder of the paper, interleaved with brief, imagined monologues by Odysseus and his family that reveal her considerable understanding of their suffering and plight and her concern for others beside herself. It is as if she needed to give voice to specific others, and in so doing she found a way to express the several sides of her own understanding. Although this kind of imaginative literary writing is not usual in a strictly academic paper, it enabled her to find a passionate voice and write more strongly and with fewer errors than she had previously done. It is interesting that the lapses in standard English syntax and punctuation occur in the one paragraph that details her personal experience. Three of the eight fragments in the seven-page paper appear in this paragraph. Most of these occurrences capture the emphatic phonology of oral speech. Only one—*That* in the last sentence of the excerpt—seems to result from a miscue in attempting a relative clause used in formal written language.

This example from Rachela's first long paper was typical of students' movement from creative to academic modes. The parallel assignments drew forth the latent competence in both modes, perhaps because students first developed something to say and had one creative assignment to verbalize that something before launching into the academic mode in which they were less sure how they should write. On subsequent assignments, Rachela gained greater control over the transitions among the different types of writing in a paper, and her mastery of sentence structure, already apparent in most of her paragraphs, improved without loss of topic focus and intonational emphasis that she knew to be critical elements of language used well.

In another segment of the course several weeks later, Rachela again chose family and the pain of separation as topics to explore. At this point, students study slavery in nineteenth century America together with the Jewish Holocaust before and during World War II. Students read autobiographies (Douglass; DuBois; Weisel); Cynthia Ozick's essay "On Christian Heroism," a taxonomy of types of agency during the Holocaust—hero, victim, murderer, and bystander—that revises the taxonomy studied earlier and that asks readers to contemplate their own capacities for heroic action; poems by nineteenth century American slaves and World War II concentration camp prisoners; and Octavia Butler's *Kindred*, a contemporary science fiction emancipatory narrative[4] in which the female hero compares slavery to the Jewish Holocaust as part of her attempt to understand her identity in terms of present conditions as affected by the past and as affecting the future. Butler uses time travel as a device for exploring connections, for understanding Douglass's life and writings from an experiential perspective, and for contrasting and comparing modes of thought, perspectives, and social conditioning in the nineteenth and twentieth centuries. Students visit the U.S. Holocaust Memorial Museum and Frederick Douglass's last home. These materials take students deeply into the complex issues of the individual's struggle for identity and meaning amid oppressive social forces and cultural realities that conflict with stated ideals.

After recording their responses to these readings and experiences, students compose comparative essays that link researched facts, authorial perspectives, and reader experience. Students focus on particular exhibits and narratives that depict what life was like during both periods of history. Calling attention first to the particular details that make these remembered events and stories resonate so powerfully, students then interpret the larger vision and moral imperatives that the authors, architects, filmmakers, and curators convey—ideas about the construction of history, community, and identity, about the horrors, consequences, roots, and possible forms of resistance to such injustices. Rachela chose to write about the inward struggle and alienation felt by both Douglass and Weisel as they grappled with a fragmented family and threatened loss of identity. She admired how, in real life, these two "heroes" were able to reconstruct, despite their harrowing experiences, a self from which to write with authority and grace, and were able to effect social and political change.

In the unit on the spiritual quest, Rachela identified most strongly with Siddhartha's recurring struggles with restlessness and despair, his quest for inner peace and fulfillment, his taking on of new and shedding of old identities and philosophies. She composed a paper detailing her own spiritual quest, creating subheadings inspired by Hesse's, for example, "The Catholic's Daughter" in lieu of "The Brahmin's Son," to describe herself in past, present, and future stages of her journey. She took solace from and expressed confidence that she, like Siddhartha, would someday experience wholeness and human connectedness across cultures and time. She also wrote a reflective essay describing her visit to a neighboring Franciscan monastery—a site of repose, sanctity, and natural beauty in the midst of the high-crime area of Washington, D.C. where she is a resident. She discovered in the monastery, in its art, architecture, and landscaping, valuable historical traditions that gave her the space and freedom to experience her own meditation and uplift.

Improvement in academic writing was not our only goal, for we reasoned that if students were to succeed after they left our course, they would need to come to a decision that college study was valuable, and they would need to discover that in particular ways that were meaningful for them. Many write of their changed attitudes, new confidence in their abilities, new perspectives, and future directions. Many sort through conflicts that they see as impeding their learning, often identifying areas where they had been confused or in conflict. In Rachela's case, she saw her divided family, her feeling of being alone, and her faith as the key areas clouding her ability to move toward the academic success she wanted. Her way in to academic learning came through struggling to relate texts to her own experience. In the at-first alien worlds of the *Odyssey*, and the Vietnam Memorial, by taking those parts of tradition she could embrace and use, she finally came to understand the healing of families as heroic struggle. Anger at her racial marginalization finally came to be tempered by a wider understanding that other groups have suffered great injustice as well. For her, this meant she was less alone, that others had made difficult journeys and had learned compassion, strength, endurance, wisdom. Her characteristic mode of learning was to imagine and write from the perspectives of various characters, as she did for the *Odyssey* and Vietnam Memorial paper. Her high motivation and deep involvement were evident in her willingness to revise her drafts, often as many as eight times with sometimes as many visits to her seminar leader or workshop leader/tutor. Like Rachela, several students each term make the search for family the focus of their intellectual inquiry as well. Other important complexes of interwoven issues included faith, occupation, gender roles, and ethics. Usually, one area is of greatest interest, with others intersecting in minor keys. Some notice that to choose and follow a way of life is a deeper, more purposeful choice than living out an unexamined image of a lifestyle.

A clearer idea of oneself and growth in writing seemed to be inseparable for our students. Rachela's final paper illustrates the very strong voice she had developed, and more importantly what lay behind it—a strong individual finding her self as she found her right to speak her self. The importance of literary models to her is evident in her use of them for renewal of her identity and for form and style. Here are some excerpts, beginning a third of the way into the paper:

The Catholic's Daughter

When I was young, I grew up in a Catholic surrounding. I went to church from sun up to sun down. I went to Catholic Schools, Sunday Classes, and read the Bible with my mother and father. The Bible teaches you things that you should follow, and your parents teach you the same rules, Catholic's believe you should not divorce, you should not commit adultery, and the church and my parents would preach the same to me. As I got older I realized that the Catholic teaching is not really written in stone, because I grew to see my family fall apart right in front of my face. My father went one way, my mother went another way, and my sister was sent to another state. It was just me and my brother, who was always sick. Basically I was all alone. The Catholic preaching taught me nothing, but the opposite. I was alone; ALONE was me.

Right now I am in a journey in my mind, but I have not taken action. All that matters is the action, and that's something that I have to do. [The next portion is a 17-line poem titled ALONE, given in part in the epigraph.]

Finding my Quest

Quest is the question? I am alone, but I'm on a quest to discover who, what, and where I come from. The Catholic way was not myself. My family is still separated. My quest is very important to me. The Quest means the searching of me the searching of my background . . . .

I start my quest as a wanderer, because of the fact that I do not know my historical background. As a wanderer I am consciously and according to Carol Pearson taking my journey, setting out to confront the unknown, which marks the beginning of a life lived at a new level (51). . . . Within a wanderer's mind, I frame my family, but as for the color pictures in that frame, there is none. I know the names of my parents, and where they come from, but do I really know my parents? I see people and they say that they're a part of me and my family, but I really do not know. The wanderer inside of me is searching very hard. . . . Similar to Pearson's notion of the Wanderer's journey, I make a leap of faith to discard old social roles, which I have worn to please and to ensure safety and try instead to discover who I am and what I want (51). In my own family I am basically self-made, a woman of business searching for the missing piece of whole. I am living on the edge of myself. Where do I stand? According to Carol Pearson, wanderers' identity comes from being the outsiders. In their spiritual life, they may experience doubt especially since they usually have been taught that God rewards a measure of conformity and traditional morality. Yet the dark night of the soul they experience often leads to a more mature and adequate faith (52). I have found this to be true for me as well.

Siddhartha

. . . For me to begin my journey according to Herman Hesse I must find my source within my own heart, I must find my source within my own Self . . . . According to Herman Hesse, "happily he looked into the flowing river. Never had a river attracted him as much as this one. Never had he found the voice and appearance of flowing water so beautiful. It seemed to him as if the river had something special to tell him, something that he did not know, something that still awaited him. Siddhartha has wanted to drown himself in this river; the old, tired, despairing Siddhartha was today drowned in it. The new Siddhartha felt a deep love for this flowing water and decided that he would not leave it again so quickly" (100). I found myself so close to this quotation deeply, because of the fact that I was one day looking through a mirror, the reflection of myself and I can hear it talking to me saying everything will soon come in for a complete landing. I resemble my father and the part of me that was speaking was my father's half... when I heard that voice I felt that my father will always be a part of me and that he's not far away. The mirror was my river and my reflection of what was soon to come....

Here, at semester's end, Rachela's voice is strong, sure, and deeply moving, often as beautiful as the prose she has read and clearly loves. The writing demonstrates huge strides toward academic prose, and she has done so with an expanded sense of the power of language in academic learning while also deepening her skill with linguistic play. What we as teachers learned from this experience is that students will become deeply engaged with the course material and will write confidently, movingly, and with authority and verve, with beauty and deep humanity, if fuller dimensions of themselves and the materials are given a place.

EXPANSION AND EVALUATION

Following the first summer of the experimental course, it was clear that our students' competence in academic writing was improving dramatically. In the fall term, rhetoric and composition instructors indicated that all but several were doing acceptable work due to two factors: (1) revision skills enabled them to make major improvements on sketchy rough drafts, and (2) willingness to use the Writing Center. In 1995, at-risk students elected to take either the 4-week summer or the full-semester fall version of the course. In the fall term, a control group of students comparable in size and at-risk criteria took the precollege writing course, taught from a well-known basic writing textbook, that had existed on our campus for 13 years. The overall GPAs for these groups were averaged and compared. Results suggested that the expanded semester program was very successful in that the fall experimental group achieved an average overall GPA .69 higher than the control group: 3.16 for the fall term experimental group vs. 2.47 for the precollege writing course group. (The average grade in our fall experimental course was 3.05, pulling the overall average of 3.16 down slightly.) The summer experimental group scored about the same as the precollege writers, even though they were taking the more difficult college writing course. Besides our course, students enrolled in history, philosophy, science, and religion, all courses requiring frequent papers or lab reports. Progress was slow initially but became rapid in the experimental group about midsemester as students growth in writing and thinking accelerated sufficiently for them to succeed, on average, at the B level, despite failing or near failing grades so many had in the first several weeks.

Because of the success of the trial full-term expansion, the control group was eliminated and all students admitted to the School of Arts and Sciences in the at-risk category were enrolled in the full-term experimental course the following year. At the same time, following up on teachers' views that the revision workshops and tutoring sessions were key to success, we started a second course format for at-risk writers in the other five undergraduate schools of the university. This version was the prototype for our current model; weekly writing workshops are led by a second instructor, who also provides tutoring as needed. To evaluate the success of the two fall-term writing courses, we collected from all students in the courses the second revised researched writing, due in late November. In the spring term, we collected the argumentative writing done in class on the last day. For each semester, all papers were coded for later identification, mixed together, and read by two experienced instructors who had not taught first-year students in that term. The fall mainstreamed students' papers were rated only slightly lower than "regular" students, but final grades were higher overall. On a scale of 3 to 1 with 3 being the highest, the comparisons of mainstreamed to "regular" students were: for a score of 3, 8% to 20%; for 2, 56% to 52%; for 1, 36% to 29%. In the spring, most of the students who had completed the hero quest experimental fall course were placed into the required college writing class with the "regular" students, with the exception of 16 students identified by their instructors as needing extra help. These students were placed in a section with workshops and tutoring attached, and they thus completed both of the test courses. Even though these 16 students were judged from their writing to be the weakest at the university at the start of the spring term, the last day in-class writing was judged slightly higher than that of all other groups, except for honors students. Of these 16 students' final in-class papers, 15% were scored at the highest level (3) as compared to 6% for "regular" students; at level 2, 40% compared to to 47% for regular students; and at level 1, 45% compared to 46% of the regular students. Of the 14 honors composition papers that were mixed in and rated, seven scored at the 3 level and seven at the 2 level. The group enrolled in both test programs, those who had one full year of writing workshops and tutorials attached to their class, earned higher final grades in the spring than either the "regular" students or the experimental group who then took the regular first-year course without benefit of workshops and tutorials.

The results indicate that both courses for at-risk students were effective in improving writing sufficiently more than to keep pace with "regular" students. The writing course with workshop tested superior in both semesters to the degree that the at-risk writers scored nearly as good or better as their peers on actual writing by the end of the semester, even on unrevised in-class writing. The sequence of hero quest course followed by writing course with workshop format was superior, and it would have been the preferred route for our program but for two main significant problems. One was the labeling of at-risk that remained in this version, which we could attempt to minimize but not erase. This difficulty became critical with expansion because the visibility of at-risk students on campus increased, bringing additional stigma and marginalization. The second problem was financial: although the mainstreamed workshop course was less expensive to run than the former two-semester sequence of precollege followed by college level course, the hero quest course was expensive, requiring small classes, a second instructor for workshops and tutoring, and two to three times as many hours as other classes for preparation and biweekly staff meetings. A two-semester, nine-credit sequence was even more costly. The cost/benefit concern seems to be, as it was in our case, a critical factor in deciding how good is good enough writing instruction.

If we could have experimented further, we would have tried the hero quest course, revised to include more argumentative writing as our regular writing course had, on a test population of mixed at-risk and other students. Then we would have tested it against the workshop version of the college writing course, which would enroll all other students, so that none would take the regular course, which clearly is inferior to the workshop version. Adding workshops for everyone has several advantages: instructional time is increased and individualized; the focus on reading, thinking, and inquiry—all as preparation for writing—is central in the seminar meetings, allowing heterogeneous classes to work better; and the workshop/leader tutor becomes a writing advisor/ally, strengthening the writer's decision-making process. The only—but significant—disadvantages are scheduling and cost. Scheduling workshops, especially when they were at first detached from course sections, proved too time-consuming to work even on our small campus. Another cost on our campus, where graduate assistants do most of the composition teaching, is staffing the expensive training program, which must be kept up year after year.

CONCLUSIONS

Our results indicate that heterogeneous classes can work well with sufficient financial and human resources, with good assessment of students' knowledge and needs, with an instructional staff given the time and money to plan and meet frequently, with a content/inquiry based approach, and with an expanded view of the kinds of writing students do. We attempted to design a course that first enabled students to count what they knew already as important to college learning and to use it build on. Doing this meant using many kinds of creative writing to enable students to find their stories, responses, and voices alongside writing in the more objective, academic modes. The process of pairing assignments helped them draw similarities and differences in the modes and thus see more clearly what they needed to do as well as to gain practice in a larger rhetorical and stylistic repertoire. The learning also engaged deeply the moral imagination, which we reported on in an earlier version of this work (see Note). There we outlined our pedagogy as developing cultural literacy, critical literacy, and "critical wisdom," which we defined as grounding critical thinking in both human circumstances and transcendent values, in which the individual is located in something larger than the self. Janis E. Haswell has extended this concept and demonstrated that students can learn to make and take their moral rulers through sustained and deep inquiry into important ethical problems centered on the topic of the Jewish Holocaust. In the final analysis, we think that success derived from beginning from students' knowledge and giving a range of assignments that (1) guided students through rich, diverse materials and locations, and (2) encouraged them to discover their own meanings and voices while also learning academic conventions. Ellen J. Langer, whose learning theory appeared in print after our experimental courses had ended, argues from a broad empirical research base that when people define their own learning outcomes in a learning environment that keeps shifting contexts and perspectives they are engaging in a "process of active self-definition" (125). It is not surprising that our students' sense of identity was strengthened over against the negative at-risk images that were thrust on them. The study of cultural traditions as resources enabled students to use the images as they needed, even to turn around negative images toward learning and positive action. They also develop a centered position from which to write with strength and flexibility because they have read and written from a wide variety of genres and points of view. In this way, they develop the internal resources they bring to class in concert with their use of outside resources provided by the class, as they work toward determining and meeting their chosen path—identity and meaning—and what they need to travel it. Susanne Langer wrote, "The limits of thought in any age are not set so much from the outside by the fullness or poverty of experience . . . as from within by the power of conception and the wealth of formative notions with which the mind meets experience" (8). We close by suggesting that the issue of mainstreaming requires more than reaction to immediate political situations in various localities. The overarching need is to imagine our way through the categorizing of people toward ways of teaching and ways of writing that are large enough to include the strengths and needs of all our students.

ACKNOWLEDGMENTS

We wish to acknowledge our debt, with gratitude, to all those who contributed to the success of this course: the students who worked so assiduously and expressed so frequently and enthusiastically what they were learning along the way; to "Rachela," (a pseudonym), for her hard work in Monica Mische's seminar, and special thanks to her for permission to use her writing in this study; to Lisa Robeson, whose ideas and teaching helped formulate the initial design; and to all the other instructors, who devoted ideas, materials, time, and unflagging energy to this course. Small portions of this chapter appeared in *The Journal of Basic Writing* 15.2 (1996): 76–94.

NOTES

[1]A review of grades earned in our regular rhetoric and composition course (ENG 101) revealed that few of the students who had previously taken ENG 100 did well despite the extra semester of study. There were many Cs, Ds, and Fs and few As and Bs compared to students who had not first placed in ENG 100. See also Peter Dow Adams for similar findings.

[2]Decades ago, Michael Polanyi made the point that students must begin their learning from their own existing knowledge and move from that point. It became a key concept in the writing-to-learn movement.

[3]Susan Peck MacDonald and Charles R. Cooper used a variation of our generalizations from noticed facts in their research. They found significantly better claim-evidence writing by students listing concrete detail from texts and making generalizations as a next step than from either students who chose or their own journal topics or who did not write journals at all.

[4]For an exploration of the relationship of the emancipatory narrative genre to identity in its responding stance to the European-American tradition, see the article that first named and described the genre: Eleanor Traylor's "Naming the Unnamed: African American Criticism," 1993–4.

WORKS CITED

Adams, Peter Dow. "Basic Writing Reconsidered." *Journal of Basic Writing* 12.1 (Special Issue: 4th National Basic Writing Conference Plenaries) (1993). 22–36.

Bakhtin, Mikhail M. *The Dialogic Imagination.* Trans. Caryl Emerson and Michael Holquist. Ed. Michael Holquist. Austin: University of Texas Press, 1981.

Bartholomae, David. "Inventing the University." *When a Writer Can't Write: Studies in Writer's Block and Other Composing Problems.* Ed. Mike Rose. New York: Guilford Press, 1985. 135–64.

Butler, Octavia E. *Kindred.* Boston: Beacon Press, 1979.

Douglass, Frederick. *Narrative of the Life of Frederick Douglass, An American Slave.* U.S. Antislavery Office, 1845. New York: Viking Penguin, 1986.

DuBois, W. E. B. *The Souls of Black Folk: Essays and Sketches.* Chicago: McClurg, 1903.

Fanthorpe, U. A. "Not My Best Side." *Western Wind: An Introduction to Poetry* Eds. John Frederick Nims and David Mason, Fourth Edition. Boston: McGraw-Hill, 2000. Plates 1 and 2, 1992.

Glau, Gregory. "The Stretch Program: Arizona State University's New Mode of University-Level Basic Writing Instruction. *WPA: Writing Program Administration* 20 (1996): 79–91.

Grego, Rhonda, and Nancy Thompson. "Repositioning Remediation: Renegotiating Composition's Work in the Academy." *College Composition and Communication,* 47.1 (1996): 62–83.

Habermas, Jurgen. *The Theory of Communicative Action. Volume 2: Lifeworld and System: A Critique of Functionalist Reason.* Trans. Thomas McCarthy. Boston: Beacon Press, 1987.

Haswell, Janis E. "Student Testimonies: Moral Instruction in the Composition Class." *Journal of Teaching Writing* 16.1 (1998): 3–41.

Heath Shivley Brice, "Work, Class, and Categories: Dilemmas of Identity." In Bloom, Lynn Z., Daiker, Donald A., and White, Edward M., eds. *Composition in the Twenty-First Century; Crisis and Change.* Carbondale and Edwardsville: Southern Illinois Press, 1996. 226–242.

Iser, Wolfgang. *The Fictive and the Imaginary: Charting Literary Anthropology.* Baltimore: Johns Hopkins UP, 1993.

Langer, Ellen J. *The Power of Mindful Learning.* Reading, MA: Perseus Books, 1997.

Langer, Susanne K. *Philosophy in a New Key: A Study in the Symbolism of Reason Rite and Art.* Cambridge: Harvard University Press, 1957.

MacDonald, Susan Peck, and Charles R. Cooper. "Contributions of Academic and Dialogic Journals to Writing About Literature." *Writing, Teaching, and Learning in the Disciplines.* Ed. Anne Herrington and Charles Moran. New York, MLA Press, 1992. 137–55.

Nussbaum, Martha, *Love's Knowledge: Essays on Philosophy and Literature.* Oxford: Oxford U Press, 1990.

Ozick, Cynthia. "On Christian Heroism." *Partisan Review* 59 (1992). Rpt. in *Major Modern Essayists.* Ed. Gilbert Muller. 2nd ed. Englewood Cliffs, NJ: Prentice Hall, 1994.

Pearson, Carol. *The Hero Within: Six Archetypes We Live By.* San Francisco: HarperCollins. 1989.

Soliday, Mary. "From the Margins to the Mainstream: Reconceiving Remediation." *College Composition and Communication* 47.1 (1996): 85–100.

Taylor, Charles. *The Ethics of Authenticity.* Cambridge, MA/London, England: Harvard UP, 1991.

Traylor, Eleanor. "Naming the Unnamed: African American Criticism." *Black Books Bulletin: WordsWork* 16.1–2 (1993–94): 64–75.

Weisel, Elie. *Night.* New York: Bantam, 1960.

Winslow, Rosemary, and Monica Mische. "The Hero's Performance and Students' Quests for Meaning and Identity." *Journal of Basic Writing* 15.2 (1996): 76–94.

Youniss, James, and Miranda Yates. *Community Service and Social Responsibility in Youth: Theory and Policy.* Chicago: U of Chicago P, 1997.

CHAPTER TEN

Mainstreaming and Other Experiments in a Learning Community

Mark Wiley
California State University, Long Beach

With some notable exceptions, most debates on whether to mainstream basic writing students tend to focus primarily on how effectively the basic writing (BW) program prepares students to succeed in the regular college-level composition course (or courses), and secondarily on how effectively the program prepares students to enter what some scholars have designated as the academic discourse community (Bartholomae "Inventing"; Bizzell). Although these debates are certainly necessary and motivated by the good intention of determining what curriculum might be best for our basic writing students, they also remain singularly focused on the BW course and ignore other factors on campus that might affect student retention and success. These factors include, among others, required general education courses besides composition, the quality of student services, and the overall campus climate. The best basic writing program in the world may still not help students succeed academically and persist to graduation if these same students are failing other courses; receiving inadequate support services in such areas as financial aid, academic advising, tutoring, and personal counseling; and feeling unwanted on campus, whether because of race, class, age, a disability, or simply because BW students are labeled, pejoratively, as "remedial."[1]

In separate essays, both Mary Soliday and Suellyn Duffey note that basic writing programs and the regular university-level writing courses do not exist in institutional isolation. The success of basic writing programs is often dependent on other campus entities; as Duffey argues, we need "to see a matrix of interlocking issues" that in addition to curricula include support services, instructor expertise, availability of funding, and other factors affecting how each student perceives his or her identity on campus (104). When evaluating our basic writing programs, we therefore need to weigh carefully the extent to which they are interconnected to other campus entities as well as evaluate the congruence of the form of literacy promoted in the BW curriculum with forms expected in curricula throughout the institution. Once we begin to examine these "interlocking issues" and various other campus structures that significantly affect students' experiences, the question of whether to mainstream or not becomes more difficult to answer definitively.

Certainly, recent published accounts of curricular experiments throughout the country have helped us imagine alternative forms and functions for basic writing. Experiments at City College of New York (Soliday; Soliday and Gleason) and at Arizona State University (Glau) do not eliminate basic writing but provide an "enriched" program and/or a "stretch" program. These approaches manipulate not only the curriculum but also the sequence and time students spend in writing courses. Depending upon the specific institutional writing requirements, basic writing students may take two semesters of composition courses to satisfy all requirements whereas previously it may have taken them three. In other approaches at Cal State, Chico (Rodby), and at the University of South Carolina (Grego and Thompson) basic writing has been replaced with small group tutorials of one form or another.

Yet CUNY's decision last year to end "remediation" on its 11 4-year colleges and the Cal State University system's new policy to drastically reduce the need for remediation over the next several years, may dramatically shift the focus from mainstreaming to one of program survival: basic writing programs (and the students in them) may no longer exist at 4-year postsecondary institutions. These attempts to eliminate basic writing may, ironically, make allies of those on either side of the mainstreaming debate. Those who defend existing basic writing programs, such as Karen Greenberg and Harvey Wiener, may find common cause with critics on the left, such as Ira Shor who calls BW "our apartheid." Actually, those on the left and right already agree that higher education must provide access and help to students who traditionally would be excluded. Instead of arguing among ourselves, therefore, it might be more advantageous for those of us who teach composition and administer writing programs to demonstrate that we do know how to work with BW students and that they do truly belong on our respective campuses.

None of the curricular experiments cited here prove that we should eliminate basic writing and mainstream all of our BW students. But they do challenge us to rethink what we mean by the term "basic writing" and to examine our local contexts to determine whether or not what we are currently doing in its name is really necessary and effective. This is the important point I take from David Bartholomae's well-known essay "The Tidy House." Basic writing has perhaps become too much a fixed structure on our campuses. Instead of serving a "strategic function" where questions about literacy and access to higher education can be debated, our programs may have become our institutions' convenient responses to a literacy crisis where student differences are ignored to make everyone the same. We need to determine whether our basic writing programs have become fixed structures reproducing reductionist forms of literacy and, worse, structures so rigid that they prevent alternatives from emerging, structures that might promulgate other forms of literacy.

Basic writers are, after all, produced in educational scenes, and if we determine that our individual programs are no longer serving our students well, then we should either change or eliminate them. But careful investigation should precede any final decisions. Consequently, a few of my colleagues and I have begun examining just how "tidy" our house may have become. Over the last several years, we have tried out various small-scale curricular experiments to learn as much as we could about all of the factors that enable our basic writing students to persist on campus and ultimately to graduate in good academic standing. These experiments were conducted within a learning community, which was initially organized on our campus in 1992, and although these experiments have so far been modest, they do include mainstreaming basic writing students and reconfiguring aspects of the entire BW program. The experiments have helped us re-imagine how we can work more effectively with students who traditionally have struggled at our university, and, just as importantly, shown us ways we can demonstrate that these students truly belong on campus. In the following section, I offer a general description of learning communities, and then describe specific features of our learning community to provide some context for the experiments we have so far attempted.

THE LEARNING ALLIANCE: AN EVOLVING LEARNING COMMUNITY

As many 2- and 4-year institutions have already discovered, learning communities are proving to be an effective and flexible institutional restructuring effort for working with students at all levels (Lenning and Ebbers), but particularly with first-year students. The idea of using learning communities to ease the transition from high school to college and to provide special assistance where and when it is most needed makes learning communities an attractive alternative either to placing basic writers into university-level writing classes with minimal support or into separate classes where they are often not allowed to begin their general education courses until they have been successfully "remediated." Several scholars have discussed learning communities at length and demonstrated their curricular innovations and successes in increasing student retention and graduation rates, yet little has been published about the impact of learning communities on writing programs and particularly on basic writers.[2]

The learning community on our campus was created to attract primarily students who qualified for the regular university-level composition course. However, as the coordinator of the composition program, I saw this learning community as a potential structure for working more effectively with our large population of basic writers. Up until recently, approximately 50% of the entering first-year students had been identified as needing one or two semesters of basic writing in a class averaging greater than 2,600 students.[3] The presence of so many basic writing students on our campus over the years has brought into strong relief the obstacles that most of our first-year students encounter to one degree or another. As our writing program has become more involved with the growth and development of our learning community, it has become the university's primary crucible for curricular innovation in experimenting with first-year general education courses. Nationally, the focus of learning communities has often been on the academic side, yet it has been clear to those of us involved with first-year students on our campus, and with basic writing students particularly, that we must seriously consider extracurricular factors, too. These factors are crucial out-of-class experiences that include contact with individual faculty and sustaining relationships with peer groups. Notable researchers, such as Ernest Pascarella and Patrick Terenzini, Alexander Astin, and Vincent Tinto cite these variables as highly influential on student growth and development, persistence, and success.

The Learning Alliance at Cal State University, Long Beach is embarking on its eighth year. As noted in its literature, this program seeks to help first-year students "make a positive transition to university life and to be academically successful." On our campus, we think of the Learning Alliance as an attempt to design a small liberal arts college within a large, impersonal, metropolitan university where most students commute and spend little time, except to attend their classes. The savvy director who designed the Learning Alliance and who still oversees its operation and evolution was originally asked by the dean of the college of liberal arts to set up a program that would turn around dismal retention rates and help students graduate in a timely manner. (The dean was also hoping to attract more majors to the liberal arts.) A few key administrators and staff, more so than any faculty, were the first to recognize the challenges facing our entering first-year students: they arrive at the university understanding little about college life and university expectations; many are the first in their families to go to college and so cannot rely on their parents for guidance; a majority work either full or part time while taking four or more college courses. These learning community organizers also had the dismal statistics to document the inevitable results: about a third of our students are on academic probation by the end of their first year; 52% are gone after their second. In response, the College of Liberal Arts sponsored the creation of the Learning Alliance, a comparatively complex learning community.

In a frequently cited definition, Faith Gabelnick, Jean MacGregor, Roberta S. Matthews, and Barbara Leigh Smith claim that learning communities

> purposefully restructure the curriculum to link together courses or course work so that students find greater coherence in what they are learning as well as increased intellectual interaction with faculty and fellow students.... [L]earning communities are also usually associated with collaborative and active approaches to learning, some form of team teaching, and interdisciplinary themes. (5)

Although Gabelnick et al. originally described five types of learning communities in the 1980s, they have since identified three fundamental underlying models that can be varied and combined to fit a given context. Anne Goodsell Love and Kenneth Tokuno describe these three models as (1) student cohorts in larger classes, (2) paired or clustered classes, and (3) team-taught programs.

In the first model, cohorts of students are enrolled in the same sections of larger courses. The number of these courses can vary from two to four. This is the simplest of the three models. In the second, student cohorts take the same classes together and are often the only students in those courses. Although faculty teach separately, they try to make intellectual connections between or across courses. These paired or clustered courses can be linked by a common theme that is explored differently but in a complementary fashion in each course. Love and Tokuno cite the example of Western Washington University where "The Narrative Voice" links oral history, literature, and health courses.

The last model is also known as a Coordinated Studies Program and is the most intricate of the three. Student cohorts travel together in several courses and can meet together in both large and small groups. Faculty form teams and plan the curriculum to integrate the content, assignments, and activities for three or more related courses. They can also teach in each other's classrooms, and there is frequent teacher-to-student contact. Seattle Community College offers a Coordinated Studies Program called "Speaking for Ourselves: You Cannot Shut Us Out." This integrated set of courses includes world cultures, non-Western art, composition, modern world literature, and a library research course (Love and Tokuno 10–11).

The Learning Alliance is a variation of model two. In the first semester, students travel as a cohort in three courses, two general education courses and a one-unit class introducing them to the university. This third class has recently been increased to two units because students wished to maintain the regular contact with staff and receive the practical information offered throughout their first semester. In their second semester, students enroll in two linked courses, but they change cohorts. Because students usually take a composition course in their first semester, it is linked with another general education class offered through the college of liberal arts. This second course also satisfies one of several of the university's general education requirements. Some of these links have paired composition with psychology, history, political science, anthropology, sociology, speech communication, and literature. Students are encouraged to build explicit connections between ideas and disciplines; involvement and active learning are emphasized along with lots of discussion, group work, workshops, and frequent writing assignments. Faculty work together to create links between their courses. Most go through summer and winter institutes to design their respective curricula, and each faculty pair meets regularly throughout the semester to assess and, if necessary, fine tune the curriculum jointly constructed. The Alliance faculty are offered a modest stipend per semester for the extra work such collaboration requires. Some of these pairs have been together since the Alliance began, whereas others may be together for a few years or for a single semester only.

The Learning Alliance differs from other learning communities because it extends beyond the first semester. In fact, students in the Learning Alliance have opportunities to be involved through their senior year. Moreover, the Learning Alliance focuses on out-of-classroom experiences in addition to the academic. We want students to get involved quickly in campus life, to meet others, and to come to know the university as a place that offers many opportunities—intellectual, social, and cultural. In their initial semester, first-year students must attend three campus events, and there are also numerous other informal social events sponsored by the Alliance throughout the academic year. In fact, the annual Christmas party has become such a popular event that even upper-level administrators come to enjoy the good food, activities, and general holiday cheer.

Alliance students receive priority registration each semester, an aspect that seems to be the main selling point for most first-year students. However, they must come in for academic advising each term during their first 2 years (the third is optional). We want to ensure that Alliance students are taking the classes they need in the proper sequence, and are receiving sound advice about what courses might fit their projected majors and professional careers. During both their sophomore and junior years, all Alliance students must contribute 10–15 hours of community service. They also have the option of enrolling in a core course that might include other non-Alliance students and that satisfies another general education requirement. One other option for juniors and seniors is to enroll in a 400-level Psychology course that will prepare them to become one of 39 peer mentors to other Learning Alliance students. The peer mentoring program has been a valuable addition because these now older and wiser students can teach first-year students about navigating that difficult transition from high school. Some of our basic writing students have become outstanding peer mentors, a gratifying outcome for a few individuals who we initially feared would not remain in school for long.

The Learning Alliance is a small learning community compared to those offered at other colleges and universities. Temple University, for instance, offers various learning communities that accommodate close to 1,000 students each fall semester. The Learning Alliance has remained small because of its complexity and extension beyond the first semester, dimensions of the program that require extra resources in contrast to single-semester LCs. Nevertheless, growth has been incremental. There were 90 students in the initial Learning Alliance cohort; now in its eighth year, close to 300 students will be coming on board. Although these numbers seem slight in terms of students served, bear in mind that Learning Alliance students continue in the program through their junior year so there are always approximately 600–800 students participating to some degree. The success of the Learning Alliance has raised eyebrows around the university. Since 1992, the annual retention rate in this learning community has averaged 89% with the probation rate at about 13%. By contrast, the retention rate for the rest of the university after the second year has been 48%, and typically over 30% of first-year students have been on academic probation by the end of their second semester.

I have offered a brief sketch of the background, structure, and overall success of the Learning Alliance to provide the institutional context within which the program's experiments with some of our basic writers began and continue. In the following section, I will describe those experiments, including an attempt to mainstream some basic writers, and explain how these experiments have affected the composition program overall.

MAINSTREAMING AND OTHER EXPERIMENTS

Cal State University, Long Beach is one of the most populous of 23 campuses in the Cal State system, the largest state university in the country. CSU policy has dictated that depending upon their scores on the English Placement Test (a test Ed White helped develop in 1978), some students might be required to take at least one, and possibly two, noncollege credit courses in basic writing. Although the Cal State system has not suffered the intense political scrutiny and bitter battles to the degree that CUNY has recently, it has mandated the long-term systemwide goal of reducing the need for remediation to 10% of entering first-year students by the year 2007. Such a dramatic reduction throughout the system is unlikely to happen, though, given the shortage of well-qualified high school teachers, the overcrowded conditions at many urban secondary schools, the growing number of students in the state whose heritage language is other than English, and the inevitable gap between what colleges and universities expect of first-year students and the knowledge and skills high school graduates actually possess. However, the anticipated rise in applications to the CSU over the next several years means that individual campuses may attempt to modify existing admission criteria to attract the most qualified students. On my campus, the preliminary discussions so far, predictably, have centered on restricting admission to "college-ready only" students. But there are also strong arguments that our campus must continue to honor its commitment to all students in our local region who qualify for admission under the present criteria. Those of us making this case also insist the campus must remain committed to diversity. Given these anticipated political struggles, it is vitally important that we demonstrate our ability to work with underprepared students and show that they indeed can be successful.

The Learning Alliance was not designed specifically as an alternative for basic writing but to meet as far as possible the academic and personal needs of all students who volunteer to join it and to help make the first year a better experience for them. Yet, even though we do not think of BW students as different in kind from other students, we recognize they may need more of the additional support such a program as the Alliance can effectively offer. As soon as the Alliance was created, the director attempted to include basic writing students. Unfortunately, there has been some resistance from other campus entities who believe "remedial" students do not belong on a college campus and resent any funding used to help them. And, ironically, resistance has even come from some BW students themselves. They are admitted into the university before taking their placement test. However, too many do not take this test until the May or June prior to enrolling in fall classes. Consequently, after they discover they must take one or two semesters of basic writing, several decide to enroll instead in a community college where tuition is much cheaper. Some of these students also fear that the classes in the Alliance may be too tough for them, or they simply fear entering a program markedly different from the courses the majority of their peers will be taking. Another significant recruiting obstacle is that because the Alliance is part of the college of liberal arts, it must primarily recruit students who declare (or who are thinking about declaring) a liberal arts major. Despite these obstacles, the Alliance has succeeded in attracting enough basic writing students to allow us to try out some curricular experiments, and so far the results of both the mainstreaming experiment and the others tried have been encouraging.

THE SUCCESS OF BASIC WRITERS

The majority of our work with basic writers in this learning community has consisted of linking sections of BW to other Alliance courses and having these basic writing students participate in the full range of activities and benefits available to all Alliance students. However, we have tried one successful mainstreaming experiment and one where we combined students from the first- and second-level basic writing courses into a single course and linked sections of this course to other disciplines. Since 1992 when we began experimenting with different configurations of basic writing, we have kept data on how successful these BW students have been in terms of retention, academic performance, and persistence to graduation.

The first small group of 11 BW students who were recruited in the Learning Alliance's inaugural 1992 year was quite successful. Six of the 11 students graduated within 5 years or less, and although four students eventually left the university before they graduated, two transferred to the University of California. None of these students was ever on academic probation. A much larger group (39 students) joined in 1994. These students were in two sections of a second-level BW class that was linked to another discipline course. The 1994 students have so far been the least successful cohort to date in terms of persistence to graduation. Ten of these students (25.5%) eventually had to leave the university due to poor grades. On the other hand, another 25% of this 1994 group graduated in 5 years or less.

When I joined the Alliance in 1995, I taught two sections of basic writing, each linked to an Introduction to Psychology course. I have continued to teach in the Alliance each fall semester since. Of the 39 students in my two 1995 sections, four graduated in 4 years or less and to our surprise their cumulative GPA was 3.3. Only four students (10.5%) were disqualified from the university due to poor academic performance. The data for 1996, 1997, and 1998 reflect similar low percentages of students disqualified for poor grades, except, of course, that the later the year, the less time students have been enrolled. Still, these numbers are very encouraging. So far, only 5% (two students) of the 39 student cohort group from my two 1998 basic writing sections have left the university because of poor grades.

AN ATTEMPT AT MAINSTREAMING

Two noteworthy mainstreaming experiments have led to major changes in our basic writing program. In 1996, 35 students in the upper half of the second-level basic writing course were invited to join the Learning Alliance and be mainstreamed into the university-level writing course. The SAT verbal scores for all basic writing students invited to join the Alliance have ranged from 480 to 330 (or as much as 15 points below the cut-off score of 151 on the EPT for the university-level composition course). These upper-level students' EPT scores were between 146–150 (a 146 EPT score correlates to approximately 430 on the SAT). These 35 students were divided among eight sections, with four instructors teaching two sections apiece. Each instructor had his or her two sections linked with another discipline course in the college of liberal arts. My two sections were linked with cultural anthropology. We also mixed into these eight experimental sections students admitted to the university as advanced scholars, so there was a broad range of student expertise represented across all sections, expertise based on high school courses taken, high school GPAs, and SAT and EPT scores. However, none of the students in these classes knew who the basic writing students were.

Our team of four instructors monitored the progress of these mainstreamed BW students throughout the term. We compared notes regularly and reviewed end-of-semester portfolios. If the basic writing students who were mainstreamed met all course requirements and their portfolios were judged satisfactory by two other instructors on our team, the students received the appropriate passing grade and full university credit for satisfying the writing requirement. Students who failed were required to repeat the university-level course the following semester. For the most part, the basic writing students were successful across all sections. Twenty-nine of those 35 students earned at least a C grade or higher in the university-level composition course. Sixteen earned an A or B. Remarkably, 3 years later, of the 35 basic writing students who in 1996 were mainstreamed, only four have left the university because of poor grades. The grade range for these same BW students in the discipline course paired with the composition course reflected a typical grade-distribution pattern: about one third received either As or Bs, another third received Cs, and the remaining one third received mostly Ds, although one student withdrew from the anthropology course. Interestingly, after their first year in college taking full course loads both semesters, the average GPA for all basic writing students who were mainstreamed was the same as the GPA for the rest of the first-year Alliance students—2.9.

The team of four writing instructors generally could perceive no clear pattern that might demarcate the performances of the basic writers from the regular students in these eight sections. Our collective perceptions were that the basic writers benefited most from the consistency of instruction they were receiving from two instructors working together. For instance, my students carried out an ethnographic study. The anthropology instructor explained how to conduct ethnographic inquiry and together the two of us helped students organize their notes and essays. I designed a rubric based on criteria both the anthropology professor and I agreed were essential for success on this assignment and shared this rubric with students while they were composing their accounts. To test our rubric, the anthropology instructor and I separately graded the ethnographies (although the grade actually only counted for my course) and then compared grades. There were a few discrepancies of more than a grade point, but these cases also proved to be instructive for us. The anthropologist and I talked about what we valued in reading these texts. For example, I found one of the basic writing student's ethnography too mired in detail and lacking in sufficient generalizations that might organize and provide perspective on the myriad particulars. I could not see the essay meriting more than a C. In contrast, my colleague rated this student's essay one of the best. She loved the detail and interpreted this texture as an attempt at "thick description." She convinced me the essay deserved a higher grade.

All faculty involved in this mainstreaming experiment recognized and appreciated the help our basic writing students received from the Alliance staff. Whenever we instructors believed one of our students might be having a problem, whether personal or academic, we could immediately contact an Alliance staff member who would make sure the student received appropriate counseling or the necessary referrals. More importantly, though, in addition to the support, students felt welcomed: all basic writing students were accepted as equals among the several hundred students participating in the Alliance. In short, BW students were motivated and encouraged to succeed. Yet, despite the success of this mainstreaming experiment, we have not tried it since. One problem was that the few students who had to repeat the course had to drop out of their cohort because their peers had moved on to other classes for which composition was a prerequisite. This was a technical problem we needed to solve before attempting to mainstream students again.

However, a much more serious problem concerned a few instructors' fears that the presence of basic writing students in their regular university-level courses would negatively affect the rigor and standards of their classes. This was a problem for at least four instructors, two of the composition teachers and a history professor in the Alliance; but it was also a problem voiced by a former Alliance faculty member who expressed his belief that the mere presence of BW students in GE courses for which the regular composition course was a co-requisite would surely bring standards down. It was clear this veteran faculty member believed he represented the view of many of his colleagues. I feared he did. One of the composition instructors felt she needed to teach to the advanced students in the class and could not slow down for the basic writers. She was frustrated by a too diverse range of student ability. The history teacher felt similarly, although he expressed his dissatisfaction as the basic writing students' inability to handle the amount and complexity of the assigned reading. This was an interesting problem because both instructors, it seemed, were really defending how they taught their respective courses and implicitly arguing that course materials and assignments should be pitched to students performing at the higher end. They seemed to desire homogeneity in student ability. Still, their protests raised a significant curricular question we have yet to answer: how complex should introductory and first-year courses be?

This same history professor had previously admitted how surprised he was when a few years earlier he had discovered that the grade distribution in this same introductory course he also taught outside of the Alliance had favored seniors and juniors in the class. First-year students in the course had regularly received the lowest grades. This professor, admirably, recognized that although he was supposed to be teaching an introductory, 100-level course, he was not actually teaching it for first-year students. The possibility of more basic writing students appearing in his introductory courses seemed to raise fears that he might have to change his teaching further by reducing and simplifying the subject matter.

Faculty resistance to the presence of BW students in their classrooms is based on stereotypes of these students' presumed deficiencies, which leads some instructors to assume they will have to lower their standards. This resistance is highly subjective. Despite empirical evidence that casts doubt on these stereotypes, some faculty refuse to question them. Consequently, anyone considering a mainstreaming experiment of one kind or another should be prepared to deal with some of their colleagues' negative attitudes toward and ingrained ways of thinking about students labeled as "remedial." We could not resolve this resistance at the time we conducted our mainstreaming experiment, and to complicate matters, another problem loomed concerning our basic writing program that required my immediate attention and energy.

WPAs in the CSU system were hearing rumors that all "remedial" students would soon have only a single academic year to complete their remediation, whether in English, math, or both (the two subjects in which they are tested). If they were unsuccessful, these students would be asked to leave the university and complete their remediation at a community college. In anticipating such a move (one that has since been mandated systemwide), I thought it more prudent, given the large number of students qualifying for basic writing on our campus, to make sure our BW program was enabling them to move to the university-level writing course as soon as possible. Having taught both levels of BW courses, I did not believe all students whose EPT scores required them to take a year of basic writing necessarily needed to.

In the fall of 1997, rather than try another mainstreaming experiment, we opted instead to combine students in the Learning Alliance from the lower-level basic writing course with students from the second level. A total of

58 BW students participated and traveled as two separate cohorts. To date, this has been the single largest contingent of basic writers who entered the Alliance at the same time. It was also a group that included students with the lowest SAT verbal and EPT scores so far. Happily, all 58 students satisfied their BW requirement after the first semester, although a couple were close calls. Yet even these "close calls" were not necessarily students with the lowest EPT scores. After 2 full academic years, only six of the initial 58 have left the university because of poor academic performance. On the other hand, eight of them have attempted to become peer mentors with four selected to be mentors in their junior year. The Learning Alliance has kept track of cumulative GPAs for all the basic writing students involved in the program since 1992. For the 6 years we have data (up to 1998), cumulative GPAs for these BW students have ranged from a low of 2.5 (the 1997 group) to 2.9.

WHAT HAVE WE LEARNED?

Although those of us involved in this learning community are not ready to draw any grand conclusions, we have seen promising trends, but also some troubling ones. We know that basic writing students in the Learning Alliance have stayed in school in percentages above the university's average for all students. Moreover, fewer end up on academic probation. Unfortunately, we do not yet have the data to compare basic writers in the Alliance with a comparable group outside of it. Some of our colleagues criticize the apparent success of the Alliance by claiming that Alliance students, because they volunteer for the program, are already "different" from the rest of the student population and therefore we can never have a comparable population to study outside of this learning community.[4]

We know that basic writing students who remain in the Alliance make regular progress toward their degrees and are successful in their coursework, but perhaps what has been most surprising are some of the dramatic changes we have been able to witness. Besides the four basic writers from the cohort of 1995 who graduated in 4 years or less with average GPAs of 3.3, 11 of those students sought to become peer mentors, with nine eventually being selected. Rarely are faculty able to witness the long-term maturation process our students often undergo because we typically only see students for a single semester. It is particularly gratifying to see how much basic writing students can develop over a relatively short time. Having these same students I taught back in 1995 now working side-by-side with me in 1998 and helping the new cohort of BW students navigate the transition to college life was a pleasure I have rarely experienced in my academic career. Beyond the statistics, teachers in the Learning Alliance can keep track of what happens to students once they leave their introductory courses. It is easier to find out what has helped them be successful in their education and conversely learn what we need to do better during their first year.

By design, our experiments with basic writing have been small scale. With the mainstreaming experiment, we learned that despite the success of most students, significant gaps exist between the literacy performances of some of the advanced scholars and some students with lower EPT scores. Certainly, this should come as no surprise, yet our experience is not an argument for not continuing the mainstreaming experiment; rather we need to make sure instructors have strategies for dealing with the various literacies students may bring to those sections. Despite the resistance from some faculty, most of us who teach in the Learning Alliance are convinced that many of our basic writing students can handle the university-level composition course. Still, although recognizing that disparities already exist across the spectrum of students testing into and exiting from the university-level comp course, we will need to decide how much of a disparity in levels of performance we are willing to live with if we want to continue mainstreaming more of our BW students. All faculty in the Alliance recognize that most students, not just BW students, need more writing instruction. Yet rather than force students into another writing course, we will work to infuse more writing throughout the undergraduate curriculum beyond the first semester, a task more easily accomplished in courses offered through the Alliance.

There have also been some important changes in the basic writing program as a direct result of these experiments. When we combined the two levels of BW in 1997, we used some of the writing program's veteran and most respected instructors. This experiment helped convince the rest of the composition faculty and pertinent administrators to eliminate the lower-level basic writing course and extend the second-level course (which is now the only basic writing course) from 3–4 hours per week. All basic writing students, regardless of EPT scores, will be eligible to advance to the regular composition course if their writing portfolios pass at the end of a single semester of instruction. As a result of the mainstreaming experiment, the composition program received permission from campus administrators to try out a lower EPT cut-off score for the university-level composition course. We lowered the score 3 points and offered students the option of taking the required writing course or enrolling in basic writing. This experiment began in fall 1998. The results so far have shown no significant difference in grades earned between students with EPT scores of 148–150 and those scoring at or above the 151 cut-off score. In fact, fall 1998 data suggest that these "former" basic writing students actually performed somewhat better, at least measured by course grades, than students who were eligible for the course based on the 151 score. The former BW students numbered over 200 and were randomly spread among all sections of composition offered. All of these changes were not meant to "dummy down" the composition program as some of my colleagues have feared. Rather, the experiments have shown what several of us in the composition program have recognized: EPT cut-off scores are arbitrary. When we provided some choice of what course to take and motivation for students to try harder, they responded positively.

One problem that, ironically, has surfaced is directly attributable to the success of the Learning Alliance. Though the director and I both agree that we want to include more BW students in the program, we are struggling against key administrators and some faculty who would rather turn the Alliance into another honors program. Our president, through an aggressive recruiting campaign over the last few years, has brought to our campus dozens of high school valedictorians and National Merit scholars. Because the Learning Alliance offers excellent teaching and because Alliance students are doing so much better overall than students outside the program, the president has sought to include increasingly more scholars in this learning community. So far, the director has been able to get her way through compromise and negotiation, and she and I recognize that if we can continue to offer convincing evidence that the Learning Alliance enables our basic writing students to succeed as well as the rest of the students, then we will have made significant progress in changing the university's attitude toward "remedial" students and in showing faculty and administrators that they do truly belong on our campus. (At least we hope so.) Consequently, the director and I are planning further mainstreaming experiments with larger cohorts of basic writers for fall of 2000. We are also going to try out some learning communities based on model one. Designated sections of BW students will form several cohorts and travel together to large lecture courses where they will mix in with the rest of the general student population. We also hope to continue increasing the number of basic writing students in the Alliance over the next couple of years, and as we do so, we will study the literacy problems these students encounter, but also remain responsive to their personal and social needs, as they move through the general education curriculum. Furthermore, we intend to continue working with faculty across the disciplines on improving the way they teach this group.

I want to be clear that I do not hold up our learning community as "the model" to be replicated. Rather, the Alliance serves as a hybrid institutional structure for curricular inquiry and for examining the campus climate. It has helped us think through what is needed to better help our first-year students make the often rough transition from high school to the university's culture. The Alliance has become the catalyst for creating a teaching community on our campus, and the basic writers in several experiments have helped us become effective teachers and more astute observers of the real needs of our students, needs that are both academic and social, sometimes idiosyncratic, but needs that a single teacher working alone in his or her classroom might never see. The debate over mainstreaming should not be reduced to an either–or question. Rather, we must consider the structures we have in place on our respective campuses: will these structures truly meet the needs of our basic writing students? In answering that question, we must also determine what sort of curriculum and pedagogy will enable our students to extend their developing literacies to meet the challenges they will face in other courses and beyond as they move into their major areas of study.

I worry that those of us working in composition, and specifically basic writing, have become a bit parochial by setting our sights too narrowly on writing pedagogy confined to a single course without considering sufficiently the writing class within the context of other courses students are concurrently taking as well as possible sequences of courses they may take subsequently. Moreover, we sometimes exaggerate the importance of writing courses in our students' lives and ignore their immediate social situation: young adults, often on their own for the first time, on an impersonal college campus. Students want to feel that they belong on campus. This is an especially crucial issue for basic writing students who are initially stigmatized as "not ready" for college. Too many first-year students do not know where to turn for help, either for academic advising, tutoring support, or counseling. Too many simply feel lost and insignificant and do not know how to make new friends. Too many will not take the initiative to go and see an instructor during office hours. These students are unconfident and afraid. The Learning Alliance has effectively enabled its first-year, and particularly its basic writing, students to cope with academic and personal problems. Our learning community is a flexible structure that allows faculty and staff to work with students in ways not previously possible, given the isolation of courses from one another and the fragmented approach to student services on campus. Compared with other academic programs on campus that have kept data over several years, the Learning Alliance has been more successful in terms of academic retention and persistence to graduation than any other program in the history of the university. It is a success worth pursuing and will probably mean the former "tidy" home where our basic writing program resided will get messier—and more comfortable.

ACKNOWLEDGMENTS

A special thanks to Bron Pellissier, the Learning Alliance Director, and to Cindy Milkovits, her Administrative Assistant, for their help in gathering the data on Learning Alliance students. I am also grateful to Bron for her continued collegiality and friendship. I want to thank Dan Tompkins at Temple University for passing along information on the learning communities he helps direct. Dan also maintains a listserv devoted to learning community efforts nationwide. Also a special thanks to Susan Marron for her helpful editorial suggestions, and to Barbara Gleason for her comments on an earlier version of this essay.

NOTES

[1]Although I realize the scholarly literature in the field shuns using the term "remedial," its rhetorical resiliency in the wider society indicates the greater political forces that shape the discourse surrounding basic writing. I use this term only in instances reflecting the views of those outside the field of composition studies who tend to view the presence of basic writers on campus as a problem. I am often indicating this attitude by using quotation marks when I use the term.

[2]Despite the little that has been published on learning communities, there is a tremendous amount of learning community activity at 2- and 4-year institutions throughout the country. At a recent national conference on learning communities in Seattle, WA, over 200 postsecondary institutions were represented. In addition to the sources on learning communities I cite in other parts of this essay, interested readers can find out more by contacting the Washington Center for Improving the Quality of Undergraduate Education. Also see their publication describing several FIPSE projects. It is called *Strengthening Learning Communities: Case Studies from the National Learning Communities Dissemination Project* (FIPSE).

[3]The percentage of first-year students identified as needing basic writing is typical of several large urban campuses in the Cal State University system. The population of the state is growing at a tremendous rate with about three quarters of a million more students predicted to be graduating from high schools over the next decade. The demographic shift in California throughout the nineties has been no less dramatic. At my campus in Long Beach, for instance, from 1990 to 1996, the White population has gone from a 58% majority to a 38% minority. In contrast, those students self-identifying as Hispanic have nearly doubled on campus, rising from 12.7% to 23% in 1996. I am not implying a cause and effect relationship between the demographic shift and the increase in the number of basic writers. In fact, the percentage of students identified as needing basic writing at CSU, Long Beach has dropped slightly the last 2 years. But because enrollment of first-year students has increased substantially (3,500 in fall 1999 and a projection of 4,600 for fall 2000) the actual number of students needing basic writing will increase. The rise in enrollment plus the rapid shift in the ethnic make-up of the student population indicate that our campus must respond

to different needs posed by students from various backgrounds—social, cultural, and linguistic—and that the large number of students identified as basic writers is part of a complex situation that has impacted the secondary schools particularly and their ability to respond adequately to the swift increase in and diversity of their student populations.

[4]Despite this criticism, a few of us in the Alliance believe a comparable population would be students who tried unsuccessfully to get into the Alliance. We will, therefore, study the success of these students beginning this year.

WORKS CITED

Astin, Alexander W. *What Matters in College: Four Critical Years Revisited.* San Francisco: Jossey-Bass, 1993.

Bartholomae, David. "Inventing the University." *When a Writer Can't Write: Studies in Writer's Block and Other Composing-Process Problems.* Ed. Mike Rose. New York: Guilford Press, 1985. 134–65.

———— "The Tidy House: Basic Writing in the American Curriculum." *Journal of Basic Writing* 12.1 (1993): 4–21.

Bizzell, Patricia. "What Happens When Basic Writers Come to College?" *College Composition and Communication* 37 (1986): 294–301.

Duffey, Suellyn. "Mapping the Terrain of Tracks and Streams." *College Composition and Communication* 47 (1996): 103–7.

Galbelnick, Faith, Jean MacGregor, Roberta S. Matthews, and Barbara Leigh Smith. "Learning Communities: Creating Connections Among Students, Faculty, and Disciplines." *New Directions for Teaching and Learning* 41 (1990): 5–18.

Glau, Gregory R. "The 'Stretch Program:' Arizona State University's New Model of University-level Basic Writing Instruction." *Writing Program Administration* 20.1–2 (1996): 79–91.

Greenberg, Karen L. "The Politics of Basic Writing." *Journal of Basic Writing* 12.1 (1993): 64–71.

Grego, Rhonda, and Nancy Thompson. "Repositioning Remediation: Renegotiating Composition's Work in the Academy." *College Composition and Communication* 47 (1996): 62–84.

Lenning, Oscar T., and Larry H. Ebbers. *The Powerful Potential of Learning Communities: Improving Education for the Future.* ASHE-ERIC Higher Education Report Volume 26, No. 6. Washington, DC: The George Washington University, Graduate School of Education and Human Development, 1999.

Love, Anne Goodsell. "What are Learning Communities?" *Learning Communities: New Structures, New Partnerships for Learning.* Ed. Jodi H. Levine. U of South Carolina: National Resource Center for the First-Year Experience and Students in Transition, 1999. 1–8.

Love, Anne Goodsell, and Kenneth A. Tokuno. "Learning Community Models." *Learning Communities: New Structures, New Partnerships for Learning.* Ed. Jodi H. Levine. U of South Carolina: National Resource Center for the First-Year Experience and Students in Transition. 1999. 9–17.

Pascarella, Ernest T., and Patrick T. Terenzini. *How College Affects Students: Findings and Insights from Twenty Years of Research.* San Francisco: Jossey-Bass, 1991.

Rodby, Judith. "What's It Worth and What's It For? Revisions to Basic Writing Revisited." *College Composition and Communication* 47 (1996): 107–11.

Shor, Ira. "Our Apartheid: Writing Instruction and Inequality." *Journal of Basic Writing* 16.1 (1997): 91–104.

Soliday, Mary. "From the Margins to the Mainstream: Reconceiving Remediation." *College Composition and Communication* 47 (1996): 85–100.

Soliday, Mary, and Barbara Gleason. "From Remediation to Enrichment: Evaluating a Mainstreaming Project." *Journal of Basic Writing* 16.1 (1997): 64–78.

Tinto, Vincent. *Leaving College: Rethinking the Causes and Cures of Student Attrition.* Chicago: U of Chicago P, 1987.

Wiener, Harvey S. "The Attack on Basic Writing—And After." *Journal of Basic Writing* 17.1 (1998): 96–103.

CHAPTER ELEVEN

Mainstreaming Writing: What Does This Mean for ESL Students?

Trudy Smoke
Hunter College, CUNY

As writing teachers, writing program administrators, and researchers in higher education, many of us are grappling with the complexities of legislated educational reform. We are making or having imposed on us definitions as to which of our students are remedial and which ESL; we are making programmatic decisions about how to best meet these students' academic needs, all the time doing what we can to maintain their access to public higher education. By examining the effect on ESL students of legislation phasing out remedial course instruction from baccalaureate programs nationwide, I hope to point out the challenges of maintaining effective programs and pedagogical approaches during this time of turmoil and instability.

To this end, I look at the sociopolitical history of remediation at the City University of New York (CUNY) in some detail and specifically examine how the January 25, 1999 resolution phasing out remedial course instruction is affecting ESL students. I describe a course that was developed at Hunter College that mainstreamed "remedial" ESL and non-ESL students into full-credit composition classes. After analyzing some of the research on the mainstreaming of ESL writers, I describe the various ways programs around the country have provided for these students and then make suggestions for implementing programmatic decisions.

DEFINING THE ESL STUDENT

Defining students as ESL has always been difficult. Ilona Leki writes in her book *Understanding ESL Writers* that sometimes "the only similarity [ESL students] share is that they are not native speakers of English" (39). ESL students in higher education can range in age from 17 to 80. They may have been in the United States for 7 days or 7 years, and in some cases were born and have lived entirely in the United States. They may be highly or poorly educated. English may be their second, third, or sixth language. As Leki writes, they may be "poor writers in English but good writers in their L1 (first language), poor writers in their L1, or illiterate in their L1; those hoping to remain in the United States; those eager to get back home; those extremely critical of life in the United States or U.S. foreign policy; and those wholly in support of anything the United States does" (39). Leki focuses more on the international ESL student, but in their book, *Generation 1.5 Meets College Composition: Issues in the Teaching of Writing to U.S.-Educated Learners of ESL*, Linda Harklau, Kay M. Losey, and Meryl Siegal introduce another complexity: the reality of the United States-educated ESL student. They critique the fact that "the field of college ESL in general, and academic writing in particular, focuses on a population of international students who enter postsecondary institutions in the United States after completing primary and secondary education abroad" (2). These are not the students that many of us find in our ESL classes in urban public institutions. According to Harklau et al., "The advent of open admissions policies and growth of nontraditional student population since the mid-1970s, especially at community colleges, has . . . [resulted in a] dramatic growth in the population of linguistically diverse students who have entered college by way of an U.S. public school education" (3).

Are students such as these, who have spent many years in U.S. schools, ESL or not? Should they be placed in ESL classes or not? Should they be mainstreamed? How do we define ESL in a changing world in which our most dramatic "enrollment increases are of U.S. educated, U.S.-resident learners of English" (Harklau et al. 3)? To what advantage or disadvantage might it be for a student to be defined ESL?

In this article, I look not only at New York, but also at California, Arizona, South Carolina, Alabama, and Indiana only as examples of what I see as a nationwide issue: the identification of ESL students. On January 3, 2000, Gerri McNenny wrote to me, "In California within the CSU system, how we define an ESL learner is still not determined (as of the last English Council for the CSU system meeting)" (personal letter). One day later, I was registering entering students in a required 3-week intensive program at my college. As I finished describing our ESL program to a student from Puerto Rico whose

English was quite limited, I was interrupted by a college counselor who said that students from Puerto Rico were not to be considered ESL and that this student would not be eligible for the college if she did not pass all tests during the 3-week program. Part of the problem for this student and many others may be that ESL has been deemed a remedial course at CUNY and in other systems, and due to political pressure, remedial courses are being eliminated by public universities nationally.

THE SOCIOPOLITICAL CONTEXT OF CUNY

Recent statistics reveal that about 78% of the nation's colleges offer remediation, whereas at CUNY, the largest urban university in the United States, only 12.4% of all university-wide instruction is remedial (Beaky). Despite these statistics, over the last several years, CUNY has been portrayed as "remediation university" and has been publicly denounced for the admission, testing, teaching, and retaining of "remedial" students (MacDonald; Traub). This negative perception of CUNY was intensified by the Mayor of New York City, who in 1998 after publicly criticizing CUNY, appointed an Advisory Task Force to look closely at CUNY and present its findings to the public[1]. The Task Force was headed by Benno Schmidt of the Edison Project, a group interested in privatizing education. As might have been expected, the report described CUNY as "adrift" and "in a state of decline" (Executive Summary 1). Moreover, at a meeting with the University Faculty Senate discussing his Task Force report, Benno Schmidt said that "the proper institutions within CUNY, which should focus on remediation among the range of their academic responsibilities and mission, are the community colleges" (Proceedings 6).

The problems of CUNY were exacerbated by what *New York Times'* writer Karen Arenson termed a "leadership void." After one chancellor resigned with a cloud hanging over her, and more than a year was spent with an acting chancellor, in 1999 CUNY appointed a new chancellor, Matthew Goldstein. Goldstein, the former president of CUNY's Baruch College, a college avowedly opposed to "remedial" programs in higher education, did immediately start to fill positions then held by an acting deputy chancellor, two acting vice chancellors, and an acting dean for student services. Arenson quotes Bernard Sohmer, the nonvoting faculty representative on the Board of Trustees as stating, "The gap in leadership has empowered the worst aspects of the [15 politically appointed] trustees, who are trying to micromanage the university." Part of this micro-management resulted in the passage of a hotly debated resolution to eliminate remedial classes from the senior CUNY colleges. The first vote passing this resolution was overturned by court decision because of the conditions in effect during that May 1998 meeting; the resolution was ratified by a small margin when a newly-constituted Board of Trustees re-voted it on January 25, 1999. The New York State Board of Regents voted to uphold the Board's resolution on November 22, 1999. To understand the ideological nature of the resolution, one has to examine the consequences it will have on the education of ESL students. We need to look at the resolution itself.

> All remedial course instruction shall be phased-out of all baccalaureate de-gree programs at the CUNY senior colleges as of the following dates: January 2000, for Baruch, Brooklyn, Queens, and Hunter Colleges; September 2000, for Lehman, John Jay, Staten Island, New York City Technical, and City Col-leges; and September 2001, for York and Medgar Evers Colleges. Following a college's discontinuation of remediation, no student who has not passed all three Freshman Skills Assessment Tests, and any other admissions criteria which may exist, shall be allowed to enroll and/or transfer into that college's baccalaureate degree programs. Students seeking admission to CUNY senior college baccalaureate degree programs who are in need of remediation shall be able to obtain such remediation services at a CUNY community college, at a senior college only during its summer sessions, or elsewhere as may be made available. This resolution does not apply to ESL students who received a sec-ondary education abroad and who otherwise are not in need of remediation.[2]

It is interesting that the first four colleges out of the 17 CUNY colleges to begin the phase out of remediation are Baruch, Brooklyn, Queens, and Hunter. These are being referred to by many as "the top tier" colleges, so this resolution in addition to whatever else it accomplishes formalizes a hi-erarchy in the City University. Additionally, the last sentence reveals a bias against United States' educated students. On the basis of this resolution, access to senior colleges will be provided only to those ESL students who received a secondary education abroad and who "otherwise are not in need of remediation," a shorthand for those who have passed the Math Assess-ment Test. Students entering CUNY take a battery of three Freshman Skills Assessment Tests (FSATs)[3] : the Reading Assessment Test (RAT), the Writing Assessment Test (WAT), and the Mathematics Assessment Test (MAT). Failing any of the three categorizes a student as remedial.[4]

What the resolution means for those students that fail these exams is that, if they have spent their entire high school career in bilingual or ESL classes in New York City high schools, they will not be admitted to the four top tier senior colleges as of Spring 2000. And in short order they will not be admitted to any CUNY senior college. These students will be required to attend community colleges until they pass the three FSATs.

Although these changes are problematic, separating students into ESL or non-ESL classes or into basic or mainstream writing has had its own complications for some time. And they have not all come from outside the institution. Even in our own field, a scholar like Ira Shor describes separate basic writing classes as "a gate below the gate" (94). Therefore, as he and others in this volume have stated, mainstreaming basic writing and ESL students into standard composition courses may have great consequence for students. It may, in fact, offer a means of admitting students into the "real" college courses as well as of maintaining access for students that because of test scores and linguistic differences could be denied a college education. Institutions may have made the decision to mainstream students for pedagogical reasons with the idea that students would gain from their interactions with students with diverse cultural, linguistic, and educational backgrounds. The decision may also make sense administratively; many have found that placing students into no- or reduced-credit courses has led to poor retention and low grades. However, even those who are convinced that mainstreaming is the best path for native speakers of English (NSEs) may not be quite so sure about whether or not it will work as well for ESL students.

HISTORICAL BACKGROUND OF PLACING ESL STUDENTS

Deciding when and how we should mainstream ESL students has been a complicated and difficult decision at my college, Hunter, a large urban commuter campus of some 19,800 students, located on Manhattan's upper east side. As part of the CUNY system, in 1969 Hunter became an "open admissions" college, which meant that standardized tests and grades would not be the sole criteria for admissions. As Tom Fox writes, open admissions "was a historical sign that change [was] possible, . . . a possibility that the university could work against social inequality" (40). However, in a short time, Hunter and many of the other senior colleges in the CUNY system were no longer truly open admissions. That role fell to the six community colleges in the system, and the 11 senior colleges had to establish criteria that would not eliminate, but would in some sense limit admissions of less-well prepared applicants from New York City high schools. Hunter went back to the grade point average (GPA) for admissions' evaluation. But in addition to the GPA, once admitted, students were required to take the FSATs, including the WAT. And this leads to the second important use of the WAT after its role in designating students as remedial or not: it is also used to distinguish between ESL and non-ESL students. At Hunter, every failing WAT test is re-read to decide if the student needs an ESL course or not. Meanwhile, Hunter, along with most other CUNY colleges, developed multilevel mathematics, reading, writing, and ESL classes to meet the needs of entering students. We could claim that no matter what the scores were on the FSATs, we had courses to help students become successful in the college. But things changed.

Two years ago, the policy at Hunter was changed so that any student who had not passed the FSATs would be limited to three treatments—a summer semester, a fall semester, and a 3-week January workshop; or a spring semester, a 3-week June workshop, and a summer semester. Students who had not passed the FSATs at the end of the third treatment would be faced with dismissal from the college. As part of this change, our lowest levels of developmental reading, writing, and ESL were eliminated, leaving us with only one reading, one writing, and two ESL levels. An exception from the three treatment policy was made for ESL: those students deemed qualified for our former intermediate, now lowest level ESL class could receive an extra semester to complete the upper level ESL course. Concomitant with this were new admissions criteria—higher GPAs, a requirement of a particular number of English and math courses completed in high school, and a strong encouragement for students to take the SATs. The reduction in the numbers of semesters students had to pass the FSATs was made despite protests in the college stating that good students would be eliminated and good programs dismantled. But these changes were part of an overall shift.

The shift seems intended to eliminate graduates of New York City high schools who have not passed the three FSATs. The Board of Trustees' resolution specifically excepts from the policy ESL students that meet a specific definition: "ESL students who received a secondary education abroad and who otherwise are not in need of remediation." This new definition of the ESL student is now used university-wide as part of the admissions and allocations process for entrance to CUNY. The definition has created a myriad of problems for continuing students already in the college and for writing directors such as myself. Of the continuing students not passing the WAT, only those defined as ESL because they received a secondary education abroad and passed the MAT will be permitted to remain in the college. Others will be dismissed and advised to attend a community college.

I am in the unfortunate position of having to talk to students and teachers about what these changes will mean for them. I do not have the power to designate them as ESL, yet I will be the one they come to see to understand this complex policy. For the past few semesters, I have been troubled about how to handle the little bit of power I have. I felt ambivalent about suggesting that students take ESL classes when I thought those classes would be lost to the college, and then I was ambivalent about suggesting that students take mainstream classes when I knew that their needs would be better met in ESL classes. Some students, with full knowledge that ESL classes meant they could stay in the college, did not want to be designated as "other," as needing a special language class. They preferred to struggle in classes with native speakers of English.

ENGLISH 110

Perhaps it was with foresight that in 1996, before the resolution barring remedial courses was passed, we in the English Department developed English 110, Composition I, a course that precedes the college-required expository writing course, English 120. Karen Greenberg[5] and Ann Raimes along with other members of the English Department designed English 110 as a mainstream, nonremedial, three-credit course for those students who had passed either the RAT or the WAT and almost had passed the other. Students write four or so papers with multiple drafts, one short research paper, and a final examination based on a reading students have in advance of the test.

In creating this course and getting it passed by the college senate, we were able to keep the doors of Hunter open for many students who would have been eliminated on the basis of the remediation policy. The course was developed for both ESL and NSE writers. Any student who scored a "6" (two 3s given by two readers on a 6-point scale in which two 4s are passing) on the WAT and who passed the RAT was placed into English 110. Although this course has only been in existence for 3 years, it has been remarkably successful in terms of numbers of students who passed the course, passed the FSATs, and who have been retained in the college. Each semester, some 500–800 students register for English 110. The pass rate for the course is always above 80%. The students in English 110 include many non-native speakers of English who attended United States' high schools for all 4 years and may even have attended junior high school in the United States but were not able to pass the WAT. Approximately 50% of the students at Hunter are non-native speakers of English, and many of these students do not pass the WAT the first time they take it and are placed in ESL classes or with the advent of English 110, into that course.

In addition to the positive aspects of English 110, there are problems as well. Some teachers in 110 are working with ESL students for the first time and find themselves confronting complex and baffling language problems. It has become apparent that both teachers and students often need extra support beyond the 3-hour-a-week class. Our writing, reading, and computer centers are oversubscribed with students in these classes. We have recently begun discussing the possibility of offering some special grammar-intensive sections for just those students. However, despite any institutional problems we may have identified, English 110[6] has helped maintain access for students, and has given them the opportunity to prove that they are able to rise to the challenge of a demanding writing course.

A CLOSE LOOK AT ONE ENGLISH 110 CLASS

The English 110 course has a student limit of 25, and includes students who might have taken and passed our upper-level ESL writing course or our basic writing course (a course we will no longer be permitted to offer as of Spring 2000) as well as students that placed directly into 110. In my most recent 110 class, I had 18 ESL students and seven non-ESL students. Some of the ESL students had recently graduated from New York City high schools, and several had attended colleges in foreign countries and were transferring credits into Hunter. After owning a business in New York for several years, one had decided to enter college to get a degree so he could return to his country. Another was what might be termed a "typical international student" who had come to New York from Japan to study in a field that was not available in his country. Two were nurses who had emigrated from Russia and wanted to become physical therapists in the United States. Several were young mothers who after high school graduation had devoted themselves to child care and were now entering college, after having spent some time living in communities in which little English was spoken.

Of the native speakers of English (NSE) students, two were graduates of non-CUNY community colleges, who had not passed the WAT. One was a recent high school graduate who had come to New York from Ohio and was living in the Hunter dormitory. Another was repeating the course and claimed that her problems in the previous class had stemmed from difficulties in getting child care for her baby, necessitating her absence and lateness in handing in papers. The rest had recently graduated from New York high schools. Of the seven, four were African-American. At first, several of the NSE students told me they thought they were in the wrong class because they did not belong in an ESL class. When I explained that 110 was a mainstream, nonremedial, non-ESL class, they could not understand why so many of their peers were non-native speakers of English.

Some of these native speakers might have dropped the class, but at Hunter, students' registrations are canceled if after receiving a warning, they do not enroll for the required developmental or the English 110 class. So they stuck it out. Interestingly, and this may reveal something about power and hierarchy, the ESL students did not complain in the same way, especially those U.S.-educated ESL students. They were glad not to be placed in ESL classes, which they claimed not to need. Most of them said that, although they realized they had some problems with their writing, they had spent most of their lives in United States' schools. They were resistant to being placed into ESL classes with international students. They may have felt that U.S.-educated ESL students are not the focus in ESL classes. For them, it seemed to be as Linda Blanton observed, "Program decisions in those joint classes usually privilege the internationals: teaching goals, textbook choices, and instructional talk are all founded on everyone's 'newness' to things 'American' and to everyone's need for greater English-language fluency" (126). Interestingly in my case, the other ESL students with experiences more similar to those of international students said that they too learned more from being in a class with native speakers of English. For some, it was their first experience speaking to people actually born in the United States, and they welcomed it.

By the end of the semester, some rapprochement had developed between ESL and non-ESL students. Nonetheless, undoubtedly some students still felt they had been placed in 110 for gatekeeping reasons, to keep them out of expository writing, and not to better prepare them for the writing required in the college. That semester students had worked on projects related to English 110 and to remediation. They investigated why the department had developed English 110, what the difference between 110 and 120 was, why students faced additional and more consequential assessment measures, whether remediation was necessary in college, and what the general state of public higher education was. Students worked together and on their own examining these issues. They read articles in the *New York Times, New York Post, Daily News*, and other popular media on CUNY and public higher education. Their anger at the misrepresentations of CUNY students in the media led many of them to produce strong, well-supported writing documenting what they had read, seen, and experienced first hand. I had made a presentation before the Board of Trustees and was quoted out of context in the *New York Times*. Students read my testimony and the paper's coverage and analyzed how reporters can slant a story by decontextualizing material. Many of them wrote letters to congressional and local representatives explaining the value of a CUNY education. A few students received replies. A few met with interviewers to discuss the political situation at CUNY. So part of the English 110 experience for them involved their reading, writing, and speaking about a real concern. At the end of the course, all the students in this class passed the WAT and/or the RAT, and they passed the course. Of the 25 students, four of them have left the college—one graduated, one transferred to a SUNY college, another to a private college, and another returned to his country. Another student dropped out of school for one semester because of child care issues, but she has returned. They have all passed English 120 and are moving through the college.

For their final evaluations, one of the NSE students who had complained about the composition of the class most vehemently at the beginning wrote that "having non-native speakers as well as English speakers in the class gives us a better insight on ways of learning English. Honestly other countries may learn the English language at a more accurate or faster pace than English speakers learning other languages. . . . Bottom line it's a great course and it should continue." Another student said that he learned to "understand about other native languages and different cultures. It showed me a sense of diversity." One ESL student wrote that ESL students should be mainstreamed with non-native speakers in a composition class because "the native speakers of English can teach non-native speakers English. Also native speakers tend to be more friendly."

CRITIQUING MAINSTREAMING

My findings with this English 110 student population are unlike George Braine's findings in his study of ESL students at the University of Southern Alabama. Braine found that ESL students preferred to be in the specially designated ESL-composition courses rather than in the mainstream courses because in those classes, they "were afraid to ask questions or speak out in class, fearing that their accents and errors in speech would cause embarrassment" (98). Braine did not make it clear whether students that preferred specially designated ESL composition classes were international or immigrant students, a factor that might be important in understanding this complex issue.

However, Braine's description of the problems of speaking up in class faced by ESL students in a mainstream class are serious ones that I have also written about describing my research linking ESL writing classes to various classes in the college (Smoke "Using Feedback"). A teacher in my program responding to my survey asking whether or not ESL students should be mainstreamed in English 110 described a similar situation in her class. She wrote that ESL students should be mainstreamed in English 110 because "the sophistication many of them bring to the course enriches it for native speakers of English, and I believe that it is important that they begin to operate within an American-language spoken/written environment." She also acknowledged that "while it is still difficult for many ESL students to follow informal classroom banter and often painful for them to join the conversation, I believe the speed and range of language is something they must face, an impetus to increase proficiency." Another teacher confirmed this when she wrote, "My ESL students said they preferred being with native speakers. But they said it 'challenged' them. ESL students in many cases performed better than native speakers." All was not so harmonious for the teacher who wrote "No! ESL students have special needs that are different from native speakers. By combining these two groups, it is difficult to meet the needs of either of them! This makes it hard for many of the students to keep up with the pace of the course." What is interesting is that those teachers with ESL experience tended to be the ones most in favor of the mainstreaming approach and the ones least troubled by linguistic differences and problems, whereas those teachers with less experience dealing with ESL students favored placing the students into specially-designated classes. My own experience teaching ESL writing may be the reason why so many of the ESL students in my class were so positive and perhaps even why they were so successful in the class.

One important element in Braine's study is that the teachers who taught the ESL sections of composition had attended a 3-day workshop taught by an ESL specialist. At Hunter, Ann Raimes, who has done much research on the writing process of ESL students (Raimes), coordinates English 110 and meets with the 110 teachers to discuss ESL issues, among others. Her work with 110 teachers is in no small part one of the reasons why many of the 110 teachers feel as comfortable as they do dealing with both native and non-native speakers in their classes. We have made a conscious effort as well to make sure that many of the 110 teachers have ESL experience. In fact, as our developmental English program has been cut back, we have moved ESL and developmental teachers into English 110. Their expertise in working with basic and ESL writers has made them effective 110 teachers and for those who are adjuncts, it has ensured their continued employment in the college. We need to do more to stress the importance of this kind of training in making English 110 work for our students.

Interactions between ESL and non-ESL teachers are also critical because they lead to discussions of pedagogical approaches and curricular design. Teachers working with a diverse student body need to learn tools that will help them emphasize curricula that stresses, for example, communicative discourse, discourse with which widely diverse groups of students may identify. Some approaches to this might include ethnographic projects involving field research and writing about speech communities that students choose to study such as the project described by Barbara Gleason in this volume. Gleason also suggests readings and films that are appropriate for students of diverse ability levels. ESL researchers such as Sarah Benesch, Stephanie Vandrick, and I (Smoke, Critical) also utilize pedagogical approaches that involve feminist theory and critical pedagogy as a means of introducing students to the complexities of our academic and sociopolitical worlds. These approaches may be useful to meet the diverse needs of students with a wide range of abilities and experiences as well.

OTHER PROGRAMS

As part of my analysis of how we can best serve our non-native speaker population, I will look at several colleges across this country to see whether or not non-native speakers of English are mainstreamed and what the ramifications of the decision are for their college and program.

Arizona State University

At Arizona State University (ASU), former Directors of Composition John Ramage and David Schwalm developed a "Stretch" program in which at-risk students, those with the lowest test scores, register for English Stretch, WAC 101, the first semester and then ENG 101 the second semester, a required two-semester composition course. The school's web site explains this by saying that they offer regular one-semester ENG 101, an honors ENG 101, summer versions of ENG 101 and now a stretched out version (WAC 101 and ENG 101). The stretch version is intended to offer support to basic writers "who may not have a lot of experience at 'academic' college-level writing. . . . Students pass stretch ENG 101 at five-percent better rate (91.8%) than 'regular' ENG 101 students (86.8%) do. . . . Regular ENG 101 students do four papers plus a portfolio; Stretch students do six papers plus two portfolios—and each paper has intense teacher involvement and feedback and goes through multiple drafts." I was concerned about how this program affected ESL students. Gregory Glau, current Director of Composition, and I had an e-mail conversation about this issue. He explained that in the spring of 1997, ASU started offering WAC 107 (the ESL version of Stretch) for those students who had a Test of English as a Foreign Language (TOEFL) score of 540 or lower. Students passing this course are supposed to register for ENG 107 (the ESL version of ENG 101), but ASU does not have the computer capability of blocking students from registering for ENG 101 courses. So far, 102 students have taken WAC 107; 84 passed (82.5%). Of those 84 who passed, 76 went on to register for ENG 107 (some might have taken ENG 101, but they are not easily tracked on the computer system), and 67 passed (88%). Glau states that it is hard to make statements about this small a population, but the special ESL sections seem to be effective. The fact that students take the TOEFL suggests that they are international students. Glau states that there is an instructor who coordinates the ESL classes, but the school realizes that more has to be done to demarginalize the ESL teachers and students. One of Glau's concerns is that the ESL classes are using a different handbook from the other writing classes, which could create additional costs and problems for students when they register for advanced non-ESL courses. ESL students are often marginalized because of their language needs, so it seems especially important to do whatever can be done to help integrate students into the mainstream as soon as possible. Arranging some meetings with both ESL and non-ESL teachers can bridge some of the pedagogical and theoretical gaps between these faculty members as well.

University of South Carolina

Rhonda C. Grego and Nancy S. Thompson developed another approach to mainstreaming less prepared writers in freshman composition classes with their Writing Studio. All students are placed into English 101, but "[s]tudents could volunteer, and others whom teachers identified could be placed (based on two first-week writing assignments and a portfolio of previous writing) in the Writing Studio" (68). The Writing Studio brings together for regular weekly sessions small groups of four to five students (from different sections of English 101). They work with an experienced small-group leader and receive intensive help on the writing they are currently doing for their 101 classes. Studio staff small-group leaders send weekly dialogue sheets about each student to the student's 101 instructor. No grade is given for the Studio, but Grego and Thompson explain that the instructors use the weekly communications as part of their calculation in students' final grades. They report that more than 90% of the students participating in the Writing Studio have passed English 101. Despite initial fears that they would be doing the "same old remedial work," students in the Writing Studio report their surprise at how helpful and beneficial the Studio has been for them (68).

When I contacted Thompson by e-mail (Grego has moved to another campus), she explained that they generally had a special section of English 101 classes for ESL students, "but international students always seem to show up in regular classes as well, which we have come not to resist" (e-mail). She said that there had been a number of ESL students in the Studio as well and that she had worked with several of them. "The ESL students are eager for help and they appreciate having a small group of native speakers to give them feedback on papers—on grammar, on generating ideas, on using language that 'sounds right' to native speakers, and perhaps as important as anything, it gives them a group of familiar and friendly native speakers to interact with each week" (e-mail). Despite the fact that the ESL students sometimes slowed down the work of the Studio group, she "always appreciated the benefits to native speakers of having international students in our group to help move beyond provincial mindsets of some students" (e-mail). The ESL students in Thompson's program seem to be only international students.

University of Arizona, Tucson

At a recent TESOL (Teachers of English to Speakers of Other Languages) conference, Susan Penfield and Yvonna Roepcke presented their model of combining non-native speakers and native speakers in freshman composition classes. They explained that historically the two groups had been separated at the University of Arizona, Tucson. In developing their model for mainstreaming the two groups of students, they discovered three principles that had to be in place for the classes to be effective. First, the students had to be able to self-select whether they wanted to be in a mainstream section or not. Second, the ratio that worked best was 2/3 non-native speakers to 1/3 native speakers. And third, the teacher needed to be experienced with ESL and/or had to have an ESL educational background. Penfield and Roepcke reported that when classes were divided 1/2 and 1/2, they were not as successful. When they surveyed the students, they found that the biggest problem students faced was scheduling and finding a class that fit their time slot availability. They also got better feedback on the class from non-native speakers than from native speakers. Some teachers reported that they had problems meeting the needs of all the students; one reported that from time to time she had dismissed the native speakers and then worked separately with the non-native speakers. Students take an essay exam and presently there is a different test for native speakers and non-native speakers. ESL instructors read all tests written by ESL students. Although they have found the mainstreamed composition classes to be effective, they are concerned that there might be grading issues down the line if faculty perceive that ESL students are being graded differently from native speakers of English.

California State University (CSU), Chico

As part of a move to restructure the freshman composition course to eliminate all remedial courses, faculty at CSU, Chico faced the challenge of having non-native speakers of English in their mainstream classes. Judith Rodby in writing about the program quotes these students as describing themselves as " 'still learning English,' 'struggling with writing and reading,' and 'having deficiencies in language' " (45). Many of these students were born in the United States or arrived when they were small children. According to Rodby, "Mostly they speak a language other than English at home with their parents and extended family, and many continue to speak their first language with their roommates on or off campus. . . . In elementary or high school, they were tracked into ESL classes, and for the most part they do not want to take ESL at the university. . . . They did not want to prepare for freshman composition, but rather they needed to do the thing itself, and to be guided in doing it" (45).

Now more than 4 years after the program was restructured, 89% of the non-native English speaker resident students pass freshman composition without taking remedial courses first. Moreover, in working with students, Rodby reports that social factors may be the best predictors of success: motivation, family support, and the belief that education will lead to better jobs play a more significant role in predicting success than do placement scores. Rodby also emphasizes the importance of pedagogy and curriculum in literacy development. She describes an assignment in which students through multiple drafts "construct the history, present, and future of their relationship to the university and the United States" (60), an assignment which provides a link between students' home culture and United States' culture. Collaborative assignments such as the one Rodby describes, and group work in summer programs, learning communities, and linked or blocked courses result in success by helping students to feel more connected to the university.

City College, CUNY

As described in much greater detail in this volume, Mary Soliday and Barbara Gleason developed their two-semester freshman composition "Enrichment" course to substitute for the two remedial courses and one college-level course that students who had not passed the WAT had been required to take. In the Enrichment program, students whether they passed the WAT or not are mainstreamed into the same classes for two semesters. They have the same teacher, same peers, and same class tutors for these two semesters building a strong academic community of learners. Like Hunter, City College has a very diverse population: some 47% of the students in these classes stated that English was not their first language and 62% had been born outside the United States. The program they developed "capitalize[d] on students' existing linguistic knowledge and literacies" (66). The program was successful for both ESL and non-ESL students. They found that "students who would have taken a non-credit writing course were competitive with students who were eligible for college-level courses. . . . [M]ost students demonstrated an ability to evaluate their own writing, to reveal growth over time in a portfolio, and to conduct research inside and outside the college library—all prominent features of the experimental curriculum" (72). Despite the success of the enrichment program, Gladys Carro, a professor of ESL, and J. F. Watts, a Professor of History at City College, because of their concern that ESL students be allowed to register for Core college courses even though they have not passed the WAT and/or RAT, recommend a different model. In their provisional report on research with ESL students, they recommend that graduates of their ESL program be enabled to take special sections of freshman composition that "have a three-hour editing component attached—making English 110 for ESLers (6 hours); and permit these students to pair with WCIV 102 (World Civilization).... [W]e believe if supported and if the courses are truly paired, students will achieve" (11). So at City College, as in many institutions, the question of whether ESL students should be mainstreamed or placed in separate sections of freshman composition has not been entirely resolved.

OPTIONS FOR ESL WRITERS

In his examination of writing program options for ESL students, Tony Silva of Purdue University compares four options: mainstreaming, basic writing, ESL writing, and cross-cultural composition. Silva finds mainstreaming to be problematic because "first year composition courses [are] designed for and dominated by native English speaker (NES) writers—the sink or swim option" (38). Although acknowledging the theoretical possibility of profitable interactions between NES and ESL students, he feels that teachers will not have the time or expertise "to deal with ESL students' cultural, rhetorical, and linguistic differences, to meet their special needs. ESL students might inadvertently be held to unrealistic NES standards" (39). He rejects basic writing courses for the same reason and adds that basic writing teachers "are typically prepared to teach inexperienced and/or educationally disadvantaged native English speakers and may not have...insight into the characteristics and needs of ESL writers" (39). Silva states that superficially the writing problems of basic writers and ESL writers may seem similar but may have different underlying causes, which may not be understood or appropriately responded to by a basic writing teacher. His endorsement of credit-bearing, requirement-fulfilling classes designed especially for ESL students is followed by the caveat that such classes require maintaining a separate program component that might be viewed as separate but unequal in some ways, particularly in relation to the segregation of ESL students from their NES peers. Along with this is the perception that ESL classes are in some way "remedial" and therefore might be devalued by both students and the institution. The final and preferable option for Silva is cross-cultural composition, "first year writing classes designed to include more or less equal numbers of ESL and NES students" (40) taught by teachers who have a background in working with both NES and ESL students. According to Silva, although these classes have the benefit of fostering cross-cultural understanding and collaboration and integrating ESL students into the mainstream of the college, they also create staffing, supervision, and registration problems.

LOCAL DECISIONS

We need to look carefully at our own institutions before we decide on the best option for placing ESL writers in composition classes. If we are situated at a university where most of our ESL students are international students or recently-arrived immigrants, separate ESL classes may be the most appropriate choice because of linguistic needs, teacher preparedness, and student desire. Although cross-cultural composition classes may be desirable because of the diversity and learning they provide, they can turn into an administrative headache if a good balance of ESL and NES students is not achievable. In colleges, such as City and Hunter, where 50% or more of the students identify themselves as speaking English as their second or third language, mainstreaming into cross-cultural composition courses in which there are equal numbers of NES and ESL students is possible. However, even in institutions such as these, we may want to offer optional separate ESL sections for those students who prefer them. Before placing students in any classes, we need to examine the students' writing and meet with them if possible. Are they comfortable speaking English? We also need to know something about their backgrounds—are they international students who have come to the United States to study English and have been here a short time and will remain only until they have completed their college education? Or are they recently arrived immigrants? Or immigrants who may have attended high school or even junior high school in the United States and who see themselves as culturally American or "half and half" as some of my students have described themselves to me? Are their language problems related more to ESD (English as a Second Dialect) or SESD (Standard English as a Second Dialect) than to ESL? And these are only a few of the possible descriptions of the L2 students attending colleges in the United States today. For most of us, the issue is far more personal than these descriptions suggest. We see the faces and hear the voices of the students. We want to offer them the best educational opportunities, and we know our powers are limited. To some degree, we must respond to our needs with local, perhaps temporary, solutions, knowing that at any time, changes may be imposed on our programs because of political and ideological shifts.

The dilemma created by this situation drew me to the notion of complexity: complexity theory acknowledges the ubiquity of change accompanied by the disorientation inherent in dealing with impermanence and unpredictability. Discussing how one maneuvers in an "ever-changing, interlocking, nonlinear, kaleidoscopic world," the author of *Complexity: The Emerging Science at the Edge of Order and Chaos*, M. Mitchell Waldrop quotes Stanford professor of population studies and economics, Brian Arthur, as saying, "You want to keep as many options open as possible. . . . What you're trying to do is maximize robustness, or survivability, in the face of an ill-defined future.... You observe the world very, very carefully, and you don't expect circumstances to last" (334). Thus, to paraphrase Arthur, what I am presenting in this chapter are some of the options, contingent and perhaps temporary, that are available to maintain access or the "survivability [of ESL and non-ESL basic writing students] in the face of an ill-defined future."

To maintain this access and survivability, particularly in an atmosphere of strong political opposition to our programs, we need to consider instructional models that may involve change and restructuring. Programs that have worked for years may have to be rethought and re-envisioned. We ought to work closely with colleagues in our own institutions to build our power bases. At the same time, we need to find out how other institutions are responding to pressures from the outside and what they have done to maintain their programs and serve their students. There are no easy answers in this paper. Even simple definitions of which students should be designated as needing special ESL considerations and which should not do not exist. Whether or not mainstreaming ESL students will work in a particular institution depends on many factors—local, political, and philosophical. After examining this issue in some depth, I believe that certain principles seem to result in more effective decision making:

1. Look closely at your ESL students—examine their writing carefully and interview them if possible. Are they mostly internationals or immigrants? How long have they been in the United States? How long have they studied English? Have they attended high school and/or junior high school in the United States? Let your decision to mainstream or not rest on local needs and local circumstances.

2. If you decide to mainstream ESL students in composition courses, make sure that your teachers have some ESL expertise. Offer workshops in ESL methodology and in dealing with linguistic differences for teachers teaching mainstreamed courses. Set up websites, chat groups, or e-mail exchanges for teachers and tutors to discuss ESL issues.

3. Develop pedagogical approaches and curricula design that are appropriate to diverse student bodies and to students with different abilities. Emphasize curricula that stress communicative discourse, ethnography, and multicultural perspectives to give diverse groups material they can identify with and find relevant.

4. Make the writing real. Students become more engaged when they are reading, writing, and thinking about issues that matter in their lives.

5. If you have a two-semester mainstreamed composition program, keep the same teacher, tutor, and students for both semesters in the attempt to build an academic learning community.

6. Try to balance the numbers of NES and ESL students in classes. Silva recommends 1/2 and 1/2. My experience and Penfield and Roepcke's suggest that 1/3 NES and 2/3 ESL is a good balance.

7. Provide options that allow students to choose an ESL section of freshman composition or a mainstreamed one. Students seem to prefer to be able to self-select whether the mainstream or ESL model best meets their needs.

8. Make sure that advisors are available at registration time to discuss options with students and help them to make decisions about which class would be the best choice.

9. Be flexible. No matter how effective your program is, it will change over time either because the needs of students change, the needs or resources of the institution change, the perceptions of the public change, or political directions shift.

10. Support what you know works. This may seem to be in direct opposition to number 9, but as much as we need to be open to change, we need to present our students, teachers, and programs in positive ways so that we will have the resources needed to sustain them and advocate for them.

NOTES

[1]The CUNY University Faculty Senate in their July 1999, *Senate Digest* stated that the Mayor's Executive Order 41 of May 6, 1998 charged the Task Force with a review of the uses of City funding by CUNY. According to the *Senate Digest*, "[The Executive Order] also called for assessing the effects of Open Admissions and remedial education, for determining the 'best means of arranging for third parties to provide remediation services,' and for recommending other appropriate reform measures. The Task Force was headed by Benno C. Schmidt, Jr. CEO of the Edison Project, a private, for-profit company that manages 52 public schools, and included Heather MacDonald of the Manhattan Institute, a conservative think tank; Herman Badillo, the newly appointed chair of the Board of Trustees; Richard T. Roberts, a commissioner in the Mayor's Office; Richard Schwartz, a former mayoral adviser; Jacqueline V. Brady, a financial specialist; and Manfred Ohrenstein, a former Democratic State Senator. The expenses of the Task Force amounted to $600,000, of which $300,000 was raised from various foundations, including the Olin, Starr, and David & Lucille Packard Foundations." (*Senate Digest*, 29, 4, p. 1).

[2]On November 22, 1999, by a vote of 9-to-6, the New York State Regents upheld the Board of Trustees' resolution to prevent students needing remedial

courses from attending senior colleges starting in January 2000. A compromise was made for a 12-month delay in implementation of the policy until September 2001 for Lehman and City Colleges, "the colleges whose overwhelmingly minority populations would be most affected by the new policy" (Karen Arenson. "Plan to Exclude Remedial Students Approved at CUNY." *New York Times* 23 Nov. 1999: A1+).

[3] As of December 2000, students no longer take the WAT and RAT as placement or proficiency instruments, CUNY now requires students who do not meet SAT or Regents requirements listed below (see Note 4) to take the nationally-normed ACT battery of tests. Students must take the ACT reading test, a 25-minute 24-item multiple-choice exam, and the ACT writing tests, a 60-minute essay exam and a 25-minute 24-item multiple-choice exam, for placement and for proficiency or exit from remedial or ESL classes.

[4] The Board of Trustees has recently refined this definition and now will consider as reading and writing proficient, entrants with verbal SAT scores of 480 and over or those with New York State English Regents' exam scores of 75 or better. These students will not be required to take remedial reading, writing, or ESL courses.

[5] Karen Greenberg has been deeply involved in the debate over whether basic writers should be mainstreamed or not. See her article "A Response to Ira Shor's 'Our Apartheid: Writing Instruction and Inequality.'"

[6] On November 30, 1999 we were told that we will not be able to offer English 110 as of Spring 2000 and that Hunter College will not accept students who have scored a "6" on the WAT. Such students will be required to attend a 3-week workshop in January or June or summer school. They will be re-tested. If they do not pass any of the exams, they will not be admitted to Hunter College unless they are designated as ESL.

WORKS CITED

Arenson, Karen W. "Leadership Void Hobbles CUNY as It Faces Severe Problems." *New York Times* 24 Mar. 1999: B1+.

Arizona State University's Stretch Program. URL: http://www.asu.edu/clas/english/composition/cbw/stretch.htm (23 June 1999).

Beaky, Lenore. "Remedial—Some Myths, Some Facts" (published by author to CUNYTALK-listserv). May 1999.

Benesch, Sarah. "Anorexia: A Feminist EAP Curriculum." *Adult ESL: Politics, Pedagogy, and Participation in Classroom and Community Programs*. Ed. Trudy Smoke. Mahwah, NJ: Lawrence Erlbaum Associates, 1998. 101–14.

Blanton, Linda Lonon. "Classroom Instruction and Language Minority Students: On Teaching to 'Smarter' Readers and Writers." *Generation 1.5 Meets College Composition: Issues in the Teaching of Writing to U.S.-Educated Learners of ESL*. Ed. Linda Harklau, Kay M. Losey, and Meryl Siegal. Mahwah, NJ: Lawrence Erlbaum Associates, 1999. 119-42.

Braine, George. "ESL Students in First-Year Writing Courses: ESL Versus Mainstream Classes." *Journal of Second Language Writing* 5.2 (1996): 91–107.

Carro, Gladys, and J. F. Watts. "Provisional Report on PSC/CUNY Grant #667276 and #668308." Unpublished CUNY Report. 15 Sept. 1997.

CUNY Board of Trustees. Resolution on Remediation. 25 Jan. 1999.

"Executive Summary of the Schmidt Commission Report." CUNY Publication, June 1999.

Fox, Tom. *Defending Access: A Critique of Standards in Higher Education.* Portsmouth, NH: Heinemann Boynton/Cook, 1999.

Glau, Gregory. "Re: Info on the ASU Stretch Program." E-mail to Trudy Smoke. 28 June 1999.

Gleason, Barbara. "Returning Adults to the Mainstream: Toward a Curriculum for Diverse Student Writers."

Greenberg, Karen L. "A Response to Ira Shor's 'Our Apartheid: Writing Instruction and Inequality.'" *Journal of Basic Writing.* 16.2 (1997): 90–4.

Grego, Rhonda C., and Nancy S. Thompson. "The Writing Studio: Reconfiguring Basic Writing/Freshman Composition." *WPA: Writing Program Administration* 19.1/2 (1995): 66–79.

Harklau, Linda, Kay M. Losey, and Meryl Siegal, eds. *Generation 1.5 Meets College Composition: Issues in the Teaching of Writing to U.S.-Educated Learners of ESL.* Mahwah, NJ: Lawrence Erlbaum Associates, 1999.

Leki, Ilona. *Understanding ESL Writers: A Guide for Teachers.* Portsmouth, NH: Heinemann Boynton/Cook, 1992.

MacDonald, Heather. "Downward Mobility: The Failure of Open Admissions at City University." *City Journal.* 4.3 (1994): 10–20.

McNenny, Geraldine. Personal Letter to Trudy Smoke. 3 Jan. 2000.

Penfield, Susan, and Yvonna Roepcke. *Combining NNSs and NSs in Freshman Composition.* Presentation at TESOL '98 Conference in Seattle. 18 Mar. 1998. Washington.

Proc. of the University Faculty Senate Spring 1999 Conference and 26th Plenary Session. *Recommendations of the Mayor's Task Force on CUNY—The Promised Objectivity: Is It There?* 8 June 1998. CUNY Publication.

Raimes, Ann. "What Unskilled ESL Students Do as They Write: A Classroom Study of Composing." *TESOL Quarterly* 19 (1985): 229–58.

Rodby, Judith. "Contingent Literacy: The Social Construction of Writing for Nonnative English-Speaking College Freshmen. *Generation 1.5 Meets College Composition: Issues in the Teaching of Writing to U.S.-Educated Learners of ESL.* Eds. Linda Harklau, Kay M. Losey, and Meryl Siegal. Mahwah, NJ: Lawrence Erlbaum Associates, 1999. 45–60.

Shor, Ira. "Our Apartheid: Writing Instruction and Inequality." *Journal of Basic Writing.* 16.1 (1997): 91–104.

Silva, Tony. "An Examination of Writing Program Administrators' Options for the Placement of ESL Students in First Year Writing Classes." *WPA: Writing Program Administration* 18.1/2 (1994): 37–43.

Smoke, Trudy. "Critical Multiculturalism as a Means of Promoting Social Activism and Awareness." *Adult ESL: Politics, Pedagogy, and Participation in Classroom and Community Programs.* Ed. Trudy Smoke. Mahwah, NJ: Lawrence Erlbaum Associates, 1998. 89–98.

———"Using Feedback from ESL Students to Enhance Their Success in College." *Ending Remediation: Linking ESL and Content in Higher Education.* Ed. Sarah Benesch. Washington, DC: TESOL, 1988. 9–19.

Soliday, Mary, and Barbara Gleason. "From Remediation to Enrichment: Evaluating Mainstreaming Project." *Journal of Basic Writing* 16.1 (1997): 64–78.

Thompson, Nancy S. "Re: Repositioning Remediation." E-mail to Trudy Smoke. 29 Mar. 1998.

Traub, James. *City on a Hill: Testing the American Dream at City College.* Reading, MA: Addison-Wesley, 1994.

Vandrick, Stephanie. "Promoting Gender Equity in the Postsecondary ESL Class." *Adult ESL: Politics, Pedagogy, and Participation in Classroom and Community Programs,* Ed. Trudy Smoke. Mahwah, NJ: Lawrence Erlbaum Associates, 1998. 73–88.

Waldrop, M. Mitchell. *Complexity: The Emerging Science at the Edge of Order and Chaos.* New York: Touchstone, 1992.

CHAPTER TWELVE

The Context Determines Our Choice: Curriculum, Students, and Faculty

Sallyanne H. Fitzgerald
Chabot College

At the opening convocation for the academic year, our community college president concluded his state-of-the-college address by announcing his goals for the coming year, one of which was to create a basic skills laboratory. As a dean with responsibility over the English basic skills program among other areas and as a basic writing researcher and teacher, my reaction was violent opposition to his proposal. First, I was opposed because of the complete change in our philosophy such a facility reflects: putting students at a computer with an online textbook to do grammar exercises is an outdated approach compared to our classes where reading and writing are taught with grammar instruction being accomplished in the context of those assignments. We do not use workbooks and do not value "seat time." We offer students the option of a two-semester basic writing sequence of reading, writing, and critical thinking courses or an accelerated one-semester course. In these courses, students write primarily argumentative essays supported with information and citations from the nonfiction, full-length text and essay collections they are reading. One text we use because it tends to reflect our curriculum is Robinson and Tucker's *Text and Contexts*. The goal of our basic writing courses is to prepare students to complete successfully a freshman composition course where they will write 8,000 words and read the equivalent of five, full-length, nonfiction texts. The freshman composition course transfers to both public and private universities as the first-semester course required for general education.

In addition to conflicting with our curriculum, the president's proposal came like a "bolt from the blue" with no faculty consultation—he was stepping into curriculum issues that are the purview of the faculty. Our English faculty are strongly invested in the curriculum that they developed collaboratively over 2 years in the early 1990s. They built it in response to research on our campus as well as that available nationally in the last 20 years using such theories as collaborative learning reflected in Andrea Lunsford's work, reading and writing ideas like those in Bartholomae and Petrosky, and, of course, the earlier work of Mina Shaughnessy in *Errors and Expectations*.

Thinking my president's was an isolated voice, I was surprised to discover at a meeting of regional, community college English Department chairs that their administrators were also proposing this lab idea, apparently in a bid to increase students and, therefore, increase funding. Unlike universities, many community colleges, especially in California, view basic skills instruction as part of their mission, so some type of basic skills lab is clearly within the scope of our responsibility; in fact, new money is coming from the state based on an accountability measure of basic skills improvement. That measure looks at the number of students who enrolled in a basic skills course and then enrolled in a higher level course in the same area of study. Because our mission is to offer basic skills and we will be funded for doing so, I was not objecting to the lab as a method of providing basic writing instruction, but rather I objected because it did not fit our current, faculty-created curriculum—the context in which we serve our students. Although such a lab might serve other community college contexts or even university ones, I agree with the authors of this text who are almost unanimous in proposing that any approach for teaching basic writing must fit the context in which it is used. Unlike some politicians and members of the public, our authors purpose ways of teaching basic writing that fit the students in their institutions—not a "one size fits all" approach.

OUR COMMUNITY COLLEGE CONTEXT

Our California community college has a curriculum that is based on the assumption that reading and writing are both processes involving a person's interaction with text. We believe that the schema built in one process can be accessed in the other. In addition, we take an approach to reading or writing text that assumes we begin at the macro level when pursuing either process. In other words, proficient readers do not begin with the word but rather read for meaning by chunking text, and writers learn to compose by having ideas to impart to readers, not by learning to choose the word and to place it into a sentence but by using whatever text makes the writer's point. This means that we encourage students to create meaning through full texts rather than restrict them to sentence or paragraph level. Because of our current curriculum, we think placing students at computers to work on word or sentence level exercises rather than to construct meaning is useless.

In addition to our curriculum, our context is characterized by whom we serve and who our faculty are. Because California community colleges admit anyone who is 18 years or older, regardless of their previous education, we have a demand for basic writing as well as other basic skills such as beginning math. At our particular campus, located on the San Francisco Bay, we enroll about 13,000 students and approximately 70% of them test into our basic writing sequence on the basis of a placement exam required for anyone who lacks a previous, acceptable college course. Many current faculty members were hired when our system grew rapidly after most colleges were built in the 1960s. So the current faculty tend to come from a period when open access and service to our students were widely accepted as part of who we are. This background of mission and faculty means that, in general, we subscribe to the idea that we have a responsibility to serve our basic writers by providing classes to help them be successful in whatever areas they are studying. Two ways that the authors of this book see as options to serve basic writers are stand-alone basic writing courses and mainstreamed courses. Mainstreaming, as defined by the authors in this text, means placing basic writers in freshman composition classes rather than in separate basic writing classes.

ONE SOLUTION TO THE NEED FOR BASIC WRITING

Rather than have basic writing classes or mainstreamed basic writers, one solution could be to eliminate the need for basic writing in higher education. A September 1998 study, *Statewide Remedial Education Policies*, written by Edward Crowe, examined remediation across the United States. He reports that "aspects of the system that must be mobilized to solve the remedial problem include high school preparation patterns; teacher education programs; school/college collaboration initiatives; state scholarship programs; higher education admissions standards; the quality of state K-16 education data systems; workforce preparation programs; and the extent to which the state system is energized by policy alignment and systemic thinking." Crowe did not examine mainstreaming or discuss initiatives for the students who come to higher education, preferring to concern himself with ways to eliminate remedial courses through interventions provided before students arrive.

BASIC WRITING CLASSES

The authors of this book, on the other hand, look at ways to help students who are enrolled in their particular context. For that reason, they tend to set up a dichotomy—either basic writing classes or mainstreamed ones. For the most part, the issue addressed in this book is not whether or not students should be in higher education, but rather once they are there, what should be done to help them succeed. Opening this text with a revision of an article he first published in the *Journal of Basic Writing*, Edward M. White explains the issue as the conflict between "egalitarianism" and "elitism," tracing its most recent history. Then, he compares studies from both coasts, which demonstrated the effectiveness of basic writing programs especially in retaining students. He declares that research shows "that placement and basic writing instruction have a powerful positive influence on the retention of students with weak preparation for college." Others in this text and elsewhere disagree with this conclusion and propose elimination of basic writing.

The desire to eliminate basic writing is articulated in a September 24, 1999 edition of the *Chronicle of Higher Education* essay by Lois Cronholm, "Why One College Jettisoned All Its Remedial Courses." She asserts, "Based on my firsthand experience as provost and then interim president of Baruch when we made and carried out that decision(to eliminate remedial courses) in 1998—and my examination of remediation from many perspectives over the past 20 years as a senior administrator at other major urban universities—I have concluded that offering pre-collegiate work in colleges and universities is a grievous error" (B6). Clearly, her opinion and that of many universities is in direct opposition to the attitude of community colleges in many states, not just in California. This opposition points to an underlying theme throughout our book: the best approach depends on the context of the college or university.

MAINSTREAMED CLASSES

Given the prevailing California community college attitude and the interest in basic skills funding, it is not surprising that in general the idea of mainstreaming basic writers at our California community college seems alien in our particular context. On the other hand, our university colleagues generally see mainstreaming as a solution to the needs of students. For example, most California universities are following the path chosen by many universities across the country of eliminating basic writing. The University of California-Berkeley, for example, no longer offers a "bonehead" English course labeled "Subject A." Instead, UC-B students take a combined Subject A and freshman composition—a mainstreamed course—if they do not place into freshman composition. California's other major public university system, the California State University, has a basic writing sequence which students place into on the basis of an exam that is required for those students whose high school grades and test scores do not automatically place them in freshman composition. At present, 50% of all entering first-year, CSU students place into basic writing. The CSU trustees have determined that by 2007 only 10% of entering first-year students attending a CSU campus will need remediation. One way to achieve this goal is to recommend students attend a community college to remediate their problems before being admitted to a CSU campus. This approach is not uniformly endorsed by faculty; in fact, the CSU English Council with representatives from each campus has spoken against the policy.

Other states, too, are mainstreaming students and encouraging basic skills remediation to occur in the community college. For example, in the early 1990s, when I was the administrator for a basic English and mathematics unit on a campus of the University of Missouri, the system began to eliminate all basic writing courses from the four campuses of that system. Today, the campuses do not offer basic writing classes as part of the general education offerings. Students are encouraged to prepare themselves for college English either in high school or at the community college although occasionally noncredit workshops are available on a campus. Some of the authors of this text mention this approach in New York which is similarly moving toward placing all basic writing instruction in the community college.

Some in community colleges also advocate mainstreaming basic writers. For example, Peter Dow Adams articulated the value of mainstreaming when he was co-chair of the Conference on Basic Writing, a special interest group of the Conference on College Composition and Communication. He explained his concern about isolating basic writers in a program that might not prepare them for success when he spoke at the opening event of the last national basic writing conference in the fall of 1992 at the University of Maryland. Adams proposed mainstreaming basic writers at his community college based on his research, which showed that on his campus students in basic writing classes did not do so well as those who were mainstreamed. Conference attendees reacted with approval or violent opposition to his presentation. Unfortunately, many of them did not hear his qualification that his proposal was for his own context, not necessarily for other settings, and was based on his research. Some of the authors of this text make the same qualification for their approaches.

VIEWPOINTS OF OUR AUTHORS

Terence Collins and Kim Lynch, in chapter 5, effectively state the case for looking at basic writing in context. In "Mainstreaming? Eddy, Rivulet, Backwater, Site Specificity," Collins and Lynch examine their local context and warn that we need to be careful of calling for something we may not want. They use two articles that both try to generalize about basic writers to prove their case with specific sites. Looking at the particular context of New York and CUNY, Mary Soliday calls for a re-examination of our philosophy of access. She traces the early origins of access philosophy and relates these beginnings to the current debates about remediation in New York spending particular efforts to situate Mina Shaughnessy and James Traub. Mark Wiley also examines a particular program and in the process finds that the differences among all writers, including basic writers, need to be addressed. He proposes an approach that is mainstreaming in its use of learning communities. He discusses the various types of learning communities, which are generally characterized by a cohort of students supported by a team of faculty in classes tied together to reinforce learning. Agreeing with Collins, Wiley asserts that it is "unwise to generalize about basic writers and about basic writing programs." Rosemary Winslow and Monica Mische describe their program as a mainstreaming one. At their eastern private university, they taught an experimental class that used the hero journey as content and attempted to help students develop not only in writing skills but in a positive self-concept as well. They make the case for mainstreaming by asserting that in developing their class they "rethought and worked out how to teach writing in the same classroom to students of varying preparation while altering their perceptions of their desires and competencies."

Like Winslow and Mische, Barbara Gleason explains the importance of a mainstreamed class curriculum, which "accounts for the diversity" among the mainstreamed students. She reflects on a class she has taught to a diverse group of students who share the fact that they are returning adults. Using two particular students, Gleason attempts to demonstrate the value of the curriculum she espouses especially when it is used in a program with the goal of "accelerated students' academic progress." She concludes with the statement that curriculum designed as hers has been will benefit both the underprepared students and those who are stronger.

Other authors also address very specific contexts. Eleanor Agnew and Margaret McLaughlin discuss a system that "contributes to creating a racially-based, two-tier system of students." Looking at their university's assessment system, they attack poor assessment, which forces students to "demonstrate they are not basic writers." Marti Singer in "Moving the Margins: A Faculty

Perspective" critiques a campus in the same state and asserts that students are marginalized as is the program on the particular campus where she teaches. She traces the changes that have happened on her campus in the basic writing program where even as things change, the world turns to bring the past back again. Trudy Smoke narrows the context she discusses to New York and to English as a Second Language students although she briefly discusses other states in an effort to examine her particular context as symptomatic of the national situation. She also offers suggestions for creating an effective program and asserts that "we need to look long and hard at our own institutions before we decide the best option for placing ESL writers in composition classes." Ira Shor attacks mainstream writing classes as an "attempt to fit students and teachers into the status quo, to develop our cooperation with the way things are, to accommodate us to the unequal culture already in place." He sees basic writing as an even more insidious problem because it is a "gate" that limits access to degrees and therefore to jobs: his argument is an economic one. He also says that "instead of bogus testing and depressant remediation we need programs based in field projects and social contexts...," and he calls for "ethnographic, context-based, socially-oriented, interdisciplinary writing and community literacy...."

CONTEXT-DRIVEN CHOICES

Although all of the authors of this text support serving the students who come to higher education rather than addressing the problem before they matriculate, these authors differ in their approaches to that end. For the most part, those who support mainstreaming see it as an approach that places students in the regular curriculum, although they also generally want a coherent program with some support. Like Shor, most of them believe that mainstreamed students need writing situated in a particular context and rich with varied assignments that tap their knowledge and social situation while empowering them to take charge of their learning. Others in this volume do not oppose mainstreaming so much as advocate for individual students in particular contexts.

Wholesale elimination of basic writing without regard to the particular context of the program seems to be the goal of some legislators and administrators whereas others in different environments see basic writing as the "cash cow." Although the authors of this text are primarily concerned with university settings, they recognize that the answer to the challenge of mainstreaming or separating basic writers lies in the situation they are examining. My concern is that too often we in basic writing see our own context as the only one, and we propose answers for our situation as if those answers are appropriate for all of our profession. In fact, the community college setting is very different from the university in the same way that California and New York, Georgia and Minnesota, large and small schools and public and private ones are also different. We even have trouble defining basic writers and usually agree that a basic writer at Harvard is not the same writer as one in a small, rural 2-year college in the southwest. Yet, we continually come back to the same point as the authors of this text: we need to serve the students who come to us with curriculum appropriate to our context—our students, our faculty, our institution. That is why I objected to our president's idea that we create a basic skills lab. We need to meet the needs of our students with a curriculum appropriate to them and one that will move them toward academic success given the institution and the faculty they have chosen. What is appropriate in one context is not necessarily what will enable students to learn in another.

As a community college administrator, I have read the chapters of this text with the same questions I have when I attend conferences such as the annual Conference on College Composition and Communication. Where do our community college students and faculty fit in the discussion? When will university people begin to understand that they do not speak for all of us in higher education or for our students? Why do my colleagues in the Conference on Basic Writing have to be reminded that basic writing is a universal term that can be applied to many contexts, not just the universities where they teach? At least, in this text, I find that the authors reflect upon their own contexts. In general, they have attempted to present what has worked for them. Community college faculty and administrators who read these reflections will need to look for what seems most similar to their own contexts to decide what to take away with them concerning the value of mainstreaming. For example, they can look to Trudy Smoke's chapter if their students are second language speakers and to Barbara Gleason if their students are working class and older adults. They can find ideas from Terry Collins and Kim Lynch if they are preparing their students to enter an elite university. Others in the text offer suggestions for focusing curriculum like Mark Wiley and Rosemary Winslow and Monica Mische. However, neither my community college colleagues nor those from universities will find all the answers here because ultimately we each must choose those approaches that best fit our unique contexts.

WORKS CITED

Bartholomae, David, and Anthony Petrosky. *Ways of Reading*. Boston: Bedford Books, 1999.
Cronholm, Lois. "Why One College Jettisoned All Its remedial Courses." *The Chronicle of Higher Education* 24 Sept. 1999: B6.

Crowe, Edward. *Statewide Remedial Education Policies*. Denver: State Higher Education Executive Officers, 1998.

Lunsford, Andrea. "Collaboration, Control, and the Idea of a Writing Center." *The Writing Center Journal* 12.1 (1991): 3–10.

Robinson, William S., and Stephanie Tucker. *Texts and Contexts*. Belmont, CA: Wadsworth, 2000.

Shaughnessy, Mina. *Errors and Expectations*. New York: Oxford UP, 1979.

About the Authors

Eleanor Agnew, PhD, is an associate professor in the Department of Writing and Linguistics at Georgia Southern University, where she is also assistant chair. She has published articles in *Assessing Writing, Journal of Basic Writing, TESOL* and the anthologies *Grading in the Post-Process Classroom* and *Attending to the Margins: Writing, Researching and Teaching on the Front Lines*. She is also a co-author of the book *My Mama's Waltz.*

Terence Collins is Morse-Alumni Distinguished Teaching Professor and director of Academic Affairs and Curriculum at General College–University of Minnesota, where he teaches basic writing. His research is on basic writing, access to higher education, and technology in education.

Sallyanne H. Fitzgerald, EdD, has experience as a teacher and administrator in three states and in high school, university, and community colleges. Her research has been primarily in basic writing, and she has published articles, chapters, and two textbooks in basic writing. Presently, she is a dean of the largest academic division at her San Francisco Bay area community college where basic writing is part of the English mission. Sally has been a member of the Conference on Basic Writing, serving in various board positions including CBW co-chair and editor of the newsletter. She organized the first national basic writing conference at the University of Missouri–St. Louis.

Barbara Gleason is associate professor at the City College of New York, where she teaches in the English Department and at the Center for Worker Education. She has published essays on program evaluation, curriculum development, writing assessment, basic writing, and phenomenology as book chapters and in the *Journal of Basic Writing, College English*, and *College Composition and Communication*. She has co-edited, with Mark Wiley and Louise Wetherbee Phelps, *Composition in Four Keys: Inquiring Into a Field: Nature, Art, Science and Politics* (Mayfield 1995) and, with Faun Bernbach Evans and Mark Wiley, *Cultural Tapestry: Readings for a Pluralistic Society* (Harper Collins 1992).

Kim Lynch teaches basic writing at Anoka-Ramsey Community College in Cambridge, Minnesota. She received her PhD in English composition from the University of Minnesota. Her research is on the writing of adult, working-class students.

Margaret McLaughlin is an associate professor in the Department of Writing and Linguistics at Georgia Southern University. Her primary research and teaching interests focus on learning support reading and writing students. With Eleanor Agnew, she conducted a longitudinal study of 61 basic writers and co-authored examinations of that study in *Attending to the Margins: Writing, Researching, and Teaching on the Front Lines* and in the Spring 1999 issue of the *Journal of Basic Writing*.

Gerri McNenny is an assistant professor at California State University, Fullerton, and teaches writing and literature and coordinates the Developmental Writing Program there. She has published articles on collaboration, working-class studies, and basic writing in *Rhetoric Review, Dialogue*, and *The Journal of Basic Writing* and is a frequent presenter at national and local conferences. Gerri has also been a member of the executive committee of the Conference on Basic Writing and served as co-chair of the CBW.

Monica Mische has taught writing and literature courses and served as assistant director of the writing program at The Catholic University of America. She has co-authored (with Rosemary Winslow) a previous version of the chapter in this book in *The Journal of Basic Writing*. At present she is completing a dissertation on using Bakhtinian theory in developing linked literature and writing courses for at-risk first-year students.

Ira Shor is distinguished visiting professor at William Paterson University for 2000–2001, on leave from the City University of New York PhD Program in English and the College of Staten Island. His most recent books include *When Students Have Power: Negotiating Resistance in a Critical Pedagogy*

(University of Chicago Press 1996), and three volumes in tribute to Paulo Freire (with Caroline Pari): *Critical Literacy in Action* (for college writing programs); *Education Is Politics*, Vol. 1(k–12); and *Education Is Politics*, Vol. 2 (postsecondary across the curriculum), from Heinemann Press, 1999–2000.

Marti Singer is an associate professor of English at Georgia State University, where she teaches graduate and undergraduate courses in both composition and American literature. She was previously the coordinator for composition and director of the Learning Center for the Department of Learning Support Programs at Georgia State. Her interests include teacher beliefs and reflective practice in the teaching of writing and literature, training graduate students for the professorate, and the psychological influences of writing style and process. She has presented many papers at CCCC regarding composition, reflection, and student voices. Her most recent publications include co-authored articles on *Preparing Tomorrow's Faculty: An Assessment Model* (forthcoming in the *Journal of Graduate Teaching Assistant Development*) and *Needs Assessment for Quality Instruction: An Interactive Report on Perceptions of Good Teaching* (in *Reaching Through Teaching: The Center for Excellence in Teaching and Learning*, Kennesaw State University). In addition, she is past president of the Association for Psychological Type and has published many articles concerning cognitive style, psychological type, and teaching.

Trudy Smoke is professor of English at Hunter College. She is the director of the First Year Writing Program in the English Department. Dr. Smoke has written several textbooks, including *A Writer's Workbook for ESL Writers*, published by Cambridge University Press, and *Making a Difference* for developmental writers, published by Houghton Mifflin. Her latest book is *Adult ESL: Politics, Pedagogy, and Participation in Classroom and Community Programs*, published by Lawrence Erlbaum Associates. Professor Smoke is a co-editor of the *Journal of Basic Writing (JBW)* and is a frequent speaker at national and local conferences.

Mary Soliday is an assistant professor of English at the City College of New York. She has published several essays about basic writing and the culture and politics of literacy in CE, CCC, JBW, and elsewhere. She is currently completing a book, *Writing Between Worlds*, about the history and politics of remedial education.

Marilyn S. Sternglass is professor emeritus of English at The City College of City University of New York. Her latest book, *Time to Know Them: A Longitudinal Study of Writing and Learning at the College Level* (1997), was a co-winner of the Mina P. Shaughnessy Prize of the Modern

Language Association in 1998 and the winner of the 1999 CCCC Outstanding Book Award.

Edward M. White is an emeritus professor of English at California State University, San Bernardino and an adjunct professor of English at the University of Arizona. He has published over 50 articles and book chapters on writing, assessment, and literature, and has written, edited, or co-edited nine books, including *Teaching and Assessing Writing*, revised edition 1994, which earned honorable mention for the MLA's Mina Shaughnessey Award, and *Assessment of Writing: Politics, Policies, Practices*, 1996. Although technically "retired," he continues to teach and write; he has book projects planned well into the new century. He, in collaboration with one of his Arizona graduate students, has published an article reflecting on the research methodology of the chapter in this book, and on the reaction to it: William DeGenaro and Edward M. White, "Going Around in Circles: Methodological Issues in Basic Composition Research," *Journal of Basic Writing*, 19.1 (2000): 23–36.

Mark Wiley is an associate professor in the Department of English at California State University, Long Beach. He directs the writing program and teaches a range of courses from basic writing to graduate classes on theories and practices of teaching composition and rhetoric. Among other publications, his most recent essay appeared in the *English Journal* (September, 2000) on the "Popularity of Formulaic Writing (and the Need to Resist)." He also co-authored and edited (along with Barbara Gleason and Louise Wetherbee Phelps) *Composition in Four Keys: Inquiring Into the Field* (Mayfield). Current projects include developing learning communities on campus, working with local high schools on aligning writing instruction with the University, and collaborating with a national group of faculty from two- and four-year colleges and universities on identifying outcomes for first-year writing programs.

Rosemary (Gates) Winslow is associate professor of English at The Catholic University of America. She directs the writing program and teaches courses in composition and rhetoric at all levels, creative writing, the teaching of writing, stylistics, and American literature. She has published over 30 articles and book chapters, including work in the *Journal of Basic Writing*, *Journal of Advanced Composition*, *Freshman English News/ Composition Studies*, *Journal of Business and Technical Communication*, *Language and Style*, and *Poetics Today*; and in *The Literacy Connection* (Ron Sudol and Alice Horning, Eds.), *Civil Society and Social Reconstruction* (George McLean, Ed.), and *Into the Field: Sites of Composing* (Ann Ruggles Gere, Ed.). She has also edited and co-authored (with Judith M. Davis) a study guide for adults learning first-year composition.

Author Index

Subject Index